lonely planet

KOREA

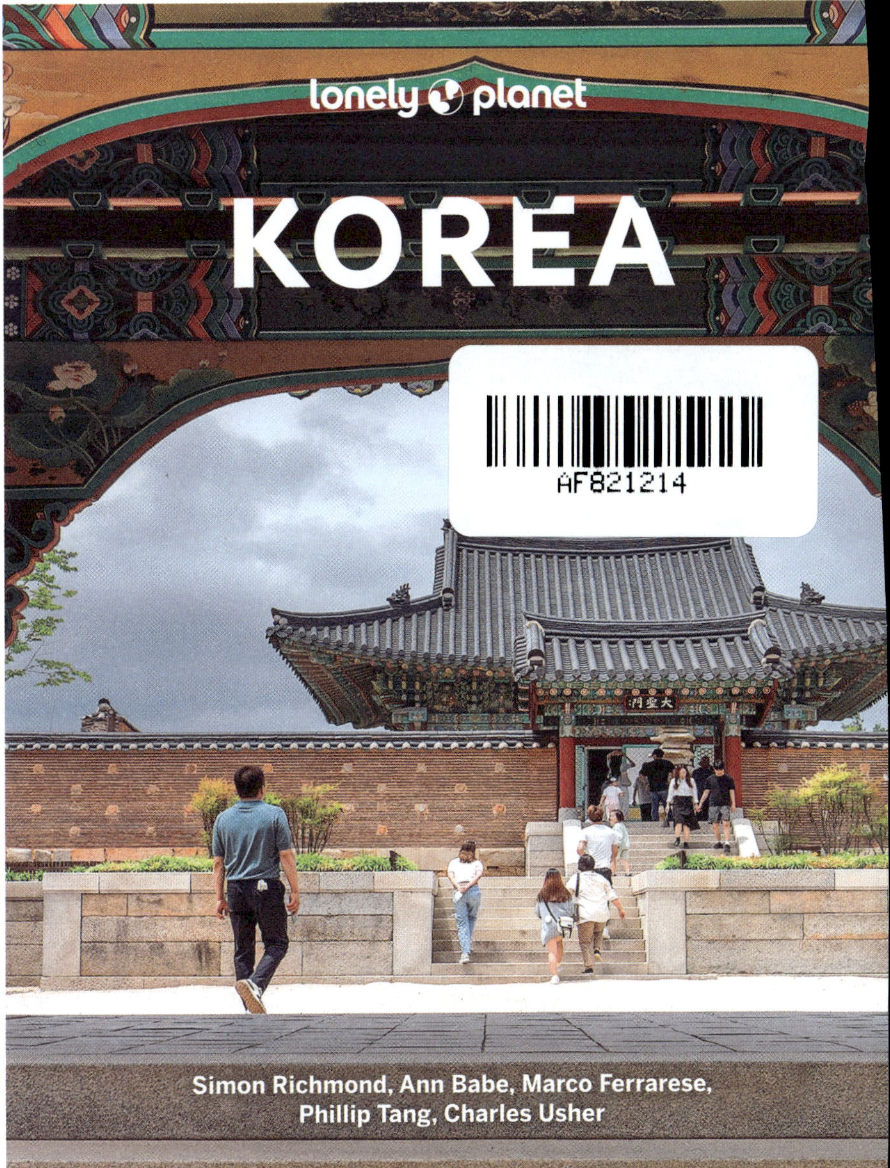

Simon Richmond, Ann Babe, Marco Ferrarese,
Phillip Tang, Charles Usher

Meet our writers

Simon Richmond

@simonrichmond

An award-winning travel writer, Simon has contributed to several previous editions of Lonely Planet's Korea and Seoul guidebooks, as well as many other titles.

Ann Babe

@ann_e_babe

Ann is a Korean-American writer and journalist who covers Korea and beyond. She's called a third of Korea's nine provinces home, and whenever she's on Jeju-do, she can't resist walking an Olle Trail (p184) route or two – or three.

Marco Ferrarese

@marcoferrarese

A Malaysia-based writer and journalist, Marco discovered Korea as a teen through the Italian dub of *Oldboy*. He's still on a mission to bag as many Korean peaks as he can.

Phillip Tang

hellophillip.com *@mrtangtangtang*

Phillip is a travel writer with a love for Latin America and Asia. Since 2015, he has returned time and again to South Korea, tracing the character of each province.

MR.SILAPHOP PONGSAI/SHUTTERSTOCK

Previous spread Naksan-sa (p88), Yangyang

MIRKO KUZMANOVIC/SHUTTERSTOCK

Wolchulsan National Park (p149)

Michelin-starred restaurants in Seoul (2025): 37

Types of kimchi: 200+

Korea's most popular instant *ramyeon*: Nongshim Shin Ramyun

TANGY, CRISPY **& DELICIOUS**

Get ready for a gastronomic experience. The flavours and textures of Korean cuisine run the gamut from tangy kimchi and steaming *jjigae* (stews) to tempting *tang* (soups), crispy *jeon* (pancakes) and moreish *mandu* (dumplings). There are noodles to slurp, quality beef and pork to barbecue and a bounty of seafood to devour. Wash it all down with some local drinks, including craft beers, *makgeolli* (rice wine) and soju.

IMAGEBROKER.COM/ALAMY

Left Jjigae Right Jeong Kwan
Below Coffee, Gangneung

→ STAR CHEF

Join the monthly vegan cooking class taught by Buddhist nun Jeong Kwan, who appeared on Netflix's *Chef's Table*, at Baegyang-sa (p152), a temple in Jeollanam-do.

FISH MARKETS

Dine on the freshest of seafood, buying direct from vendors at Jagalchi Fish Market in Busan (p122), Noryangjin Fisheries Wholesale Market in Seoul (p70) and Sokcho Tourist Fish Market in Sokcho (p82).

FROM LEFT: PHOTOHWAN/SHUTTERSTOCK, THE_DAVE/SHUTTERSTOCK

↑ SMELL THE COFFEE

Gangneung (p90) is Korea's artisan coffee capital with scores of appealing cafes and an annual coffee festival featuring the nation's top baristas.

Best Korean Dining Experiences

- **Tuck into tasty street food at Seoul's busiest *meokjagolmok* (food alley) at Gwangjang Market.** (p70)
- **Stir fry *dakgalbi*, Chuncheon's chicken and rice-cake dish, on Myeongdong Dakgalbi St.** (p84)
- **Savour *jjimdak*, a soy-braised chicken and vegetable dish, on Andong's Jjimdak Alley.** (p110)
- **Slurp noodles along Damyang's Guksu Geori (Noodle Street).** (p145)
- **Enjoy pork belly at Seomun Market's Samgyeopsal Alley in Cheongju.** (p206)

UNESCO World Heritage Sites in South Korea: 17

Grand palaces in Seoul: 5

Regional branches of National Museum of Korea: 13

FROM DYNASTY **TO DEMOCRACY**

Thousands of years of history and heritage await you on the peninsula. Korean culture stretches back to prehistoric times. On your travels you'll encounter everything from funerary monuments of the Neolithic and Bronze Ages to the beautifully decorated Joseon-dynasty palaces of Seoul and museums that tackle some of the most traumatic events of Korea's 20th century.

Left Secret Garden, Changdeokgung (p44) **Right** National Museum of Korea (p71) **Below** Unification Observatory (p99)

MANITTO/SHUTTERSTOCK

→ NATIONAL MUSEUM

Seoul's National Museum of Korea (p71) is the country's most visited museum and a superb introduction to local history and culture.

MUSEUM WITHOUT WALLS

The Silla capital Gyeongju (p114) is scattered with astonishing tumuli, ancient royal tombs and and the beautiful Donggung Palace and Wolji Pond.

FROM LEFT: DOYPUI/SHUTTERSTOCK, ©KOREA TOURISM ORGANIZATION – KIM JIHO

↑ VISIT THE DMZ

Feel the tension and appreciate the natural beauty along this fearsome border with North Korea at Imjingak (p230), Cheorwon (p97) and Goseong's Tongil Security Park (p99).

Best Historical Experiences

- **Learn about the 1980 uprisings in Gwangju.** (p142)
- **Step back in time at Gangneung's Ojukheon, one of Korea's oldest Joseon-dynasty homes.** (p94)
- **Admire centuries-old rural architecture in Hahoe Folk Village.** (p108)
- **Stroll through a World Heritage–listed garden at Changdeokgung.** (p44)
- **Wander through Jeju's oldest wooden building, Gwandeok-jeong.** (p179)

OUTDOOR PLAYGROUND

In South Korea, you're never too far from the great outdoors. Breathtaking mountain landscapes are threaded with hiking trails, dotted with ancient temples and covered with swathes of forest. There are beautiful lakes and mighty rivers. The crinkly coastline is indented with beaches, dunes, craggy cliffs and extensive mudflats. Human-made landscapes in the shape of gorgeous gardens, tea plantations and fields of grain are also part of the pretty picture.

Jeju-do

Adventure island

For the actively inclined, this subtropical island is a dream come true. Summit Halla-san (pictured left), South Korea's highest mountain, learn to surf, walk one of the 27 routes of the Jeju Olle Trail, and dive alongside Jeju's *haenyeo* (female freedivers).

1hr 15min from Seoul

▶ p166

TSUGULIEV/SHUTTERSTOCK

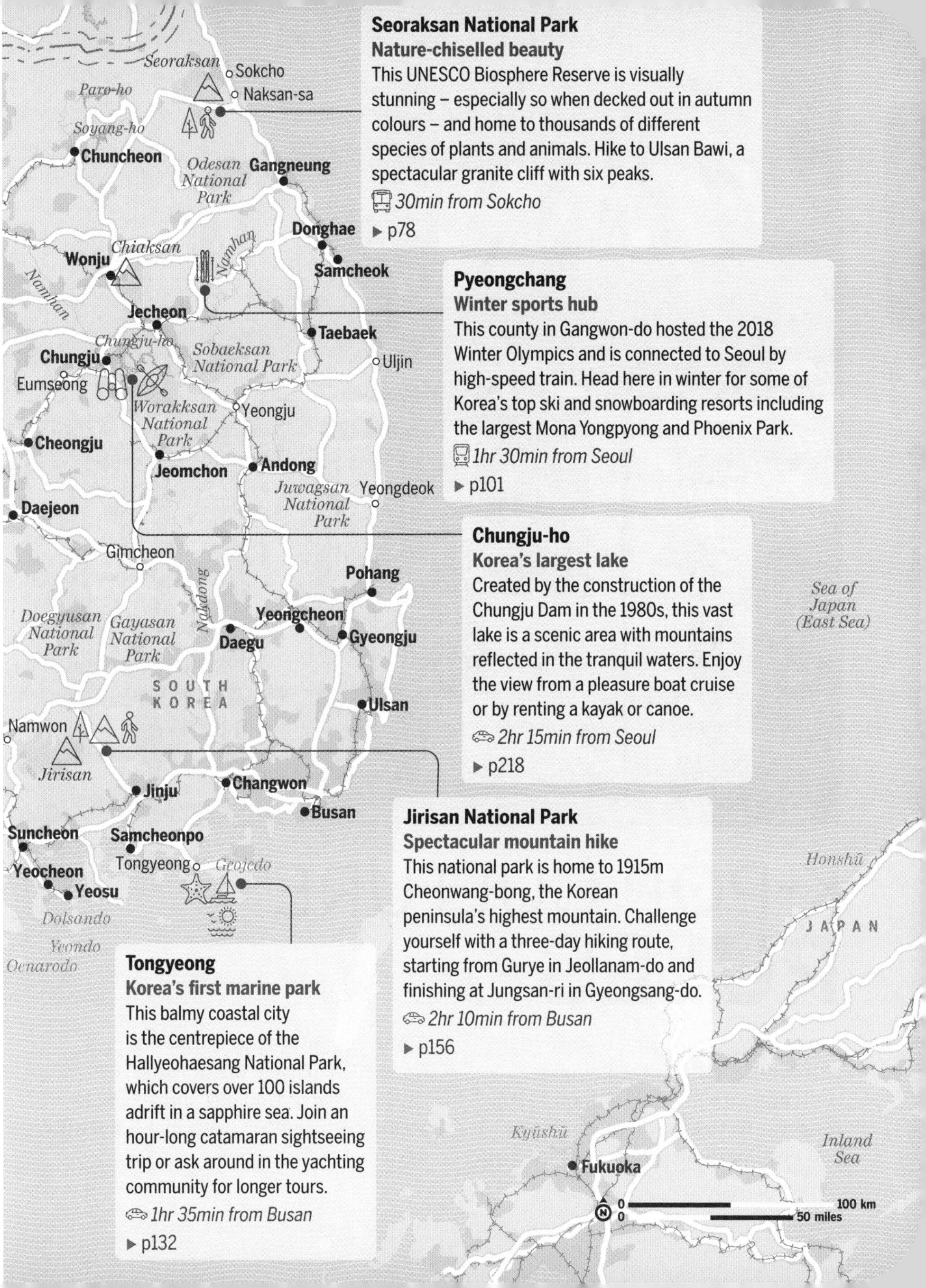

Seoraksan National Park

Nature-chiselled beauty

This UNESCO Biosphere Reserve is visually stunning – especially so when decked out in autumn colours – and home to thousands of different species of plants and animals. Hike to Ulsan Bawi, a spectacular granite cliff with six peaks.

30min from Sokcho

▶ p78

Pyeongchang

Winter sports hub

This county in Gangwon-do hosted the 2018 Winter Olympics and is connected to Seoul by high-speed train. Head here in winter for some of Korea's top ski and snowboarding resorts including the largest Mona Yongpyong and Phoenix Park.

1hr 30min from Seoul

▶ p101

Chungju-ho

Korea's largest lake

Created by the construction of the Chungju Dam in the 1980s, this vast lake is a scenic area with mountains reflected in the tranquil waters. Enjoy the view from a pleasure boat cruise or by renting a kayak or canoe.

2hr 15min from Seoul

▶ p218

Jirisan National Park

Spectacular mountain hike

This national park is home to 1915m Cheonwang-bong, the Korean peninsula's highest mountain. Challenge yourself with a three-day hiking route, starting from Gurye in Jeollanam-do and finishing at Jungsan-ri in Gyeongsang-do.

2hr 10min from Busan

▶ p156

Tongyeong

Korea's first marine park

This balmy coastal city is the centrepiece of the Hallyeohaesang National Park, which covers over 100 islands adrift in a sapphire sea. Join an hour-long catamaran sightseeing trip or ask around in the yachting community for longer tours.

1hr 35min from Busan

▶ p132

K-POP CULTURE RULES

Hallyu, the Korean Wave of pop culture, reflects the nation's contemporary mindset. Attend K-Pop concerts, festivals and dance classes, and visit locations where your favourite K-Movies and K-Dramas were filmed. Korea also delivers big time on cutting-edge technology and visionary architecture and art, with major festivals devoted to what's new.

Left Shopping, Seongsu district
Right National Museum of Modern and Contemporary Art (p65)
Below Busan One Asia Festival

→ ART CAPITAL

Incredible exhibitions are regularly staged at Seoul's National Museum of Modern and Contemporary Art (p65) and Leeum Museum of Art (p65), as well as other galleries.

YLLYSO/SHUTTERSTOCK

KOREA'S BIENNALES

Gwangju's arts festival (p142) is Korea's most famous biennale. Also look out for the Jeju Biennale *(jejubiennale.org)* and Seoul's Mediacity Biennale *(mediacityseoul.kr)* and Biennale of Architecture and Urbanism *(seoulbiennale.org)*.

FROM LEFT: YLLYSO/SHUTTERSTOCK, YONHAP/NEWCOM/ALAMY LIVE NEWS

↑ BIG IN BUSAN

Busan One Asia Festival *(bof.or.kr)* showcases a range of *hallyu* content, while the latest K-Movies are screened at Busan International Film Festival (p129).

Best Contemporary Korea Experiences

- **Be dazzled by the space-age architecture of Dongdaemun Design Plaza.** (p57)
- **Go shopping in Seoul's Seongsu district to discover the latest in fashion.** (p47)
- **Dress in rental *hanbok* (traditional Korean clothing) and stroll around Jeonju Hanok Village.** (p140)
- **Enjoy the contemporary art of the Arario Museum in Jeju-si.** (p181)
- **Marvel at Busan Cinema Centre, which features the world's longest cantilever structure.** (p130)

Temples are havens of calm and quiet reflection amid Korea's often non-stop activity.

The templestay program provides opportunities for visitors to stay in these beautiful places either for a few hours or a couple of days.

SACRED & SPIRITUAL

The state religion of the Joseon dynasty, Confucianism, lives on as a kind of ethical bedrock in the minds of most Koreans. There are around 20,000 Buddhist temples scattered across Korea, many located in gorgeous mountain and forest settings. And around 30% of Koreans identify as Christian, which accounts for the proliferation of churches.

Best Spiritual Experiences

- **Admire Gyeongju's Bulguksa, an outstanding example of Shilla architecture.** (p119; pictured)
- **Pay respects to the 'spirit tablets' of Joseon royalty enshrined in majestic Jongmyo.** (p44)
- **Explore World Heritage–listed Haein-sa, home to one of the world's largest Buddhist woodblock scriptures.** (p135)
- **Explore Buddha's kingdom at mountain hermitage Seokguram.** (p121)
- **Seek serenity in the grounds in Naksan-sa.** (p88)

ARTYOORAN/SHUTTERSTOCK

CALM KOREA

Urban Korea bristles with human activity and distraction. This said, it is possible to find pockets of calm, even in Seoul, and it's very easy to slip off the radar in rural parts of the country. And there are thousands of islands to escape to, where the crowds fade away.

TOP: SEUNG HEO/SHUTTERSTOCK; BOTTOM: SIMON RICHMOND/LONELY PLANET

→ KOREAN GARDENS

Soak up the beauty of the traditional Korean gardens at Les Jardins de Médongaule (*medongaule.com*) and experience serenity at Romyzian Garden.

Best Calming Experiences

- ▸ **Explore Korea's only coastal sand dunes at Sinduri.** (p222)
- ▸ **Commune with Korea's oldest pines in the Anmyeondo Recreational Forest.** (p224)
- ▸ **Explore the evergreen islands of the Shinan Archipelago.** (p160)
- ▸ **Take in the drama of a black volcanic sand beach and soaring cliffs on Udo.** (p194)

← HEALING FORESTS

Get a dose of natural medicine in the verdant woodlands of Jeju-do (p192) including Jeju Gotjawal Provincial Park, Bijarim Forest and Jeolmul Recreational Forest.

Above Jeju Gotjawal Provincial Park (p193)
Left Les Jardins de Médongaule (p92)

Jangma, Korea's monsoon season, lasts from mid-June through the end of July – be prepared for heavy rain and high humidity.

Buy a folding fan, handheld motor fan and mentholated wet wipes to cool down during Korea's humid summers.

↗ Gangneung Danoje Festival

Ancient ceremonies for peace, prosperity and bountiful harvests are celebrated for one week starting on the fifth day of the fifth lunar month (usually in June).

▶ Gangneung, p95

↗ Healing Forests

Escape the heat in the shade of Jeju-do's woodlands, where visitors are encouraged to get off their devices and connect with nature.

▶ Jeju-do, p192

JUNE

JUNE
Average daytime max: 21°C

JULY

Korea in SUMMER

School holidays are from mid-July until late August. There are public holidays on 6 June (Memorial Day), 17 July (Constitution Day) and 15 August (Liberation Day).

↓ Hang Ten

Jungmun Beach on Jeju-do and Yangyang on the peninsula's north-east coast are hotspots for riding the waves and learning to surf.

▸ Jungmun Beach, p173

▸ Yangyang, p88 (pictured)

↗ Boryeong Mud Festival

In the last week of July and early August head to Daecheon Beach to wallow in mud pools and take part in stacks of muddy fun and games.

▸ Daecheon Beach, p203

Days of rainfall: 13 (Jeju-do)

AUGUST

JULY
Average daytime max: 26°C

Demand for accommodation at beach resorts peaks between mid-July and mid-August. View tours and overnight adventures in advance at lonelyplanet.com.

Packing Notes

Pack a hat, plenty of sunscreen and have an umbrella handy for shade and rain showers.

Busan International Film Festival

South Korea's top movie festival, held in September in the architecturally stunning Busan Cinema Centre, attracts stars from across Asia and beyond.

▶ Cinematic Busan, p128

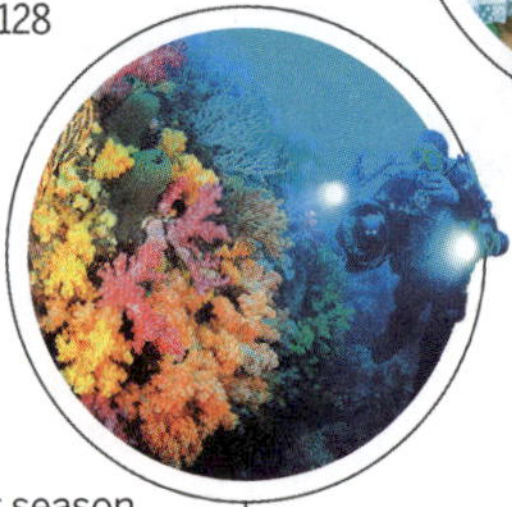

← Mask Dance Festival

This 10-day festival in Andong, kicking off at the end of September, brings together world-class dance troupes from Korea and further afield.

▶ Andong, p109

↗ Active Jeju

Autumn is the best season for diving and snorkelling off Jeju-do as well as for striking out along one of the island's Olle walking trails.

▶ Snorkelling, p172

▶ Hiking, p184

Baekje Cultural Festival

Korea's longest running history and culture festival, going since 1955, is held in Buyeo in even-numbered years and in Gongju in odd-numbered years.

SEPTEMBER

SEPTEMBER
Average daytime max: 25°C

OCTOBER

Korea in AUTUMN

FROM LEFT: SIMON SHIN KWANGSIG/SHUTTERSTOCK, KOBBY DAGAN/SHUTTERSTOCK, TRABANTOS/SHUTTERSTOCK, EKATERINA MARKELOVA/SHUTTERSTOCK
BACKGROUND: GOODBYEWYNTER/SHUTTERSTOCK

If you like hiking, this is the season when the mountains run through a palette of rustic colours – head to national parks including Seoraksan and Jirisan.

▶ Seoraksan National Park, p78
▶ Jirisan National Park, p156

↗ Gwangju Biennale

Held from September until November in even-numbered years, Korea's leading international art show is a two-month carnival of the avant-garde.

▶ Gwangju, p142

↗ Chuseok

The three-day Harvest Moon Festival is a major holiday when families gather and visit their ancestors' graves to make offerings of food and drink.

Days of rainfall: 9 (Seoul)

NOVEMBER

OCTOBER
Average daytime max: 20°C

Book ahead for accommodation and transport around Chuseok, when many Koreans are on the move. View tours and overnight adventures in advance at lonelyplanet.com.

Packing Notes

Have clothing layers and a warm and waterproof jacket on hand for chillier nights.

↘ Spicy Chicken

Warm up a cold winter's day with a sizzling hot plate of *dakgalbi* – this spicy chicken stir-fry is best sampled in Chuncheon, its birthplace.

▶ Eating & drinking in Gangwon-do, p77

Snow Festival

Marvel at giant ice sculptures and enjoy sledding fun at the Taebaeksan Mountain Snow Festival held every January.

Snow on Halla-san

Even though Jeju-do is sub-tropical, be prepared for snow if you choose to tackle 1950m Halla-san, South Korea's highest peak.

▶ Halla-san, p175

↖ Hit the Slopes

Some of Korea's top ski and snowboarding resorts are located in the mountains of Gangwon-do, including the largest, Mona Yongpyong.

▶ Mona Yongpyong, p101

DECEMBER

DECEMBER
Average daytime max: 1°C

JANUARY

Korea in WINTER

FROM LEFT: RAY BHLEE/SHUTTERSTOCK, SUCHART BOONYAVECH/SHUTTERSTOCK, NOOMNA NAKHONPHANOM/SHUTTERSTOCK, SUNGMIN/GETTY IMAGES
BACKGROUND: EMMET LEE/SHUTTERSTOCK

Warm up in a Jjimjilbang

Traditional Korean saunas are great places to relax, particularly so in winter – try Dongdaemun Sparex in Seoul.

▶ Dongdaemun, p56

↗ Nami Island

Made famous by the TV drama *Winter Sonata*, this landscaped island of art and gardens is a visual treat when blanketed in snow.

▶ Nami Island, p86

↓ Seollal

During Seollal, which falls on 7 February in 2027, 27 January in 2028 and 13 Feburary in 2029, Koreans visit relatives, honour ancestors and eat traditional foods.

Days of rainfall: 5 (Pyeongchang)

FEBRUARY

JANUARY
Average daytime max: 1°C

Demand for accommodation peaks during the Lunar New Year (late January to early February). Book tours and overnight adventures in advance at lonelyplanet.com.

Packing Notes

Bring thermal underclothes, a down jacket, sturdy waterproof boots, gloves and a warm hat.

Wonderful Wildflowers

Blossoming trees are not the only spring horticultural pleasure in Korea: head to the mountains and national parks to see an amazing variety of wildflowers.

↙ Buddha's Birthday

In late April or early May, masses of colourful paper lanterns are strung in temple courtyards across Korea to celebrate the Buddha's birthday.

↓ Blossom Forecast

The earliest cherry blossoms are seen on Jeju in mid-March, with Seoul and northern Korea hitting peak bloom in early April.

↗ Jongmyo

Held at Seoul's Jongmyo shrine on the first Sunday of May, this ceremony honours Korea's royal ancestors and includes a magnificent costumed parade.

▶ Jongmyo, p44

MARCH

APRIL

MARCH
Average daytime max: 14°C

Korea in SPRING

May is one of the most pleasant months in which to visit Korea, with good weather and plentiful accommodation options.

FROM LEFT: PKPHOTOGRAPH/SHUTTERSTOCK, VARIOUS IMAGES/SHUTTERSTOCK, SERGIO CAPUZZIMATI/SHUTTERSTOCK, YONHAP/NEWCOM/ALAMY, ST_TRAVEL/SHUTTERSTOCK
BACKGROUND: HABIBUR383/SHUTTERSTOCK

↘ Chuncheon International Mime Festival

The lakeside city hosts street performers, magicians, acrobats and quirky shows featuring top mime artists from across the world.

▸ Chuncheon, p84

↖ Suncheon Bay National Garden

In mid-May canola blooms create fields of gold at this vast southern coastal garden that contains a staggering 3.15 million flowers.

▸ Suncheon, p155

Days of rainfall: 8 (Busan)

MAY

APRIL
Average daytime max: 18°C

Demand for accommodation peaks during the cherry blossom season (early April). Book tours and overnight adventures in advance at lonelyplanet.com.

Packing Notes

Bring your raincoat and warm clothes as the weather can still be wintry and wet.

SEOUL & NORTHERN KOREA
Trip Builder

TAKE YOUR PICK OF MUST-SEES AND HIDDEN GEMS

Spend three or four days enjoying the capital's highlights, then head east to the lovely lake district surrounding Chuncheon. Cross the peninsula's central mountainous spine for the coastal delights of Sokcho, Yangyang and Gangneung.

Trip Notes

Hub towns Seoul, Chuncheon and Sokcho

How long 11 days

Getting around Subways, trains and buses will get you anywhere in Seoul and easily out to Chuncheon. Join a tour to visit the DMZ. Renting a car will give more flexibility in visiting the Garden of Morning Calm and places around Gangwon-do.

Tips Pick up your rental car at Gimpo Airport or in Chuncheon to avoid having to drive through central Seoul.

CLOCKWISE FROM BOTTOM LEFT: SAHACHATZ/SHUTTERSTOCK, CHARLES USHER/LONELY PLANET, TRABANTOS/SHUTTERSTOCK

The DMZ & Imjingak Resort
Join a tour, or travel independently to Imjingak (pictured above), to get as close as you can to the fascinating and forbidding no-man's land separating North and South Korea.
45min from Seoul

Seoul
Visit museums and royal palaces, hike the Seoul Wall, explore Bukchon's picturesque *hanok* neighbourhood, shop and eat street food in Myeong-dong (pictured below), and party in Hongdae and Itaewon.
1hr from Incheon

Seoraksan National Park

Hike to the jagged ridge of Ulsan Bawi, a spectacular granite outcrop in one of Korea's most beautiful national parks.

35min from Sokcho

Sokcho

Take a circuit of serene Yeongnang Lake, grab lunch at Sokcho Tourist Fish Market, pay a visit to Abai Village, then pad across Sokcho Beach to Bada Hyanggi Trail.

2hr from Chuncheon

Chuncheon

Ride Korea's longest cable car across Uiam Lake to the upper levels of Samak-san, dig into *dakgalbi*, Chuncheon's most famous spicy chicken dish, and visit LEGOLAND Korea.

45min from Seoul

Naksan-sa

Stand at the foot of the 16m tall statue of the Goddess of Mercy in this venerable temple, then take in the gorgeous coastal surroundings.

20min from Sokcho

Gangneung

Sip your way around this coastal city's many artisan coffee shops, lounge on its long sandy beaches (pictured below) and visit one of the oldest Joseon-dynasty homes in Korea.

1hr 30min from Sokcho

Nami Island

Sail out to Nami Island, a beauty spot on the Bukhan River famous for its avenues of soaring pines and gingko trees as well as charming art exhibits.

30min from Chuncheon

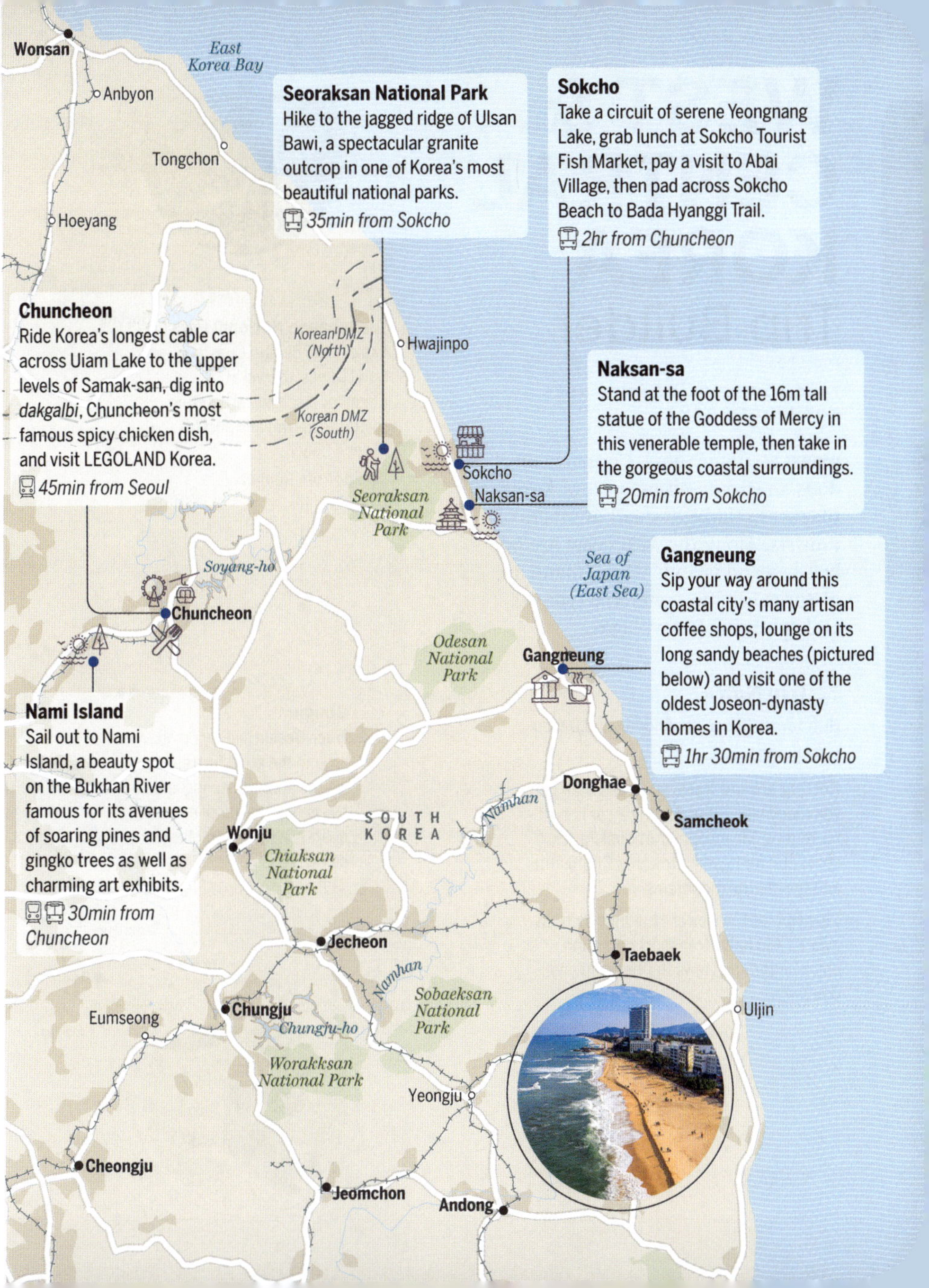

WEST & CENTRAL KOREA
Trip Builder

TAKE YOUR PICK OF MUST-SEES AND HIDDEN GEMS

South of Seoul, Chungcheong-do is an easy-to-access part of Korea that sees relatively small numbers of tourists. Along the west coast are fine beaches and islands while inland are historical sights, venerable temples and charming folk villages.

Trip Notes

Hub towns Cheongju, Andong and Daegu

How long 12 days

Getting around Trains and buses can get you many places but renting a car is best for touring Taeanhaean National Park's coast and for heading towards Chungju-ho and the central mountains.

Tips Opt for the slower Mugunghwa train over KTX to halve transport costs and enjoy hinterland views to Cheongju and Gyeongju.

Taeanhaean National Park
Explore the Sinduri Coastal Sand Dunes, marvel at Cheollipo's seaside arboretum (pictured above) and surf off Mallipo Beach.
2hr from Gongju

Gongju
Trace Baekje history on hikes around the great fortress wall of Gongsan-seong and by visiting the burial mounds of Korean royalty (pictured below).
1hr 15min from Seoul

CLOCKWISE FROM BOTTOM LEFT: STOCK FOR YOU/SHUTTERSTOCK, PTERA/SHUTTERSTOCK, LIES OUWERKERK/SHUTTERSTOCK

Chungju-ho
Take a pleasure boat cruise across the tranquil waters of Korea's largest lake and enjoy gorgeous views of the surrounding mountains.
1hr 15min from Cheongju

Hahoe Folk Village
Stay overnight and watch a traditional *byeolsingut talnori* mask dance performance (pictured above) at this World Heritage Site of thatched roof homes.
1hr from Andong

Andong
Seek out Andong Market Jjimdak Alley, a street dedicated to the city's famous chicken dish, and try the local firewater Andong soju.
1hr 30min from Chungju-ho

Cheongju
Visit the Early Printing Museum, the Culture Factory and MMCA Cheongju in this youthful city with an appealing small-town vibe.
40min from Gongju

Bulguksa
Meditate in the precincts of this World Heritage Site temple, which rises amid pine forest on a series of stone terraces.
1hr from Gyeongju

Gyeongju
Walk around the capital of the Silla kingdom for almost a thousand years, home to more tombs, temples, pagodas, Buddhist statuary and palace ruins than anywhere else in South Korea.
55min from Andong

SOUTHERN KOREA
Trip Builder

TAKE YOUR PICK OF MUST-SEES AND HIDDEN GEMS

Starting in Busan, the nation's second-largest city, this itinerary soon leaves urban Korea behind to explore green and rural Jeolla-do. Stacked with places of historical note and scenic beauty, there are opportunities to sail to islands, dine in seafood restaurants and learn about artistic traditions.

Trip Notes

Hub towns Busan, Gwangju and Jeonju

How long 14 days

Getting around Buses connect every major city and most of the countryside. Within cities, and especially in Busan, punctual and frequent bus services are ideal for getting around without worrying about parking.

Tips The Visit Busan Pass offers 24 (₩55,000) or 48 hours (₩85,000) of access to more than 30 city attractions plus discounts at over 200 additional establishments.

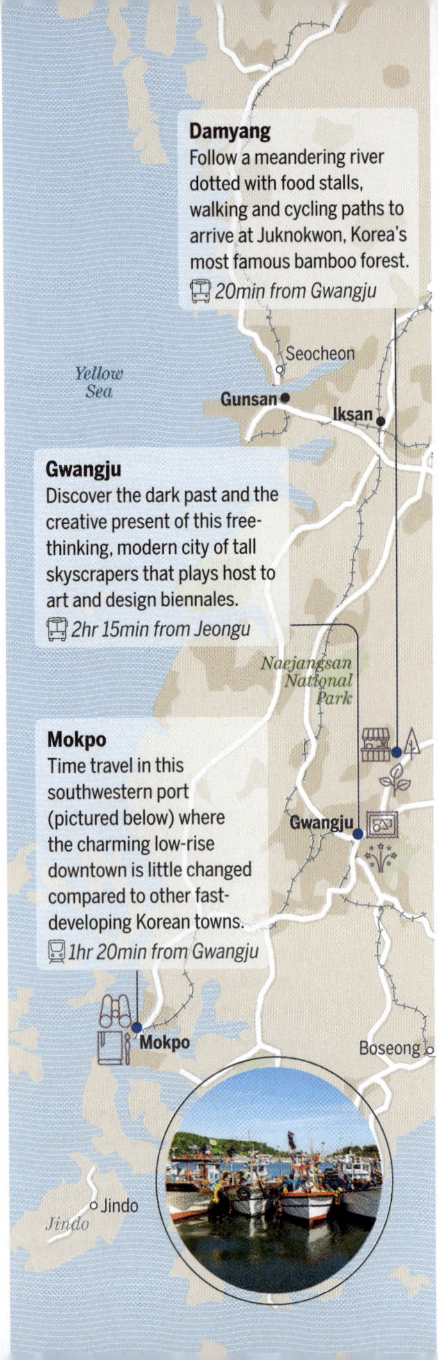

CLOCKWISE FROM BOTTOM LEFT: PHOTO_JEONGH/SHUTTERSTOCK, FINN STOCK/SHUTTERSTOCK,NGHIA KHANH/SHUTTERSTOCK

Jeonju
Wander the atmospheric cobbled lanes of the touristy yet picture-perfect Hanok Maeul at the heart of Jeollabuk-do's provincial capital, pausing at cafes and boutiques as you go.
3hr 40min from Busan

Jirisan National Park
Hike the Korean peninsula's highest mountain within Korea's largest national park – the traverse of Jirisan's main ridge typically takes three days and two nights.
1hr from Suncheon

Busan
Browse the incredible array of seafood at Jagalchi Fish Market (pictured above), then explore gorgeously colourful Gamcheon, the poster child of Busan's cultural villages.
15min from Busan train station

Suncheon
Immerse yourself in the greenery of this Jeollanam-do city where nature comes to the fore and the entire downtown has been transformed into perfectly manicured gardens.
2hr 15min from Busan

Tongyeong
Climb aboard a sailing boat in this balmy coastal city to tour some of the over 100 islands in the beautiful Hallyeohaesang National Park (pictured right), Korea's first marine park.
1hr 35min from Busan

JEJU-DO
Trip Builder

TAKE YOUR PICK OF MUST-SEES AND HIDDEN GEMS

Korea's largest island offers fascinating volcanic landscapes, Korea's highest peak and dozens of sandy beaches. Located 85km off the southern tip of the peninsula it has a balmy (but windy) climate, unique culture and history, fierce freediving women, and superb walking trails.

Trip Notes

Hub towns Jeju-si and Seogwipo

How long 12 days

Getting around Driving on Jeju-do is fairly easy, with English signs on roads and English-language GPS systems in rental cars. Buses will get you lots of places. Several routes circle the island, circumnavigate Halla-san and run between Jeju-si and Seogwipo.

Tips The Jeju Olle Trail, which spans 437km along 27 routes, is the premier way to walk the island.

CLOCKWISE FROM TOP LEFT: STOCK FOR YOU/SHUTTERSTOCK, TRABANTOS/SHUTTERSTOCK, SIMON SHIN KWANGSIG/SHUTTERSTOCK

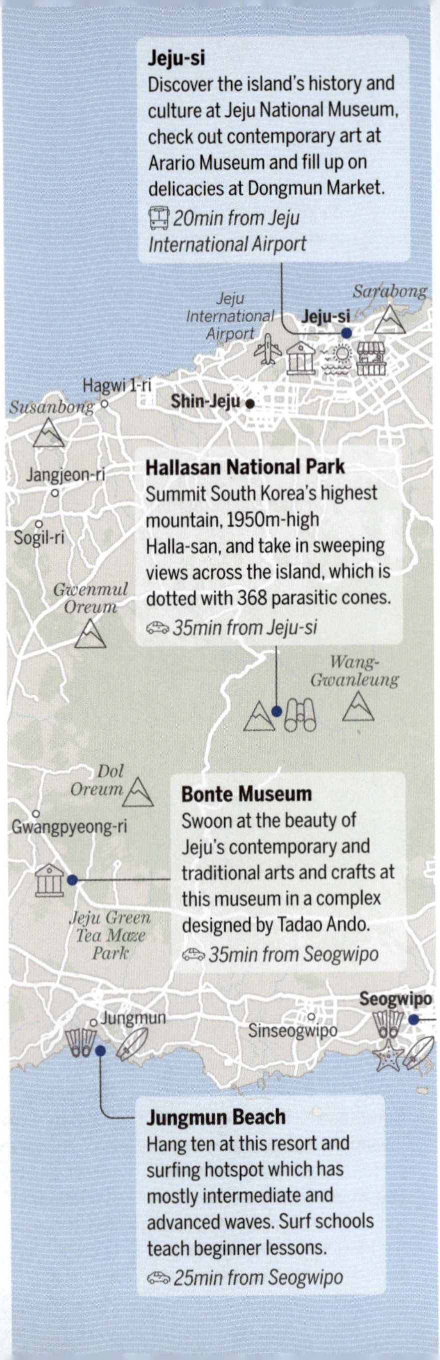

Hado-ri

Head to this attractive beach along the northeastern coast to find the excellent Haenyeo Museum where you can learn all about Jeju's amazing women divers.

1hr from Jeju-si

Udo

Hop on a ferry to this island where you can sample peanut *makgeolli*, ice cream and burgers, and hike one of the scenic Olle trails (pictured below).

15min from Seongsan-ri

Seongsan-ri

Spend the night in this coastal village to wake up the next morning in time for a sunrise hike up World Heritage–listed Seongsan Ilchul-bong, an extinct tuff volcano (pictured below).

1hr 30min from Jeju-si

Seogwipo

Go diving off the islands of Seopseom, Munseom and Beomseom where the waters are warm and you can see soft corals, kelp forests and tropical fish (pictured right).

1hr from Jeju-si

7 Things to Know About KOREA

INSIDER TIPS TO HIT THE GROUND RUNNING

1 Chaebol

You will already know their products but once you're in Korea it will become apparent how pervasive and powerful *chaebol* (mega-business conglomerates) are. Controlled by families or groups of wealthy individuals, corporations such as Hyundai, LG, Samsung and Lotte are reckoned to account for as much as 90% of Korea's gross national income with their businesses extending into nearly every economic sector.

2 Dining Lingo

Here are some words and phrases that will come in handy when dining out:

jeogiyo – how to get a waiter's attention; literally means 'hey over here!' but is not considered rude

igeo jom deo juseyo – say this if you'd like your *banchan* (side dishes) refilled

mul jom juseyo – 'please bring me some water.'

jeon chaeshikjuijaeyo – 'I am vegetarian.'

ddaro gyesan hae juseyo – 'please split the bill.'

▶Learn more on p248

3 Braving the Elements

Consider carrying these items with you:

Folding umbrella with UV blocking For sudden showers and sun shade.

Cooling wipes and pocket warmers Buy these from convenience stores to deal with summer sweats and winter chills.

4 How Old Are You?

It may seem impolite but Koreans will ask this question to gauge social standing. Young people are expected to show respect to their elders.

1, 2 & 4: P LITLE P/SHUTTERSTOCK, 6: NYANGMASTER/SHUTTERSTOCK

5 Public Etiquette

Politeness is a cornerstone of Korean culture and language. To be invited into a Korean's home is an honour. Be punctual and bring a small gift for the host. Wear smart clothes and remove your shoes before entering the home. Show respect to elders. Use two hands or your right hand alone to offer or receive something.

▶ See more about etiquette on p247

7 Names

Koreans give their family name first followed by their birth name, for example Lee Myong-bak. There are around 280 traditional Korean family names, with Kim, Lee and Park being the most common, accounting for around half the population. Each surname is associated with a clan name, which indicates its regional origin.

6 Competitive Society

In Korea everything seems to be well organised and fast moving. The locals even have an expression for the phenomenon: *ppalli ppalli* meaning 'quickly'. Underlying this approach to life is the highly competitive nature of Korean society, with the stress starting from birth and rarely letting up – even in retirement as seniors battle it out on golf courses or climbing mountains.

From corporate manoeuvres to elementary-school maths class, everything is competitive. Take, for example, the country's hyper-competitive education system. To get into a top Korean university, high-school students go through a gruelling examination process, spending over half the day or more memorising reams of data for the annual college entrance test known as the Suneung.

Vast amounts of money for private education are required to be competitive at school. *Hagwon* (after-school academies) are rife. As a result, higher education is no longer a social leveller, instead it exacerbates social divisions.

Read, Listen, Watch & Follow

READ

Welcome to the Hyunam-dong Bookshop (Hwang Bo-reum; 2023) A woman quits the corporate world to open a bookstore.

Human Acts (Han Kang; 2014) Multidimensional examination of the 1980 Gwangju uprising.

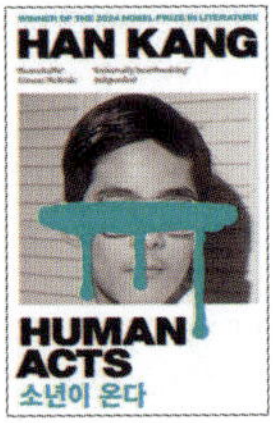

Whale (Cheon Myeong-kwan; 2004) Epic magical-realist tale shortlisted for the International Booker Prize.

Korea: A New History of South and North (Victor Cha & Ramon Pacheco Pardo; 2023) Great overview of modern history.

LISTEN

Love Yourself: Tear (BTS; 2018) First album by the seven-piece boy band to top the US Billboard chart.

Psy 6 (Six Rules), Part 1 (Psy; 2012) EP including 'Gangnam Style', which became a global sensation, bringing K-Pop to new audiences.

The Korea Society Podcast *(koreasociety.org)* Covers a fascinating range of topics – from diplomacy and politics to cooking and crime fiction.

Stories from Korea *(bbc.co.uk/programmes/p090qy63)* Podcasts on many aspects of Korean culture and society from the BBC.

KEVIN MAZUR/GETTY IMAGES FOR MTV/PARAMOUNT GLOBAL

Born Pink (Blackpink; 2022; pictured above) This K-Pop quartet is the most successful Korean girl group internationally.

WATCH

Parasite (2019) A poor family inveigles their way into a wealthy family to devastating effect.

Squid Game (2021–2025) Netflix series in which players risk their lives for money.

Winter in Sokcho (2024) French drama based on a novel by a Swiss-French-Korean writer.

No Other Choice (2025; pictured top) Dark satire about a man's plan to murder his way back into work.

The Last of the Sea Women (2024; pictured bottom) Documentary about female freedivers on Jeju-do.

CAPITAL PICTURES/ALAMY

BFA/HASISI PARK/APPLE TV+/ALAMY

FOLLOW

Korea.net
(korea.net) Government portal about all things Korean.

Koreana
(koreana.or.kr) Quarterly magazine of the Korea Foundation.

Korea Tourism Organisation
(knto.or.kr) Official account for national organisation.

KBS
(world.kbs.co.kr) Key public service media of Korea.

10 Magazine
(10mag.com) Online English magazine with focus on Seoul.

興禮門

SEOUL & AROUND

CULTURE | HISTORY | ENERGY

RESEARCHED BY ANN BABE, SIMON RICHMOND & CHARLES USHER

SAYAN URANAN/SHUTTERSTOCK

SEOUL & AROUND
Trip Builder

If it happens in South Korea, it happens in Seoul, the country's political, cultural and economic capital. Gaze down on royal palaces from ancient city walls, then dive into Seoul's world of K-Pop beats, trendy boutiques and neon-washed nightlife alleys.

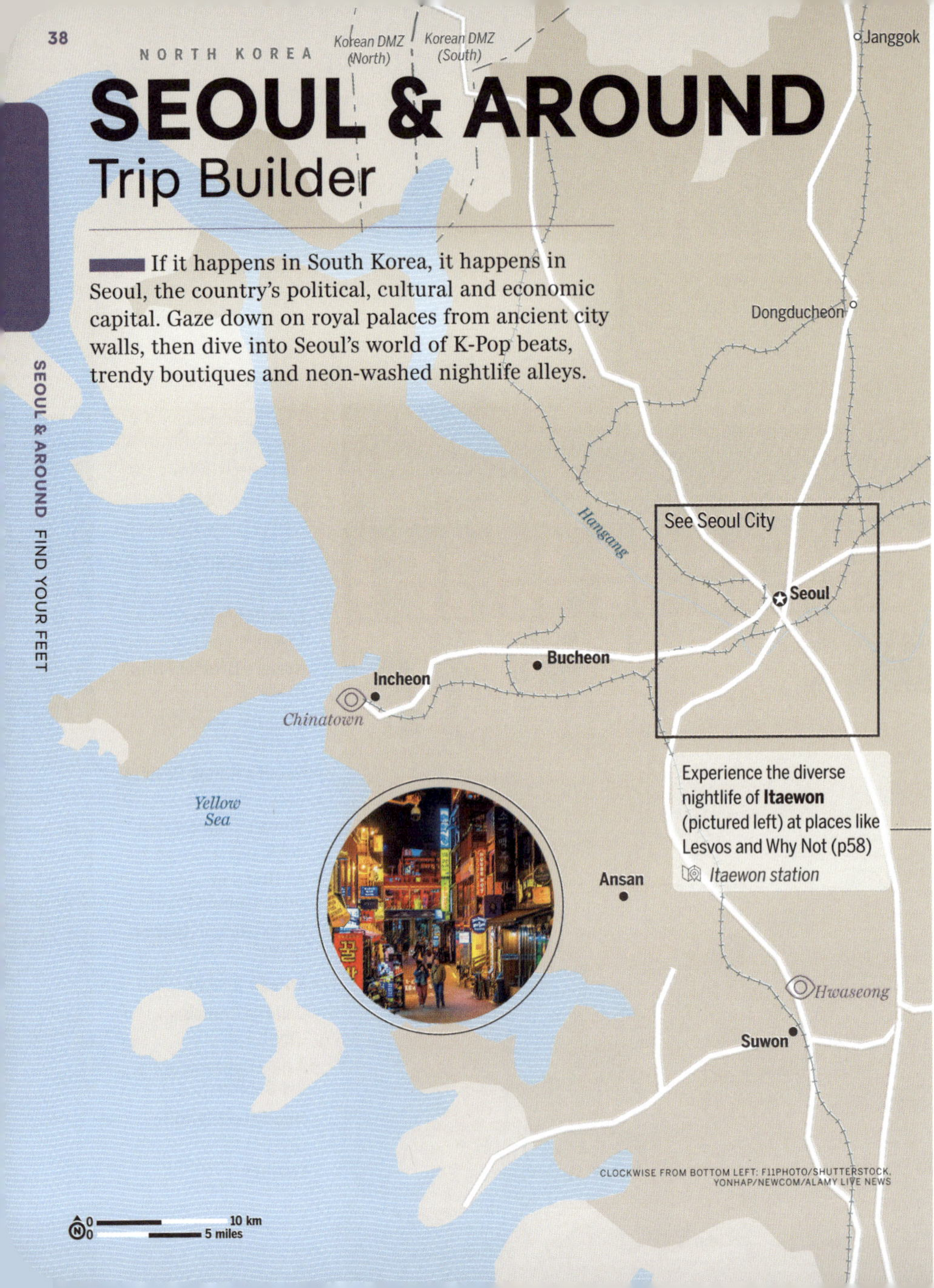

Experience the diverse nightlife of **Itaewon** (pictured left) at places like Lesvos and Why Not (p58)
Itaewon station

CLOCKWISE FROM BOTTOM LEFT: F11PHOTO/SHUTTERSTOCK, YONHAP/NEWCOM/ALAMY LIVE NEWS

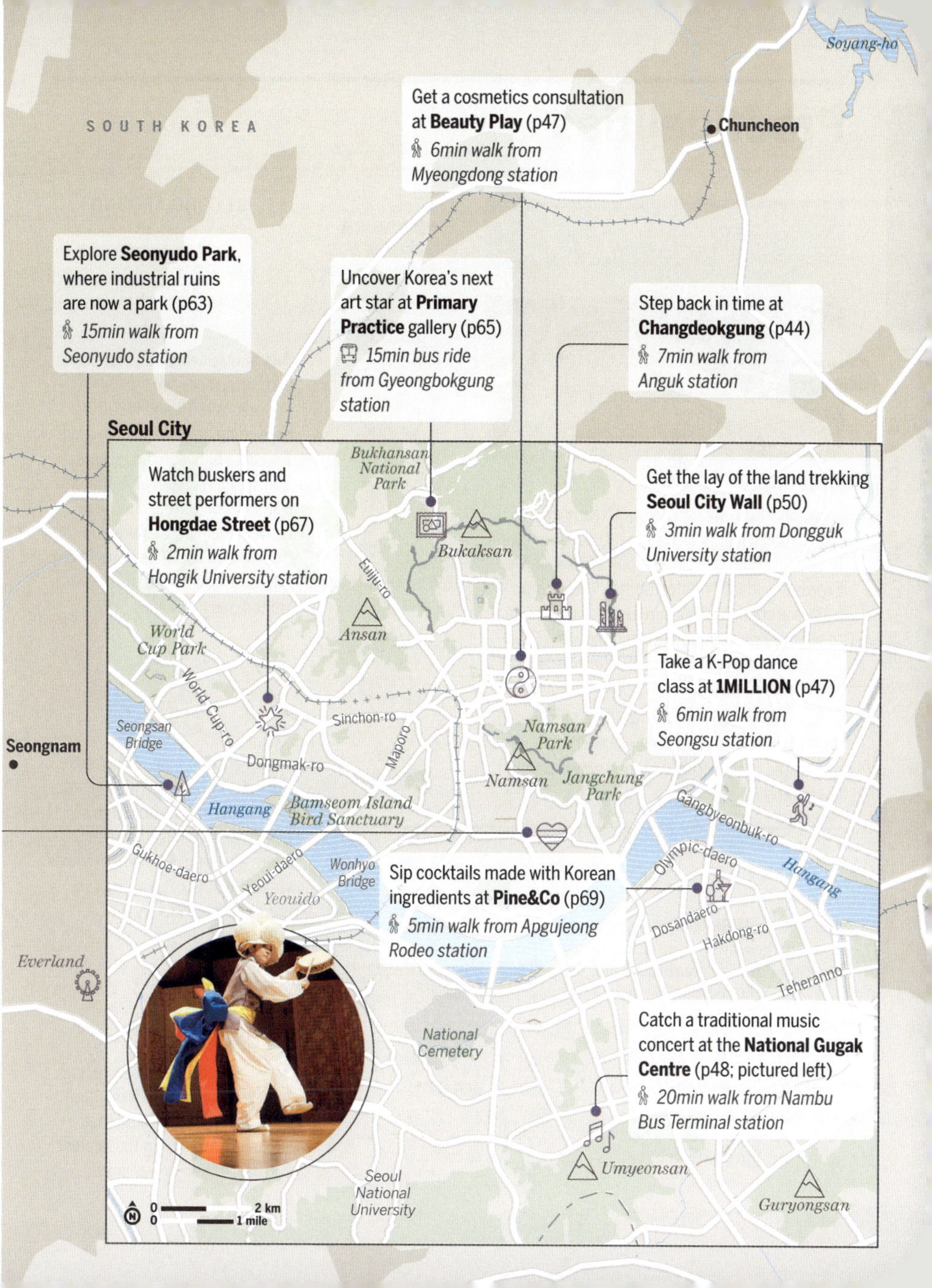

SOUTH KOREA
Soyang-ho
Chuncheon
Get a cosmetics consultation at **Beauty Play** (p47)
6min walk from Myeongdong station
Explore **Seonyudo Park**, where industrial ruins are now a park (p63)
15min walk from Seonyudo station
Uncover Korea's next art star at **Primary Practice** gallery (p65)
15min bus ride from Gyeongbokgung station
Step back in time at **Changdeokgung** (p44)
7min walk from Anguk station
Seoul City
Bukhansan National Park
Watch buskers and street performers on **Hongdae Street** (p67)
2min walk from Hongik University station
Get the lay of the land trekking **Seoul City Wall** (p50)
3min walk from Dongguk University station
Bukaksan
Euiju-ro
Ansan
World Cup Park
World Cup-ro
Take a K-Pop dance class at **1MILLION** (p47)
6min walk from Seongsu station
Seongsan Bridge
Sinchon-ro
Namsan Park
Seongnam
Dongmak-ro
Maporo
Namsan
Jangchung Park
Hangang
Bamseom Island Bird Sanctuary
Gangbyeonbuk-ro
Gukhoe-daero
Yeoui-daero
Wonhyo Bridge
Sip cocktails made with Korean ingredients at **Pine&Co** (p69)
5min walk from Apgujeong Rodeo station
Olympic-daero
Hangang
Yeouido
Dosandaero
Hakdong-ro
Everland
Teheranno
National Cemetery
Catch a traditional music concert at the **National Gugak Centre** (p48; pictured left)
20min walk from Nambu Bus Terminal station
Umyeonsan
Seoul National University
Guryongsan
0 2 km
0 1 mile

Practicalities

ARRIVING

Incheon International Airport Nearly all international flights arrive here. The express train to Seoul station is ₩13,000; buy a ticket at the Express Train Information Centre. The all-stop train is around ₩5000. Limousine buses travel to different neighbourhoods for about ₩17,000. Ticket booths are at the bus platform. A taxi will cost about ₩55,000.

Gimpo International Airport Most domestic flights land at Seoul's smaller airport. It's connected to the airport railroad and subway lines 5 and 9.

HOW MUCH FOR A

Palace admission
₩3000

Barbecue serving
₩15,000

Latte
₩6000

WHEN TO GO

MAR–MAY
Mild temperatures and flowers; yellow dust can create poor air conditions.

JUN–AUG
Hot and humid; late June through July sees frequent rainfall.

SEP–NOV
Warm days, cool evenings, clear skies – Seoul's best travel season.

DEC–FEB
Cold snaps alternate with milder days; occasional snowfall.

GETTING AROUND

Bus and subway Fares for buses and the subway are typically between ₩1500 and ₩2000, depending on distance travelled. Transfers between the two are free. Buy a rechargeable Tmoney transport card from a kiosk or convenience store. Trains run from roughly 5.30am to midnight. Buses run from 4am to 11pm with limited overnight lines.

Taxis Fares for standard orange taxis start at ₩4800 for the first 2km. A late-night surcharge of 20–40% is applied between 10pm and 4am. Black deluxe taxis start at ₩7000. Pay with cash, credit card or Tmoney.

Walking Seoul's city centre is highly walkable and throughout town, you're rarely more than a 10-minute walk from the nearest subway station or bus stop.

EATING & DRINKING

There's almost nothing you won't find in Seoul. One must-try original is *tteokbokki* (pictured top). The rice cakes began as a mild palace food; their current, spicy version was born in the Sindang neighbourhood in the 1950s. The dish encapsulates Seoulites' approach to eating – there's as much satisfaction in street food as there is in fine dining, though there's certainly that, too, especially in Gangnam. The city's meticulous cafes give it arguably Asia's best coffee culture, while its cocktail scene is taking Korean ingredients to exciting new places.

Best craft cocktails
Zest (p69; pictured bottom)

Must-try haute Korean
Onjium (p70)

TOP: 4KCLIPS/SHUTTERSTOCK
BOTTOM: CHARLES USHER/LONELY PLANET

CONNECT & FIND YOUR WAY

Wi-fi Most places offer free wi-fi, even buses and the subway, but connections on transport can be spotty. Rent a pocket wi-fi device or SIM card at the airport. The latter comes with a local phone number, handy for restaurant reservations.

Navigation Google Maps doesn't provide walking or driving directions in Korea. Use Naver Maps to get around.

MONEY

Seoul is largely cashless, but carry a few thousand won in bills to use in traditional markets. You'll save money by sticking to Korean food, which is considerably cheaper than international offerings.

WHERE TO STAY

Seoul's lodging options range from cheap *yeogwan* (inns) to budget-shattering luxury hotels. Start your search by picking a neighbourhood that suits your style.

Neighbourhood	Pros/Cons
Jongno	Historic sites, good public transport and *hanok* (traditional) guesthouses. Gets tourist crowds.
Myeong-dong	Centrally located, lots of options. Budget places involve an uphill hike.
Hongdae	Seoul's biggest nightlife area. Great for after-hours fun but can be loud.
Gangnam	High-end lodging, shopping and dining. Takes longer to reach major sites.
Itaewon	International and LGBTIQ-friendly. Feels less typically Korean than other areas.
Dongdaemun	Good transport links and markets for food and shopping. Busy at night.

DISCOUNT TRAVEL CARD

The Discover Seoul Pass (discoverseoulpass.com) provides free or discounted entry to many of the city's top attractions. The digital version includes a five-day eSIM.

01 Heart of OLD SEOUL

PALACES | TRADITION | ARTS

Seoul's regal heart is Jongno-gu, a district defined by majestic palaces, a secret garden, a royal shrine and other Joseon-dynasty sights that recall the country's last and longest ruling kingdom. In between are celebrated *hanok* and the city's centre of traditional arts and crafts.

ALARAX/SHUTTERSTOCK

How To

Getting there Take subway line 3, getting off at Gyeongbokgung station for Gyeongbokgung, Jongno 3-ga station for Jongmyo and Anguk station for Changdeokgung, Insadong and Bukchon.

Getting around If you're able, walk between sights, as this is a pedestrian-friendly area with plenty of tiny alleyways to go down.

When to go The palaces and royal shrine are beautiful year-round. Changdeokgung is closed Mondays; Gyeongbokgung and Jongmyo are closed Tuesdays.

MIRKO KUZMANOVIC/SHUTTERSTOCK

Majestic Palaces

Of the five major royal palaces in Seoul, Gyeongbokgung and Changdeokgung are the most impressive. **Gyeongbokgung**, meaning 'palace of brilliance and fortune', is the city's largest and oldest. Much besieged over its history, because of fire during the Japanese invasion and demolition during the Japanese occupation, its many halls, pavilions and quarters have been largely reconstructed. Walking through its massive grounds full of ornate architecture, it might be easy to imagine what court life was like here when it was the principal royal residence – particularly if you're dressed up in traditional *hanbok*, as is the popular way to tour, and catch one of the spectacular changing-of-the-guard ceremonies.

JAIONE_GARCIA/SHUTTERSTOCK

Bell Street

Jongno's name comes from the major east-west street Jong-no, which means 'Bell Street', where the Bosingak bell pavillion is located, from which the opening and closing of the city wall gates were signalled. Today Bosingak is a popular gathering spot to ring in the New Year, when the bell (a replica) tolls 33 times to wish for prosperity.

Top left Changing of the guard, Gyeongbokgung **Left** Huwon (p44) **Above** Bosingak bell pavillion

Even prettier than Gyeongbokgung, however, is **Changdeokgung** ('palace of prosperous virtue'), World Heritage–listed for its layout harmonising architecture with nature, including its serene Secret Garden. Covering almost 60% of the palace grounds, **Huwon** is a 'rear garden' of woodlands and glades punctuated by ornamental ponds and pavilions. It's where Joseon royalty relaxed, studied and wrote poems, and where military exercises and banquets were held. The garden's most famous vista is that of the lotus-dotted Buyongji Pond. If you can, try visiting Changdeokgung for a special guided moonlight tour, when the palace grounds, alive with traditional dance and music performances, are at their most magical.

Royal Spirits

Dating to 1395, **Jongmyo**, World Heritage–listed as the oldest and most authentic Confucian royal shrine to have been preserved, houses the 'spirit tablets' of Joseon royalty. While royal bodies were buried in tombs, their spirits resided in 'tablets' – or *sinju* – wooden

Joseon Dynasty Sights

Jongchinbu
Behind the MMCA's main gallery stands the office of royal genealogy.

Sajikdan
This stone altar surrounded by low stone walls and ornate wooden gates dates back to 1395 and King Taejo, founder of the Joseon dynasty.

Dongsipjagak
Once part of Gyeongbokgung's eastern wall, damaged during the Japanese occupation, this watchtower was separated from the rest to make room for a road.

Stone Pagoda of Wongak-sa
Tapgol Park was the site of the temple Wongak-sa, destroyed in 1504. This 10-tier marble monument remained.

Gongpyeong Historic Sites Museum
An exhibition hall with Joseon-era relics excavated during city maintenance.

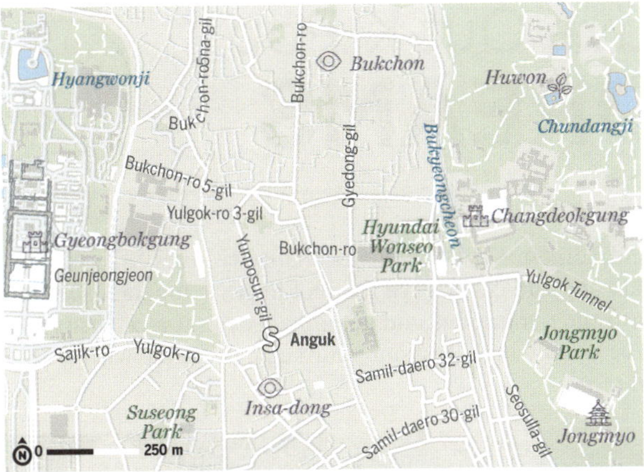

Left Stone Pagoda of Wongak-sa
Below Insa-dong storefront

boxes with small holes bored in the top, bottom and sides. At Jongmyo, the spirits of 49 kings and queens are said to be enclosed in the main hall, Jeongjeon, locked in 19 windowless rooms.

Arts & Crafts

Take a stroll through **Insa-dong**, Seoul's centre of traditional arts and crafts, to find Korean folk souvenirs galore – everything from *tal* (wooden masks) and *buchae* (handheld fans), to calligraphy inks and brushes, *hanji* (Korean paper) and lacquerware. For *hanbok* (traditional clothing), there are designers like **Dolsilnai** and **Leesle**, and for *bojagi* (patchwork wrapping cloths) and other fabric crafts, **Kukje Embroidery**.

Bukchon is another crafts area, with many arts workshops offered at centres, many of them housed in lovely *hanok* like the **Bukchon Traditional Crafts Centre**, which runs a program of the day, such as needle- and patch-work, dyeing and ceramics. At **Kumbakyeon** (금박연), you can learn gold-leaf gilding; at **Dong-Lim Knot Workshop**, ornamental knotting; and at **Gahoe Minhwa Museum**, folk painting.

As much as Insa-dong and Bukchon are known for arts and crafts, they're also known for teahouses. Stop for a soothing cup of *cha* at a teahouse like **Beautiful Tea Museum**.

02 Live Out K-Pop DREAMS

MUSIC | DANCE | FASHION

Pulled to Seoul in the Korean Wave's undertow? The city gives K-Pop fans a chance to cross the velvet rope and experience the idol lifestyle for themselves. Shop the latest fashions in trendy boutiques and get a makeover at a celebrity-approved salon. Once you've got the look, test out your stage presence with a dance class or vocal lesson.

NEWSCOM/ALAMY

How To

Getting there The closest subway station to the Ktown4u Academy is Samseong; for 1MILLION, it's Seongsu; for HiKR Ground, it's Jonggak.

When to go Your best chance of idol-spotting might be at Dongdaemun Design Plaza during Seoul Fashion Week. Check seoulfashionweek.org for dates.

Cost Private classes at Ktown4u Academy cost ₩100,000. Group classes at 1MILLION are ₩30,000. Services at Jenny House start at ₩110,000.

YLLYSO/SHUTTERSTOCK

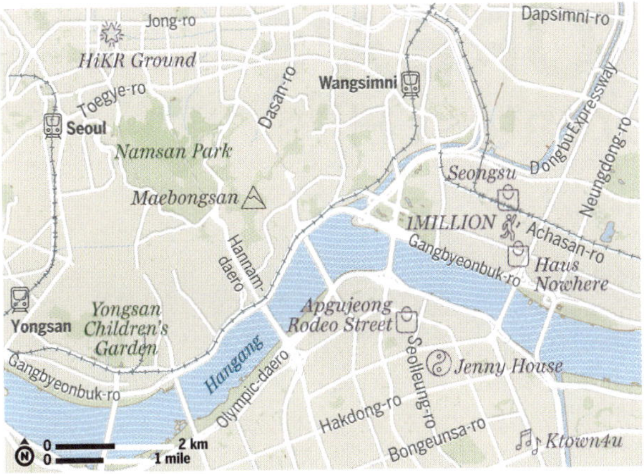

Top left HiKR Ground
Bottom left Haus Nowhere, Seongsu

Vocalist, Rapper or Dancer?

K-Pop groups have designated roles, so let your preferred position guide your idol experience. Always dreamed of being the lead vocalist? The **Ktown4u Academy** (ktown4uacademy.com) offers private classes where a singing coach will take you through your chosen song, giving tips on things like breathing techniques. See yourself more as a group's main dancer? Sign up for a session at **1MILLION** (1milliondance.com), where professional dancers and choreographers teach an array of classes. If you're new to dance or have two *wen-bal* (left feet), the popular Step by 1M introductory class is a great way to get started. Put your skills together at **HiKR Ground** (hikr.visitkorea.or.kr), a tourist info centre and K-Pop playground with five themed stages where you can set the lighting and choose the music for an impromptu photo or video shoot.

Or Visual?

The 'visual' is an idol group's best-looking member and style leader. If that sounds like you, treat yourself to a hair and makeup session at **Jenny House** (jennyhouse.co.kr). The posh salon has styled celebs like Miss A's Suzy and *No Other Choice* star Son Ye-jin. Round out your new look with a swing through the boutiques of **Apgujeong**, Seoul's high-fashion hub, or **Seongsu**, its new trendiest neighbourhood. Both have branches of **Haus Nowhere**, mind-bending retail spaces that are home to celeb-favourite eyewear brand Gentle Monster.

Find Your Style

You don't have to drop a ton of money at a salon to find your idol look. At the K-Beauty experience space **Beauty Play** (beautyplay.kr), you can get a makeup consultation and sample cosmetics from dozens of smaller Korean brands. It also runs classes on topics ranging from skincare to finding your personal colour. Classes are conducted in Korean, but some English explanation can usually be provided. The best part? All of Beauty Play's classes and experiences are free. Beauty Play has two locations, in Myeong-dong and in Hongdae.

03 KOREA'S Greatest Hits

TRADITION | MUSIC | THEATRE

The universe may have begun with the big bang, but Korean music most definitely predates BigBang (the idol group, that is). K-Pop is only the latest iteration of a performing arts heritage that goes back centuries, encompassing everything from royal court music and operatic storytelling to Buddhist dance. Catch a traditional show at one of Seoul's performing arts centres, and be transported to Korea's past.

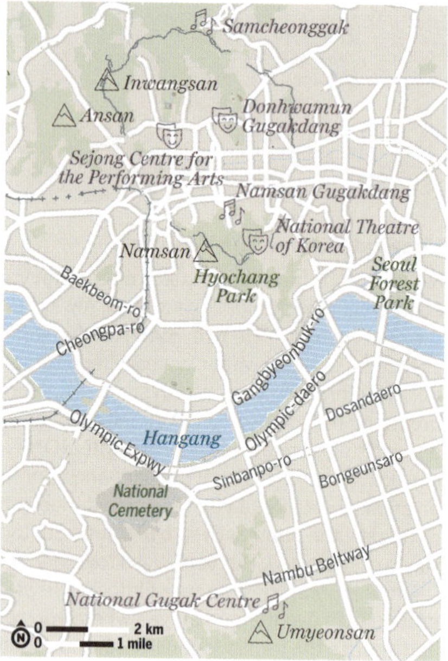

How To

Getting there Other sites are within walking distance of a subway station, but to reach Samcheonggak you'll need to catch a taxi or take bus 1111, 1112 or 2112 from Hansung University station to Seoul Dawon School, then walk 15 minutes.

Top tip Some venues lack an English-language website for ticket purchases. If you can't book online or in person, call Korea's 1330 travel helpline and an interpreter will help you book by phone.

Musical Medleys

Traditional performance still makes its presence felt in modern Seoul, sometimes in unexpected places. Ride the subway and you'll hear a recording of traditional instruments indicating arrival at a transfer station. Turn on the TV, and you might see an ad with a folk singer pitching cellphones.

For an introduction to the breadth of Korea's traditional performance styles, book a spot at one of two weekly events. Every Saturday, the **National Gugak Centre** (gugak.go.kr) holds a concert that runs through a half-dozen different genres, from court dances to regional folk songs. High in the forested foothills of Bugak-san, **Samcheonggak** (samcheonggak.or.kr) was once an exclusive retreat where *gisaeng*, trained female artists, entertained the elite. It's now a restaurant and cultural space that, each Wednesday, hosts an event combining dinner

Traditional Genres

Pansori Epic dramas sung and acted by a solo singer accompanied by a lone drummer.

Pungmul Folk music rooted in agricultural communities that combines drumming and acrobatic dancing.

Samulnori A modern adaptation of folk music that's performed with four percussion instruments.

Seungmu A beautiful dance with Buddhist roots, performed by a dancer in a conical hat and white top with long sleeves.

Jeongak Music performed at formal events like banquets or Confucian ceremonies.

Sanjo Solo instrumental music that's often played on a *gayageum* or *geomungo*, types of zithers.

Talchum Masked dance dramas that typically use humour to satirise the powerful.

and five different traditional performances.

Throwback Theatres

For something more focused, the **National Theatre of Korea** (ntok.go.kr) is home to companies that present *changgeuk* (traditional opera), dance and orchestral music performed with instruments like the *geomungo*, a type of zither, and the *daegeum*, a bamboo flute. Downtown's **Sejong Centre for the Performing Arts** (sejongpac.or.kr) also has a traditional orchestra that plays a few times a year. The twin **Namsan Gugakdang** and **Donhwamun Gugakdang** (sggt.kr) traditional theatres are small spaces where you'll be treated to intimate encounters with time-honoured melodies and movements.

Above Performance, National Gugak Centre

04 Hike the Seoul CITY WALL

HISTORY | ARCHITECTURE | WALKING

Completed in 1396 during the reign of King Taejo, Hanyangdoseong (Seoul City Wall) was built to defend the capital, then called Hanseong. Today, the stone fortifications – which connect Seoul's four inner 'guardian' mountains of Bukaksan, Naksan, Namsan and Inwangsan – are a top visitor attraction. Hiking trails take you up close to the historic wall and provide awesome views.

CHAN008/SHUTTERSTOCK

How To

Getting there and around You can hike the Wall's entire 18.6km route in a single (exhausting) day. It's better to split the circuit up over two days, or choose one of the four sections to focus on.

When to go Best walking seasons are late April and May and early November.

Top tip Pick up a free map and walking guide at the **Seoul City Wall Museum**.

STEVE JANGS/SHUTTERSTOCK

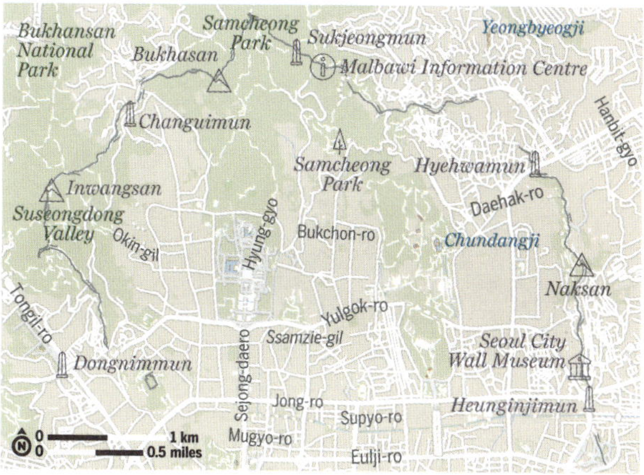

Hiking the Wall

Between 5m and 8m in height, the wall runs around downtown Seoul, with just under 80% of it restored. The shortest and least strenuous route is 2.1km over Naksan between the sub-gate **Hyehwamun** and **Heunginjimun**, one of the four original principal gates in the wall. Here the fortress wall cuts a graceful, sinuous curve through the city and provides beautiful vistas.

Although just 342.5m high, **Bukaksan**'s rocky terrain and steep granite outcrops make it a tough climb. For over half a century, most trails up and across Bukaksan were strictly off-limits to protect the presidential compound **Cheong Wa Dae**. Now that the 'Blue House' has been decommissioned, all routes on the highest of Seoul's four guardian peaks are open to the public.

If you're up for the challenge, try the 2.5km route that rises steeply from **Changuimun**, the old subgate in Buam-dong. The trail hops over the peak above Cheong Wa Dae to the **Malbawi Information Centre** near **Sukjeongmun**, the main north gate, which can also be accessed from **Samcheong Park**. The wall is in excellent condition and there's a vivid sense of its original purpose as the city's last line of defence – especially in the sections where barbed-wire-topped fences and guard posts remain as vestiges of the mountain's prior high-security status.

Top left Heunginjimun
Bottom left Hanyangdoseong at Bukaksan

Summit Inwangsan

From the top of **Inwangsan** (339.9m) you can clearly see how the old city nestled inside its guardian mountains. For the least amount of climbing start at **Changuimun** and follow the Seoul City Wall west.

Another popular route is the **Seonbawi Trail** from the historic arch **Dongnimmun** beside **Independence Park**. Along this you will pass **Inwangsa** (인왕사), a Buddhist temple, before reaching the *musok* (animist religion) shrine **Inwangsan Guksadang**. Climb up above the shrine to find **Seonbawi**, a rock formation that resembles a robed monk praying. Women wanting to become pregnant come here to ask for blessings.

■ By Simon Richmond
@simonrichmond

Seoul's Hanok Revival

K-ARCHITECTURE IS MAKING A COMEBACK IN THE CAPITAL

Among the most popular areas of Seoul today are the *hanok*-lined streets and alleys of Bukchon and Seochon. Here and elsewhere in the city you can eat, drink, shop and stay overnight in these appealing traditional wooden buildings – many vintage and renovated, others newly constructed.

Left Eunpyeong Hanok Village
Centre View of Eunpyeong Hanok Village from the development's cafe
Right Baek In-je House

PHOTO CREATOR CH/SHUTTERSTOCK

Back in the 1990s, *hanok* were under threat of disappearing almost completely from Seoul. Few locals considered these old-fashioned residences, which were difficult and often costly to maintain, to be worthy of preservation. This process had been ongoing since the start of the 20th century when Japanese colonisers destroyed Seoul's monumental palaces and surrounding residential districts, replacing them with modern concrete and stone buildings.

Hanok, which translates as 'Korean house', began to be used to refer specifically to vernacular wooden homes in the late 19th century, to distinguish them from Western-style buildings that were shooting up following the opening of the then Hermit Kingdom to international trade. Today, the legal definition is a 'wooden building with its main structure that consists of columns, beams, Korean-style roof frames, reflecting the traditional style of Korea'.

The *hanok* revival took off in the early 2000s, as foreign visitors began to show an interest in all things traditionally Korean, roughly at the same time as locals started to gravitate to retro Korean styles and put a new spin on them in a trend known as 'newtro'. City governments around Korea, including Seoul's, started providing subsidies for building new *hanok* and for restoring old ones.

Seoul Hanok 4.0

In 2001, protection for Bukchon's handful of remaining *hanok* was strengthened as part of Seoul's first *hanok* development policy. Plans were fine-tuned in 2008 to focus on preservation and promotion, and again in 2015 to develop living conditions to make *hanok* villages more inhabitable.

CHERRYDONUT/SHUTTERSTOCK

RAISAMACOUZET/SHUTTERSTOCK

A result of these policies has been **Eunpyeong Hanok Village**, a 2014 development in the northwest of the city. Here you can view contemporary, two-storey wooden buildings that blend *hanok* architecture with modern design and convenience. In Bukchon is the flagship store of beauty brand **Sulwhasoo**, an award-winning renovation of a 1930s *hanok* that's ingeniously integrated with a neighbouring concrete building from the 1960s. Around it are proliferations of stylish *hanok* conversions for rental homes and boutique-style guesthouses such as those managed by Nostalgia (nostalgiaseoul.com) and Stayfolio, a Korean-based homestay platform.

> The hanok revival took off in the early 2000s, as locals started to gravitate to retro Korean styles.

In 2023 the city launched its Seoul Hanok 4.0 plan. The aims of this latest policy are encapsulated in the motto 'new *hanok*, daily *hanok* and global *hanok*' – to expand design support for *hanok*, to build more new *hanok* villages across the city and to promote Korean culture internationally.

The most ambitious reimagining of the *hanok* is not in Seoul but 180km southeast in Yeongwol-gun, Gangwon-do. Here **The Hanok Heritage**, Korea's largest *hanok* hotel, opened in 2025. Special technology was developed to strengthen the wood used in the hotel's construction, allowing a scale and grandeur that is more palatial than usual humbler, Confucian influenced *hanok* abodes. In short, the future is looking bright for modern *hanok*.

What is a Hanok?

The most common form of *hanok* are one-storey wooden homes topped with clay-tiled roofs. The walls are insulated with mud and straw. Rooms look onto a *madang* (courtyard). Furniture was sparse and life was lived on the floor, above the *ondol* (underfloor heating system).

Unlike the ostentatious manor homes of Europe, even the *hanok* of the upper class – for example, **Seokpajeong**, an elegant late Joseon villa in Buamdong and **Baek In-je House**, a grand *hanok* from 1913 in Bukchon – were designed to blend with nature. They are typically left unpainted, their earth tones and cosy scale providing a warm, intimate feel.

Korea's Cultural
HAN ICONS

01

02

03

04

01 Hangeul (한글)
Korea's phonetic writing system, created under the leadership of King Sejong the Great in 1446 and much celebrated because it democratised literacy.

02 Hanja (한자)
Before hangeul, the Chinese characters used to write the Korean language, still seen in places like signage, newspaper headlines, calendars and birth records.

03 Hanbok (한복)
Korean traditional clothing, consisting of a top *(jeogori)*, along with a skirt *(chima)* for women and trousers *(baji)* for men.

04 Hanok (한옥)
Korean traditional house, characterised by *ondol* (underfloor heating), wood and other natural materials, *kiwa* (roof tiles) and, traditionally, separate spaces for men and women.

05

06

07

08

09

05 Hansik (한식)
From the quintessential kimchi, to *bap* (cooked rice), *banchan* (side dishes) and beyond, *hansik* is 'Korean food'.

06 Hanji (한지)
Handmade from mulberry tree bark, Korea's traditional paper is known for its beautiful textures and surprising strength. It was used to cover doors and windows, and for craft arts.

07 Hanyak (한약)
Korean traditional herbal medicine, which treats ailments by restoring the body's energetic balance.

08 Hangang (한강)
Korea's 'Great River', flowing west-to-east through Seoul. Not the country's longest in length, but its biggest by volume and flow rate.

09 Hanryu (한류)
More recognisable in its romanised form of *hallyu*, it's the Korean Wave that's sweeping the world, from Albania to Zimbabwe.

01 MIUNMIUNAN/SHUTTERSTOCK, 02 SKYXVOLT/SHUTTERSTOCK, 03 YOOJIWHAN/SHUTTERSTOCK, 04 SUN_SHINE/SHUTTERSTOCK, 05 VVOE/SHUTTERSTOCK, 06 SOBEAUTIFUL/SHUTTERSTOCK, 07 TUPUNGATO/SHUTTERSTOCK, 08 SPARKLINGLEMON123/SHUTTERSTOCK, 09 MAXBELCHENKO/SHUTTERSTOCK

05 24 Hours in DONGDAEMUN

FASHION | SHOPPING | HISTORY

Perpetually on-the-go Dongdaemun offers multi-storey shopping malls, piled high with on-trend fashions and open around the clock; iconic architecture, both historic and otherworldly; and plenty of places to eat and relax, including one of Seoul's largest *jjimjilbang* (traditional Korean saunas).

How To

Getting there Dongdaemun or Dongdaemun History & Culture Park are the most convenient subway stations.

When to go At night DDP (Dongdaemun Design Plaza) is often used as a giant canvas for projected image and light shows.

Top tips Between April and November on Sunday, an excellent farmers and craft market is held in DDP's Oulim Square (@marchefriends). Check the DDP website (ddp.or.kr) to see if rooftop tours of the building are running.

Live Performances

Between April and December every Thursday at 7pm there's a professional performance of traditional Korean music, dance or theatre at **Gwangmudae** (@Gwangmudae), a theatre hidden away on the 10th floor of the N building of Dongdaemun Shopping Complex.

01 Dongdaemun (meaning Great East Gate) is the common name for **Heunginjimun** (pictured below), one of eight historic entrances through Seoul City Wall. The gate's last full reconstruction was in 1869.

02 Dongdaemun Grilled Fish Alley is lined with small, no-frills restaurants (open daily 8.30am to 8.30pm) specialising in tasty charcoal-grilled *samchi* (Spanish mackerel), plaice and other fish.

03 For insights into the architectural ingenuity of **Dongdaemun Design Plaza** (DDP; pictured far left) join the free English tour at 1.30pm Tuesday to Sunday, starting from the M3 entrance off Miraero Bridge.

04 Central Asia Street (중앙아시아거리; pictured right) is a small area stacked with restaurants such as **Star Samarkand** serving food from Russia and the 'Stans.

05 After a long day of shopping and sightseeing relax at **Dongdaemun Sparex** (blog.naver.com/sparex4400). Open 24 hours it includes dry and wet saunas, ice and clay rooms, and a sleeping area.

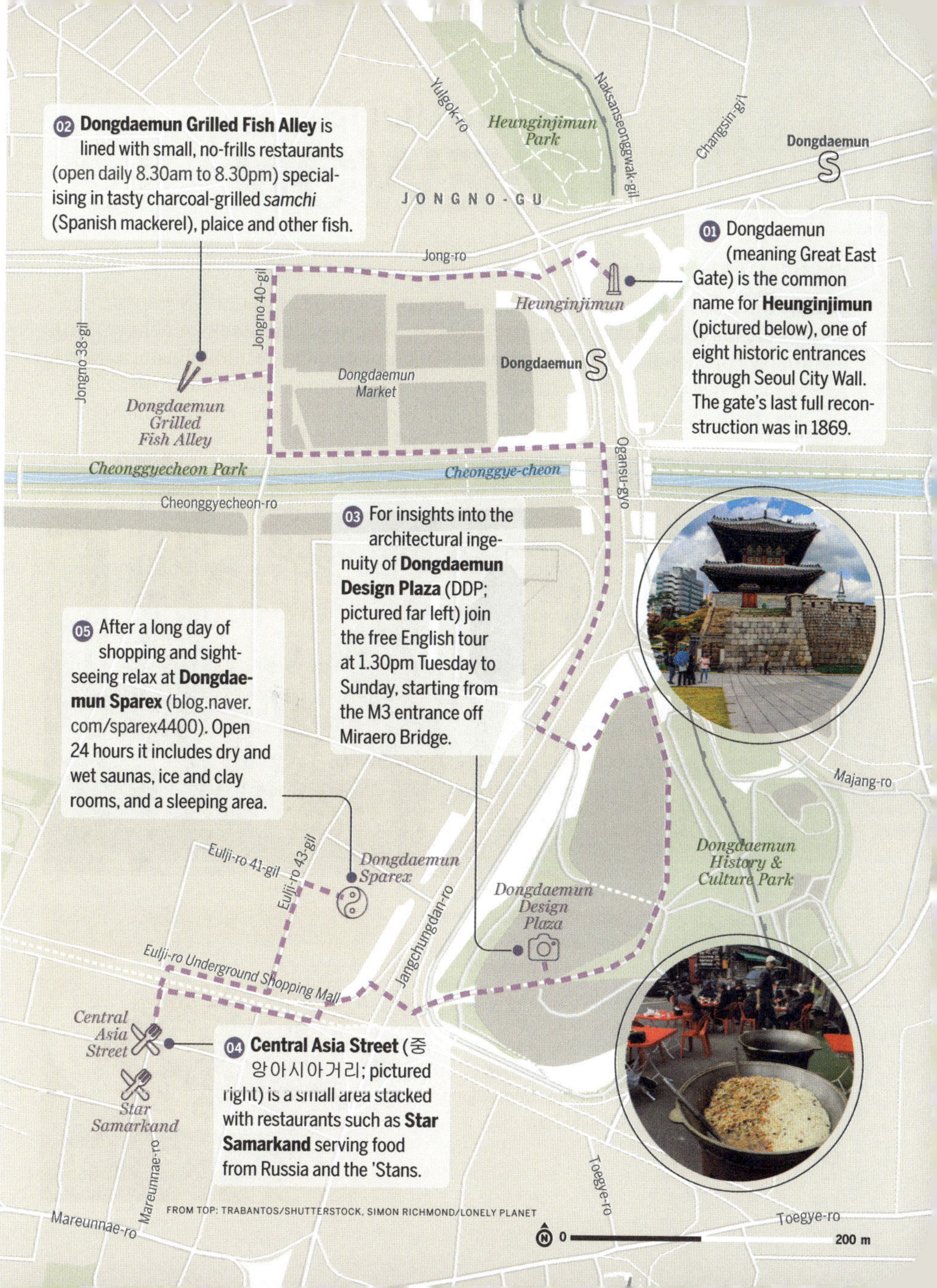

FROM TOP: TRABANTOS/SHUTTERSTOCK, SIMON RICHMOND/LONELY PLANET

06 International ITAEWON

MULTICULTURAL | VIBRANT | FOOD

Koreans sure do love a global food trend, and the restaurant scene of Seoul's ultimate district of diversity, Itaewon, is hard to top. Itaewon delivers with a culinary cornucopia of Latin, Southeast Asian, European, Middle Eastern, North African and beyond – with more than a few only-in-Korea fusion surprises along the way. It's a dynamism that's found in the district's entertainment scene, too.

F11PHOTO/SHUTTERSTOCK

How To

Getting there Take subway line 6, and get off at Noksapyeong station for Haebangchon and Itaewon station for Itaewon.

Getting around While the main Itaewon-ro is flat and walkable, things get hilly in Haebangchon on the way to Sinheung Market. Be prepared.

When to go Many restaurants are closed Mondays, as well as during an afternoon break time from around 3pm to 5pm.

GONTABUNTA/SHUTTERSTOCK

Top left Itaewon nightlife
Bottom left *Mapo tofu*

World Flavours & Global Music

Itaewon St spots The area around Itaewon-ro is Seoul's most international dining district. North of Itaewon-ro, stop at **XOLO Pub Mexicano** for Mexican-Korean fusion like *birria ramyeon*; one of the many Irish or British-style pubs; **Ya Shanghai** for *mapo tofu* and *dim sum*; or a Turkish kebab stall. Cross to the south side of Itaewon-ro, and sit down to a loaded platter of American brisket at **Linus' BBQ**; *borscht* and other Russian fare at **Troika**; or South African meat pies at **Braai Republic**. Clustered around **Seoul Central Mosque** is an amazing array of Muslim restaurants, like **Lazzat** for halal Uzbek and Central Asian cuisine. And around **Quy Nhon St** (Bogwang-ro 59-gil) are a plethora of *pho* shops.

Back-alley dining In the alleys of hilly Haebangchon, **Sinheung Market**, a former textiles centre, is now a buzzy cultural space full of fine-dining restaurants, rooftop lounges, and wine and cocktail bars with an intimate speakeasy vibe. Stop at **Ginn-Laoo** or **Pad Kapaw** for authentic and immaculate northeastern Thai fare, or **Vin Vin** for a modern European menu starring seafood, beef tartare and other protein-forward plates.

Global sounds Itaewon's diversity extends to its music scene, with jazz playing at venues like **All That Jazz** and **Boogie Woogie**; rock at **Pet Sounds**; and visiting international DJs at **Cakeshop** and **Faust / Tanz Bar**.

Inclusive Nightlife

Itaewon hosts Korea's most international, inclusive and LGBTIQ+-friendly nightlife.

Lesvos
Since 1996, this lesbian bar has been a safe space for sexual minorities and women in Korea.

Rabbithole Arcade Pub
Located in Haebangchon, this basement venue offers weekly drag shows and a welcoming vibe.

Kockiri
A hip gay bar that plays disco and caters to a diverse clientele. Its beautiful terrace is a plus.

Why Not
The perfect place to begin the night before hitting the clubs next door. Known for being foreigner-friendly.

Queen
Now in a new location, popular among foreigners for its fun atmosphere that doesn't really get going until 2am.

KOREAN SNACKS

01

02

03

04

05

06

01 Tteokbokki
Rice cakes cooked in a spicy sauce made from *gochujang*, sugar and other ingredients. The undisputed king of street food.

02 Sundae
Blood sausage stuffed with glass noodles and usually served with a mix of salt and chili flakes for dipping.

03 Eomuk
Also called *odeng*, these fishcakes are often folded and skewered. Use the brush or spray bottle to apply soy sauce.

04 Twigim
Squid, sweet potato and mixed veggies are the most common varieties of these deep-fried snacks, Korea's take on tempura.

05 Hotteok
Especially popular in winter, these griddled pancakes are traditionally filled with a mix of brown sugar, nuts and cinnamon.

06 Bungeo-bbang
Their name means 'carp-bread', but they're not seafood, just crispy fish-shaped treats filled with sweet red bean paste.

07

08

09

10

12

11

07 Mandu
Korean dumplings, served either fried or steamed. The most common fillings are ground meat *(gogi)* and kimchi.

08 Hot dog
What Koreans call a corn dog. Some varieties include cheese or a coating of fries. Topped with ketchup, mustard and sugar.

09 Dalgona
A childhood classic, this honeycomb candy saw its popularity spike after making a dramatic cameo in *Squid Game*.

10 Dak-gangjeong
Bits of fried chicken tossed in a spicy and sweet sauce, sometimes with crushed peanuts and chewy fried rice cakes.

11 Gyeran-bbang
Eggs and a pancake-like batter are cooked together in a mould; these 'egg-breads' might be topped with ham or parsley.

12 Hway-ori-gamja
Spuds are cut into a long spiral, then skewered, deep-fried and seasoned to make these 'tornado potatoes'.

01 GOWITHSTOCK/SHUTTERSTOCK, **02** JIHUN SIM/SHUTTERSTOCK, **03** IKA HILAL/SHUTTERSTOCK, **04** CHANGJU KANG/SHUTTERSTOCK, **05** GY D'ZIGN/SHUTTERSTOCK, **06** PENNY RICHARDS/CC BY-SA 4.0/WIKIMEDIA COMMONS, **07** INK N PROPELLER/SHUTTERSTOCK, **08** KAMPOL JONGMEESUK/SHUTTERSTOCK, **09** KIRILL ALEKSANDROVICH/SHUTTERSTOCK, **10** HELLO_JI/SHUTTERSTOCK, **11** AUTSAWIN UTTISIN/SHUTTERSTOCK, **12** VANIA ZHUKEVYCH/SHUTTERSTOCK

■ By Charles Usher
@charlesreclausher

Call it a Comeback

TRABANTOS/SHUTTERSTOCK

SEOUL'S RISE AND REINVENTION

Seoul's journey over the past 75 years is an astonishing success story. Decimated by the Korean War, the city rebuilt in a mad developmental rush. Once rebuilt, it set about reinventing itself, emphasising nature and design to create a more liveable metropolis. Sites across the city tell the story.

Left Cheonggye-cheon
Centre Haneul Park
Right Oil Tank Culture Park

The four decades following the Korean War (1950–53) were a period of incredible growth and change in Seoul. The city's population boomed, doubling to nearly 3 million in the first postwar decade, as people flooded the capital in search of work. Seoul couldn't keep up with the influx, and shantytowns popped up around the city. Refugees and impoverished arrivals erected shacks along the banks of the Cheonggye-cheon downtown and improvised settlements called *dal-dongnae*, or moon villages, on mountain slopes at the city's edges.

To cope with its ballooning population – 5 million by 1970, 8 million by 1980 – and spurred by the growing economy, Seoul entered a period of frenzied development. There was no time for consideration of the environment or civic beauty. It was build first, ask questions later. Utilitarian low-rises and cookie-cutter high-rises went up across the city. The Cheonggye-cheon was paved over and an elevated highway constructed in its place. The Han River became a spillway for industrial waste, and its scenic island Seonyudo, once the realm of poets, was given over to a water treatment plant. On the west side, hulking oil tanks were built to store kerosene and diesel, and the orchid-filled island Nanjido was turned into a landfill, with mounds of trash reaching 100m high.

Second Lives

That was the first, necessary stage of Seoul's turnaround. The second began in the late 1990s when, finally secure in its prosperity, Korea began focusing on making its cities more liveable. In Seoul, this often meant undoing what had just been done. The signature example is the

TRABANTOS/SHUTTERSTOCK

©KOREA TOURISM ORGANIZATION – CHOI RIN

Cheonggye-cheon. After the city tore down the elevated highway and restored the stream in the early 2000s, the waterway became a haven for wildlife, a favourite urban retreat for Seoulites and one of the city's most popular tourist destinations.

You can see the fruits of similar efforts across town. Next to the Seoul World Cup Stadium, the city buried the Nanjido dump and built **Haneul Park** on top. It planted oak and wild pear trees, and it created an artificial wetland to provide a habitat for otters, frogs and birds. The adjacent oil storage facility was reborn as **Oil Tank Culture Park**, the tanks transformed into concert and exhibition venues. Seonyudo's water treatment plant was decommissioned, and the entire island was turned into **Seonyudo Park**, which has won international awards for a design that incorporates the old infrastructure. The Han River itself has been the subject of a long-term restoration project, with large portions of its banks made into popular green spaces like **Yeouido Hangang Park**. Measures to develop forest and wetland along the river are ongoing.

> Making cities more liveable meant undoing what had just been done.

Even some poor postwar neighbourhoods have received similar treatment. In 2006, the city set out to revitalise northeastern Seoul's **Ihwa Maeul** *dal-dongnae* through public art, and artists and college students spent six months filling its walls with murals. The project turned the area into an unlikely tourist destination, and while some residents expressed displeasure with the neighbourhood's new character and crowds, over time the makeover has been embraced – yet another example of Seoul's ability to reinvent itself.

The Miracle on the Han River

After the Korean War, Seoul was in ruins and South Korea was one of the world's poorest countries. A decade on, the national GDP remained a paltry US$4 billion. Driven by a combination of shrewd government planning and intense effort across the workforce, the country achieved an extraordinary turnaround: a renaissance that came to be known as the Miracle on the Han River. By 1990, GDP was a respectable US$283 billion, and by 2006, it had reached US$1 trillion. Today, South Korea has the world's 12th-largest economy, something that would have been unthinkable just a few decades ago.

07 Asia's Contemporary ART CAPITAL

MUSEUMS | GALLERIES | ART FAIRS

Korea's growing cultural clout has seen Seoul emerge as a major contemporary art destination. Buyers fly in for international art fairs, and venues such as MMCA Seoul keep the city flush with boundary-pushing work. Meanwhile, art aficionados can hunt for the Korean art world's next big thing in dozens of edgy galleries.

©KOREA TOURISM ORGANIZATION – LEE BUMSU

How To

Getting there The MMCA, Art Sonje Centre, Kukje Gallery and Arario Gallery are all a short walk from Anguk station. Use Hangangjin station for the Leeum and Samseong station for Coex.

When to go Frieze Seoul and Kiaf Seoul are both usually held in September, while October brings the Seoul Street Arts Festival, when public performances are held along the Cheonggye-cheon. Unfold X, which combines tech and art, takes place in November or December.

©KOREA TOURISM ORGANIZATION – IR STUDIO

Top left Seoul Museum of Art
Bottom left COEX

Must-see museums The crown jewel of Korean art museums is the **National Museum of Modern and Contemporary Art** (MMCA Seoul; mmca.go.kr). Start your visit with *MMCA Collection: Korean Contemporary Art*. Inaugurated in 2025, it's the museum's first permanent exhibition and offers a crash course in modern Korean art's most important figures, such as the genre-defying Yang Haegue and current art-world darling Kim Ayoung, who blends video, sculpture and AI. The **Seoul Museum of Art** (sema.seoul.go.kr) has expertly curated exhibitions that range from Korean artists' solo shows to international examinations of the occult. Other major institutions with must-see shows dedicated to Korean artists include the **Leeum Museum of Art** (leeumhoam.org) and the **Amorepacific Museum of Art** (apma.amorepacific.com), both in Yongsan-gu.

Galleries galore From the MMCA, it's easy to hop between the area's excellent galleries. Many shows at the **Art Sonje Centre** (artsonje.org) bring together domestic and international artists, putting Korean work in a global context, while the **Kukje Gallery** (kukjegallery.com) and **Arario Gallery** (arariogallery.com) also host top-tier shows. Further afield, two galleries currently generating buzz are **Primary Practice** (primarypractice.kr), focused on emerging Korean artists, and the new **Frieze House Seoul** (frieze.com), affiliated with the major international art fair.

All's fair Speaking of Frieze, in 2022, Seoul became the contemporary art fair's first Asian outpost. To really immerse yourself in art, time your trip to coincide with Frieze Seoul, usually held concurrently with the Kiaf Seoul (kiaf.org) art fair. Both take place at **COEX** (coexcenter.com), in Gangnam.

The New Korean Artists

Korean contemporary art isn't a monolithic genre, and the artists at the forefront of Korea's art scene have long since cast aside the imposing shadow of Paik Nam-june. While technology and its effects on society is still a contentious topic among Korean artists, so are issues like reinterpreting histories, subverting cultural norms, questioning dominant ideologies and asserting the autonomy of one's sexual identity. Video and installation art are particularly popular among the country's Millennial and Gen Z artists, whose rise has shaped the direction of Korean art toward increasingly conceptual examinations of perception and reality in the digital age.

■ **Andy St Louis** is Director of Frieze House Seoul. *@seoulart friend*

08 Non-Stop NIGHTLIFE

COCKTAILS | BEER | NIGHTLIFE

Seoulites play as hard as they work, and the city is at its most vibrant after dark. Join the late-night crowds to sample traditional alcohols, sip some only-in-Seoul cocktails and explore the city's diverse nightlife offerings.

CHARLES USHER/LONELY PLANET

How To

Getting home The Seoul subway runs until midnight on weekends and 1am on weekdays. Night buses run all night but are infrequent, and routes are limited. Get the Kakao T app to reserve or summon a taxi.

Cost Expect to pay about ₩8000 for a pint at a craft brewery, ₩10,000 for a basic cocktail and ₩25,000 for a top craft cocktail.

Top tip Don't tip. It's not part of bar culture in Korea.

4K-CLIPS/ALAMY

Cha-Cha-Cha

A customary Seoul night out unfolds in three stages. The first stage, or *il-cha*, is dinner, often Korean barbecue washed down with soju, beer or *somaek*, a combination of the two. *Yi-cha*, stage two, is a bar for more drinks and maybe some *anju* (bar snacks). The last stop, *sahm-cha*, is the *noraebang*, or karaoke room. By that point, any inhibitions are hopefully gone, so grab the mic and let 'er rip. If you want to show off, get one of the glass-walled rooms at **Luxury Su Noraebang** (sunoraebang.com) that overlook bustling **Hongdae Street**.

CHARLES USHER/LONELY PLANET

Nightlife Neighbourhoods

These spots each have a vibe all their own.

Hongdae This is Seoul's centre of alternative culture, popular with students and arty types. Head here to watch street performers along

Convenience Store, Corner Pub

Having a beer or some soju outside a convenience store is a common pastime in Korea, and many shops have patios with tables largely for this purpose. Not only is it cheap but, with plenty of snacks at hand and built-in people-watching, it's a fun alternative to the bars.

Top left Hongdae Street
Left Performers, Hongdae Street
Above Luxury Su Noraebang

Hongdae Street (Eoulmadang-ro), catch live music at venues like **Jebi Dabang** and **Club FF** or dance at **NB2**, **MODECi** and other clubs.

Itaewon The city's most international neighbourhood draws a fun mix of expats and young Koreans. Follow a stylish crowd to **Glam Lounge** or score cheap drinks at the American-style pub **Thursday Party**. Seoul's best gay scene is in the bars along Usadan-ro 12-gil.

Gangnam Sophisticated cocktail bars pepper the side streets near Sinsa and Apgujeong Rodeo stations. Drop by **Villa Records** for 'molecular' spins on classic recipes or go down the rabbit hole for whimsical concoctions at **Alice Cheongdam**.

Euljiro Bars and machine shops share neon-lit alleys, giving this central neighbourhood a unique atmosphere. Options run the gamut from **Seendosi's** artistic-industrial space and **Euljiro Brewing's** craft pours to **Tabacchi** for wine and gelato sets and **Nogari Alley** for street beers.

Tips from a Makgeolli Maker

On your trip to Seoul, you'll meet *makgeolli*, a gently sweet, lightly fizzy fermented rice wine. Seek out traditional versions from 9% to 14% ABV for deeper texture and savoury notes. Drink it from traditional ceramic cups and pair it with crispy *jeon* (savoury pancakes). Korea also makes clear rice wine called *cheongju*, or *yakju*, that's best sipped with seafood. Skip the mass-produced soju in green bottles and try craft versions at 40–50% ABV for nutty, fruity elegance. Pour and receive drinks with two hands, never pour your own and say '*jan*' or '*geonbae*' when toasting.

■ ***Joe Kim*** is founder of Baekusaeng Makgeolli. *@baekusaeng.mak*

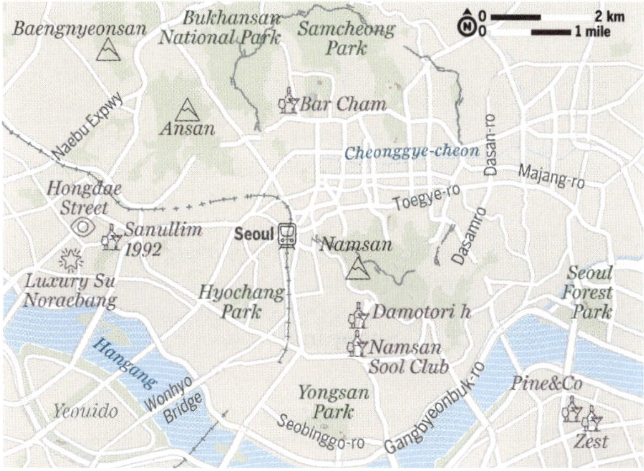

Left Baekusaeng Makgeolli
Below Villa Records

Korean Cocktail Bars

Recent years have seen the rise of the Korean cocktail, with skilled bartenders using traditional ingredients to craft drinks you won't find anywhere else. In Apgujeong, the wizards at **Zest** combine ingredients like Jeju millet soju, soy sauce and upcycled corn silk to produce cocktails that have made the bar one of the best in Asia. Make a reservation through Catchtable (catchtable.net) at least two weeks in advance. A few blocks away, **Pine&Co** works similar wonders. Try its Nuruk cocktail, made with a traditional fermentation starter and toasted barley. In Seochon, **Bar Cham** has drinks inspired by, and using ingredients from, the country's various regions: chestnut with bourbon for Chungcheong-do, the native *deodeok* plant and angelica-infused gin for Gangwon-do.

Modern Jumak

Sample more Korean flavours at modern *jumak* that specialise in traditional alcohols. In Itaewon, **Namsan Sool Club's** English-speaking sommeliers will guide you through more than 100 types of *makgeolli* (milky rice wine), soju and more. Nearby, **Damotori h** offers sampler sets of craft *makgeolli* from around the peninsula to help you find your favourite. In Hongdae, the rustic **Sanullim 1992** stocks some 250 different traditional bottles and serves excellent food pairings.

Listings

BEST OF THE REST

Markets

Namdaemun Market
Next to the eponymous gate, Korea's oldest and largest market has thousands of shops selling everything from souvenirs to eyeglasses. Food alleys are devoted to noodles and braised hairtail.

Noryangjin Fisheries Wholesale Market
Half of the capital's seafood passes through this market near Yeouido, from tuna and blue crabs to octopus and fermented skate. On-site restaurants prepare fresh *hoe* (sliced raw fish) and seafood soups.

Gwangjang Market
Gorge on *bindaetteok* (mung-bean pancakes), *yukhoe* (raw beef) and a sea of other Seoul food at one of the city's best *meokjagolmok* (food streets). Then head to the upper floors for vintage and clothing bargains.

Tongin Market
Stop at this Seochon market to grab a midday meal at Lunchbox Cafe, where you can buy tokens (₩5000 for 10) to spend on helpings of dishes from the various food stalls.

Jungang Market
This covered market arcade, the beating heart of the hip Sindang district, has stalls serving *haemul pajeon* (seafood pancake), *hotteok* (glutinous rice dough pancakes with cinnamon and honey filling), *hoe* and Tex-Mex tacos.

Dongmyo Flea Market
One of Seoul's coolest (not to mention most sustainable) shopping locations surrounds Dongmyo Shrine where you'll encounter piles of used clothing on the street and shops trading in quality hand-me-down fashion.

Yangnyeongsi Herb Medicine Market
Browse hundreds of specialised stalls selling all manner of roots, seeds, barks, dried flowers, fruits and vegetables, and check out the exhibition on traditional medicine at the Seoul K-Medi Centre.

Shopping

Notdam
Sells gorgeous *bangjja* (brassware) of the sort that once graced royal tables and is now a fixture of Seoul's Michelin-starred restaurants. Near Gangnam-gu Office station.

Eating

Hadongkwan ₩₩
This Myeong-dong institution has been making simple, perfect *gomtang* – beef and rice soup seasoned with scallions and black pepper – for nearly 90 years.

Wooara ₩₩₩
At this *omakase* (chef's choice) spot near Gwanghwamun, refined multi-course meals starring Korean beef and seasonal ingredients are served with impeccable presentation in elegant private rooms.

Onjium ₩₩₩
Contemporary fine dining in a sophisticated setting in Seochon, with an open kitchen, counter seating and views of Gyeongbokgung.

Drinking

Coffee Hanyakbang ₩
Down what might be the narrowest alley in Seoul, this Euljiro cafe creates a time-warp aesthetic with old pharmacy fixtures and lots of mother-of-pearl.

Gopchang Jeongol ₩

This Hongdae basement bar runs on nostalgia, with DJs playing classic 1960s to '90s pop that frequently inspires impromptu singalongs.

Suyeonsanbang ₩₩

Once home to novelist Yi Tae-jun, this is one of Seoul's most charming *hanok* teahouses. Sit on the verandah with a view of the garden while relaxing with traditional drinks and sweets.

Parks

Gyeongui Line Forest Park

Built atop a former railroad, this long, narrow green space sits between Hongdae and the trendy Yeonnam neighbourhood. It's surrounded by shops, cafes and restaurants and offers unparalleled people-watching.

Olympic Park

Created for the 1988 Summer Games, this massive park in southeastern Seoul contains Olympic facilities, museums, nearly 200 sculptures and the remains of an ancient earthen fortress.

Seoul Forest

Bounded by the Han River and the Jungnang Stream, this extensive and leafy park includes a sika deer enclosure, butterfly garden (May to October), insect garden, ponds and public art.

Bukhansan National Park

Summit Seoul's highest peaks in this 76,922 sq km reserve bestriding the city's northern reaches. Hike lower slopes for abundant nature, rushing streams, serene temples and Joseon dynasty fortifications.

Cultural Treasures

Sungnyemun

Also known as Namdaemun, this is the oldest and largest of the historic City Wall gates, though it had to be restored following a 2008 arson attack. Near Seoul station.

JEJIM/SHUTTERSTOCK

Chinatown, Incheon

National Museum of Korea

In Yongsan, survey centuries of Korean culture and art at the country's most visited museum, spanning three floors and some 270,000 national treasures, dating from prehistoric times to the Joseon dynasty.

Jogye-sa

Learn about Buddhism at one of Seoul's most active temples, the hub of the Jogye Order and epicentre of the spectacular Lotus Lantern Festival in spring.

Day Trips

Incheon

There's lots to explore in this seaside city: Korea's biggest Chinatown, the historic Open Port area and a futuristic development built on reclaimed land. *1¼hr by subway*

Suwon

The star attraction of this city is Hwaseong, a grand Joseon-era fortress. Spend a day walking its walls, exploring gates and guard towers. *1¼hr south of Seoul by subway*

Everland

Korea's largest amusement park has rides galore, but the complex also includes a water park, traditional garden and a superb art museum. *1½hr from Seoul by bus*

GANGWON-DO

MOUNTAINS | BEACHES | ART

RESEARCHED BY SIMON RICHMOND

TANYA JONES/SHUTTERSTOCK

GANGWON-DO
Trip Builder

South Korea's lightly populated and mountainous northeastern province shares a long border with North Korea. It's an adventure playground of incredible national parks, soft sand beaches and heritage attractions including venerable temples, beautiful gardens and wonderful art museums.

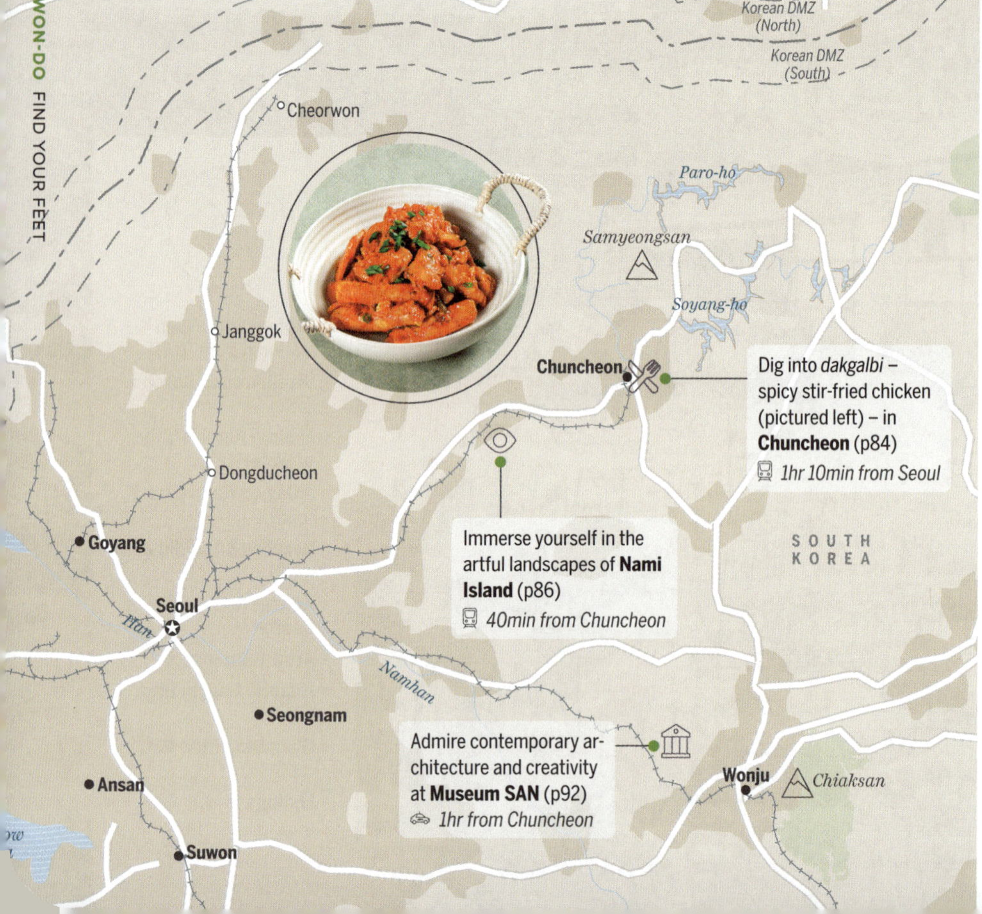

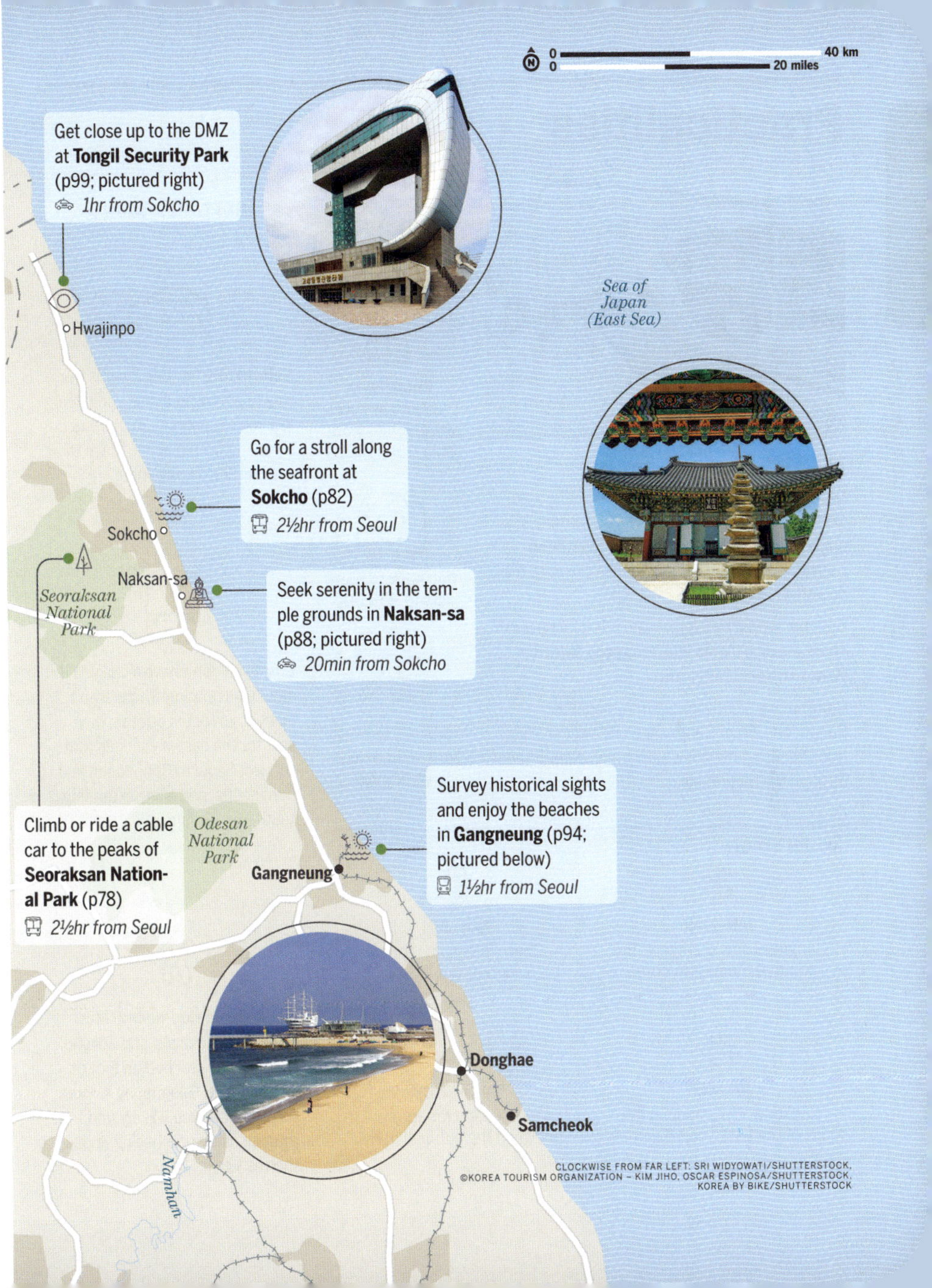

CLOCKWISE FROM FAR LEFT: SRI WIDYOWATI/SHUTTERSTOCK, ©KOREA TOURISM ORGANIZATION – KIM JIHO, OSCAR ESPINOSA/SHUTTERSTOCK, KOREA BY BIKE/SHUTTERSTOCK

Practicalities

KINSTORY/SHUTTERSTOCK

ARRIVING

Chuncheon Well-connected to other cities by express and intercity buses, whose terminals are beside each other near **Namchuncheon** train station. Chuncheon station is closer to the downtown area.

Sokcho Served by express and intercity buses. There are also flights into **Yangyang International Airport** 19km south.

Gangneung KTX trains zip from Seoul to Gangneung. From Gangneung, a slower seaside track heads south. A few slow trains depart Seoul through the mountains.

HOW MUCH FOR A

Chuncheon cable-car ride adult/child from ₩23,000/17,000

Day pass to Nami Island ₩19,000

Snow crab meal for two in Sokcho ₩150,000

GETTING AROUND

Self-driving Renting a car is the way to go. Without one, you'll feel like you're spending more time travelling from place to place than ever settling in anywhere.

Bus If you don't have a car, you'll mostly be bussing. There aren't many train routes out this way, save for the east–west lines that connect Seoul to Chuncheon and Gangneung, and a line extending south from Gangneung.

Walking and ride-hailing Most sights in Chuncheon and Sokcho can easily be reached on foot or by city buses. Gangneung is more spread out so you'll likely find yourself using ride-hailing apps such as k.taxi.

WHEN TO GO

JAN–MAR
Gangwon-do's ski resorts are some of the best in Korea.

APR–JUN
Cherry blossoms fringe Gangneung's lagoon.

JUL–SEP
Cool down splashing in the surf of the East Sea's beaches.

OCT–DEC
Peak season for autumn foliage in the national parks.

TOP: LET GEO CREATE/SHUTTERSTOCK
BOTTOM: SHINE RYU/SHUTTERSTOCK

EATING & DRINKING

Sokcho is famous for its fresh seafood and delicacies such as *ojingeo sundae* (pictured top) – a sausage made by stuffing squid with various ingredients including rice; *abai sundae*, made by stuffing pig intestines with pig blood, cabbage and rice; and *dak gangjeong* – extra crispy fried chicken, coated in a sweet sauce and garnished with peanuts or *deodeok* root.

Chuncheon is synonymous with *dakgalbi*, a stir-fry of spicy gochujang-marinated chicken, cabbage, sweet potato, spring onion and rice cakes. Another staple is the buckwheat noodle dish *makguksu* (pictured bottom).

Best craft beer
Gamja Island (p100)

Must-try dakgalbi
Myeongdong Dakgalbi St (p84)

CONNECT & FIND YOUR WAY

Wi-fi Freely available across Gangwon-do. You will need internet access for navigation apps on your phone.

Navigation Large swathes of Gangwon-do can feel very much off the beaten path, with looming mountains seeming to always block your path. Be patient; go slow and don't try to pack too much in.

WHERE TO STAY

While Sokcho and Gangneung are the largest cities along the East Sea coast, there are scores of smaller towns and villages that are less busy and are pleasant places to stay.

Place	Pros/Cons
Chuncheon	The province's largest inland city. Fast transport links to Seoul. Beautiful lakeside location.
Sokcho	Fine beaches, busy fish markets and easy access to Seoraksan National Park. No train station.
Gangneung	KTX link to Seoul. Excellent beaches, pumping coffee scene and several heritage attractions. Best city hub for nearby ski resorts of Pyeongchang.

CHEORWON VOUCHERS

Whenever you pay for an attraction in Cheorwon, you'll get vouchers that can be used like cash at other attractions and businesses in the town.

MONEY

Keep your admission ticket when you visit some of Chuncheon's major attractions to qualify for a discount at another attraction either the same or the following day.

09 Explore Seoraksan NATIONAL PARK

HIKING | LANDSCAPES | TEMPLE

Covering 173.7 sq km, Seoraksan National Park is a UNESCO Biosphere Reserve. It is visually stunning – especially so during autumn – and home to thousands of different species of plants and animals. The park's main entrance at Seorakdong, near Sokcho, gives access to Oeseorak (Outer Seorak).

CHEONGHAE/SHUTTERSTOCK

How To

Getting there and around Frequent buses run from Sokcho to the Seorakdong entrance.

When to go Upper peaks close to visitors from 15 November to 15 December and 15 March to 15 May.

Top tip Borrow hiking gear, including boots, poles and small backpacks, for free from the **Seorakdong Park Information Centre**.

Templestays Both **Sinheung-sa** and **Baekdam-sa** offer templestay programs. Apply in advance at templestay.com.

JESSE33/SHUTTERSTOCK

Ride the Cable Car

About 1km before the Seorakdong entrance, in a small village packed with accommodation and eating options, is the well-conceived **Seoraksan National Park Visitor Centre** (free) with displays on the park's history, flora, fauna and geology.

Between the centre and the Seorakdong entrance is the **Seoraksan Cherry Blossom Tunnel**, a particularly beautiful walk when the trees are in spring bloom.

A short walk beyond the Seorakdong entrance is the **Seorak Cable Car**. The five-minute ride whisks you up to within a short climb of the natural fortress rocks of **Gwongeum-seong** (860m) for out-of-this-world views. Tickets are for specific timed departures – it's a good idea to book them as soon as you arrive in the park otherwise

CJ NATTANAI/SHUTTERSTOCK

Waterfall Hikes

Park Yongkyu, a volunteer interpreter at the Seorakdong Park Information Centre, recommends the 3.5km course along the Cheonbuldong river valley from the **Biseondae rock** to the **Cheondang** waterfall. 'It's most beautiful in autumn. Another easy hike of around 2.5km is to **Yukdam Pokpo** (falls), and the 40m-high **Biryong falls**.'

Far left Seoraksan National Park in autumn
Left Daecheong-bong (p80)
Above Seorak Cable Car

you may have to wait a while for an available departure slot.

Giant Buddha Statue

About 700m beyond the cable car is venerable **Sinheung-sa**. Founded in 652 CE, the temple has been destroyed and rebuilt many times over the years. First you'll pass the 14.6m-tall bronze **Tongil Daebul** (Great Unification Buddha), dedicated to the hope of reunification between North and South Korea. A little further on, beside the stream and off to the right, is the temple's main prayer hall, its entrance gate guarded by polychromatic statues of the Four Heavenly Kings.

Along Dinosaur Ridge

The ascent to the park's highest peak **Daecheong-bong** (1708m) is a solid tramp of five to seven hours, traversing 10km to 14km, depending on the route you take. Hardcore hikers will want to follow **Dinosaur Ridge**, an undulating stretch with some of Korea's toughest trekking – and most jaw-dropping views.

Ulsan Bawi

From Sinheung-sa it's a roughly three-hour round-trip hike (7.6km) to reach the park's most iconic feature: **Ulsan Bawi**, a spectacular granite cliff with six peaks, the tallest of which is 873m. About 1km from the cliff, you'll arrive at **Gyejo-am**, a Buddhist grotto hermitage dating to 652 CE. Outside, balanced on a ledge is **Heundeul Bawi**. Although *heundeul* translates as 'wobbly', hikers try in vain to shift this giant boulder. The final climb to Ulsan Bawi (including an 808-step metal staircase) is hard going, but well worth it for the panoramic views all the way to the coast.

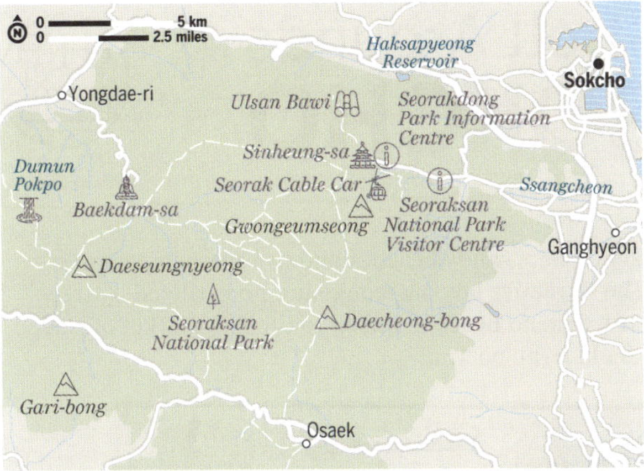

If you'd like to time your arrival at Daecheong-bong to catch the sunrise, as many Korean hikers do, there are mountain shelters along the way. These shelters fill up quickly, so it's crucial to make a reservation in advance via knps.or.kr. You will need to bring your own bedding and food.

The quickest way up Daecheong-bong is from the park's southern **Namseorak entrance**, though the climb is still very steep and difficult, and goes through thick forest, so you lack the wow factor of the main route to the peak. Plan on four hours up and three hours down.

Escape the Crowds

The relatively uncrowded river valleys in the northwestern section of the park are stunners to explore. From the park entrance near **Yongdae-ri**, take a shuttle bus, or hike 6.5km, to the serene temple of **Baekdam-sa**, which faces east and is best appreciated in the morning.

From the temple, you can ramble along the Suryeomdong Valley for an hour or two, or even connect to **Outer Seorak** (seven hours, 14km).

Alternatively, from **Namgyo-ri** there's a splendid 2½-hour hike in the Sibiseonnyeotang Valley to the waterfall of **Dumun Pokpo**.

Left Ulsan Bawi **Below** Baekdam-sa

FROM LEFT: TRABANTOS/SHUTTERSTOCK, LEE WA DA/SHUTTERSTOCK

10 Stroll Around SOKCHO

MARKETS | BEACH | LAKES

Easily walkable, Sokcho offers sandy beaches and fish markets teeming with aquatic abundance. The attractive lagoon Yeongnang-ho is ringed by tree-lined paths, while southward, Sokcho Beach is linked to the fish market of Daepo Port by the coast-hugging Bada Hyanggi Trail.

MASTAPIECE/SHUTTERSTOCK

How To

Getting around A fun way to reach Abai Maeul is to board the *Gaetbae*, an old-school ferry pulled across the narrow stretch of water by steel rope.

When to go April through November are the best months to visit.

Top tip The best view of Sokcho's other lake **Cheongcho-ho** is from the former **Chilsung Boatyard**, revamped into an art exhibition space and an excellent coffee roasters and bakery-cafe.

Sokcho Tourist Fish Market

As well as fish, this covered **market** sells all kinds of goods on several levels. Gathered together here are stalls offering all the local culinary specialities, from *dak gangjeong* (fried and glazed pieces of chicken) to sponge-like breads made with *makgeolli* (rice wine) and rice flour. The fish market is in the basement.

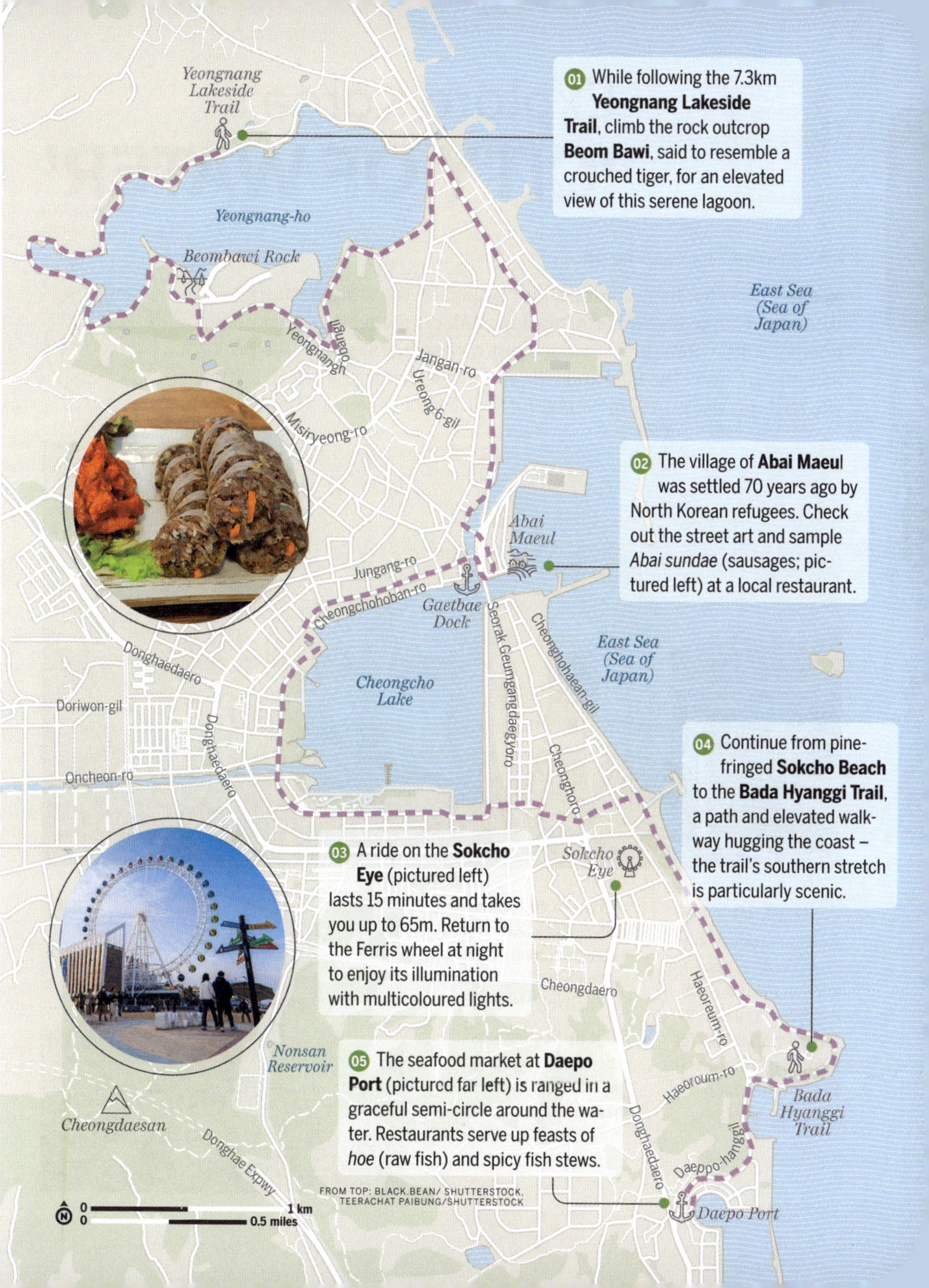

FROM TOP: BLACK.BEAN/ SHUTTERSTOCK, TEERACHAT PAIBUNG/SHUTTERSTOCK

01 While following the 7.3km **Yeongnang Lakeside Trail**, climb the rock outcrop **Beom Bawi**, said to resemble a crouched tiger, for an elevated view of this serene lagoon.

02 The village of **Abai Maeul** was settled 70 years ago by North Korean refugees. Check out the street art and sample *Abai sundae* (sausages; pictured left) at a local restaurant.

03 A ride on the **Sokcho Eye** (pictured left) lasts 15 minutes and takes you up to 65m. Return to the Ferris wheel at night to enjoy its illumination with multicoloured lights.

04 Continue from pine-fringed **Sokcho Beach** to the **Bada Hyanggi Trail**, a path and elevated walkway hugging the coast – the trail's southern stretch is particularly scenic.

05 The seafood market at **Daepo Port** (pictured far left) is ranged in a graceful semi-circle around the water. Restaurants serve up feasts of *hoe* (raw fish) and spicy fish stews.

11 Explore Korea's 'CITY OF WATER'

MOUNTAINS | LAKES | FOOD

Cocooned by mountains and lapped by the shimmering lake of Uiam-ho, Gangwon-do's provincial capital, Chuncheon, is an outdoor hotspot. Glide high on Korea's longest cable car, hike up to the peaks of Samak-san, cycle the lake and ride rollercoasters at LEGOLAND. When you're done, dig into some *dakgalbi* (stir-fried chicken and veggies).

SIMON RICHMOND/LONELY PLANET

How To

Getting around Chuncheon's attractions are fairly scattered. Rent a bicycle from next to the **Memorial Hall for Ethiopian Veterans in the Korean War** or use local buses or taxis.

When to go The **Chuncheon International Mime Festival** in May attracts performers from around the globe.

Top tip Restaurants along **Myeongdong Dakgalbi St** serve the best renditions of the classic Chuncheon chicken dish.

SIMON RICHMOND/LONELY PLANET

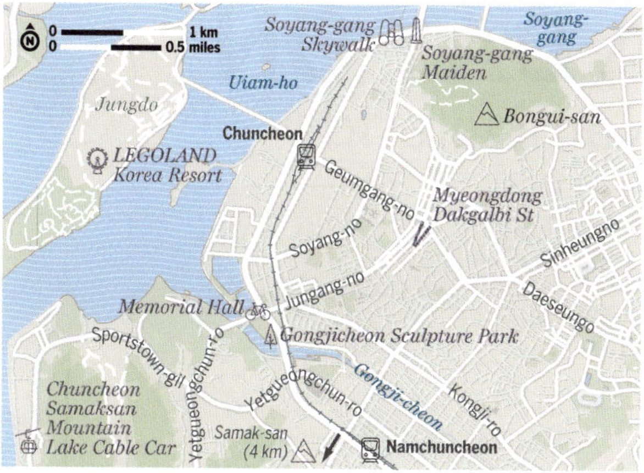

Top left Soyang-gang Skywalk
Bottom left Chuncheon Samaksan Mountain Lake Cable Car

Mountain high Glide high above Uiam-ho on the 3.61km **Chuncheon Samaksan Mountain Lake Cable Car** for breathtaking views of the lake and surrounding mountains. For an additional thrill, pay extra to ride in a 'crystal cabin' with a transparent floor. From the top station, follow the 800m-long Skywalk path to the observatory Skydeck for more panoramic views. A round-trip takes around an hour.

Three peaks There's no way to connect to hiking trails on **Samak-san** from the cable car's top station, so if you want to explore the mountain, plan on doing so separately. So named because of its three peaks – Yonghwabong (654m), Cheongunbong (546m) and Deungseonbong (632m) – Samak-san might have relatively low altitude but its trails are rocky and steep. It takes around two hours to climb to the highest peak from the Deungseon Falls' ticket booth, passing several temples and a fortress along the way.

Riverside stroll Take a leisurely stroll beside the Gongjicheon waterway until you reach the **Gongjicheon Sculpture Park**, where the stream meets the river. Here, locals picnic in the shade of trees among the park's many art pieces.

Beside the lake Continue to Uiam-ho heading in the direction of the **Soyang-gang Skywalk**. This 156m long, glass-floored pier is especially attractive at night when illuminated with multicoloured lights (note it closes at 5.30pm from November to March). Nearby stands a 7m-tall bronze statue of **Soyang-gang Maiden**, the heroine of the 1969 Korean hit song, who waits by the river for her lover to return.

Plastic Fantastic

Family fun is guaranteed at **LEGOLAND Korea Resort**, a multicoloured theme park with attached theme hotel on Jungdo, an island in Uiam-ho. If you've been to any of the other global theme parks of the Danish plastic construction toy company, you'll know the score: Korea's version serves up the same appealing mix of gentle fairground rides and a couple of small-scale white-knucklers alongside scores of LEGO constructions and character models. Most amazing are the detailed reconstructions of Korean landmarks, including an 11m-tall replica of Seoul's Lotte Tower. Book online for discounted tickets.

12 A DAY ON Nami Island

GARDENS | ART | ZIP WIRE

Nami Island, in the Han River 28km west of Chuncheon, is a beautifully landscaped garden featuring soaring metasequoias, avenues of ginkgo trees and art. The 'visa' ticket to the self-styled 'Naminara Republic' includes a return ferry ride – thrill-seekers will want to upgrade for the zip line, which whisks you to the island from an 80m tower in about 1½ minutes.

How To

Getting there Nami Island is around 30 minutes west of Chuncheon by train and bus. The island is small enough to walk around; you can also rent a bicycle or ride a miniature tourist train.

When to go Visit in early November for stunning autumn colours. The island also looks beautiful covered in snow in winter.

Top tip To experience Nami without the day-trip crowds, stay overnight at its comfortable, art-decorated **Hotel Jeonggwanru**.

Arboreal giants Gorgeous at any time of year, Nami Island is most famous for its avenues of majestic metasequoias, pines and ginkgo trees which achieve their golden-leafed peak in early November. This botanical beauty saw it cast as a location in the Korean TV drama *Winter Sonata* first broadcast in 2002. A hit across Asia, the drama pushed Nami into the international spotlight.

Sculptural art Ever since its inception as a tourist destination, the development of Nami's landscape has gone hand in hand with the promotion of arts and culture. Sculptural art abounds, with notable contributions from the Chinese artist Yu Qing Cheng – you will not be able to miss his giant bronze statue **Maternal Love**, featuring a big-breasted mother and child. Look out too for statues of Nami's founder, Minn Byeong-do, and the

TONOITOO/SHUTTERSTOCK

Island History

Nami Island was created in 1944 when the Bukhan River was dammed. This half-moon-shaped, 430,000-sq-metre island is named after General Nami who was executed, aged 28, in 1468 after being falsely accused of treason. The general's traditionally designed grave mound is a feature of the island.

Nami was bought in 1965 by the successful book publisher Minn Byeong-do. He planted the island with flowers and trees and began to develop it into a tourism destination and a showcase for children's book art and music. In 2006, the 'Naminara Republic' was declared, giving the island its own passport and flag.

lead characters from *Winter Sonata*.

Go-to galleries Among the trees are several galleries, the largest one showcasing art from the **Nami Concours**, the island's international picture book competition held every two years. In the **Song Museum Magic Hall** is a collection of ancient and ethnic musical instruments from around the world.

With plenty of restaurants, cafes and scenic spots to picnic in, it's easy to spend the whole day here. Linger a little after sunset, when the avenues and pathways are illuminated by coloured lights.

Above Nami Island in autumn

13 BEACHES & Buddhism

RELIGION | BEACH | SURFING

Founded in 671 CE, and set amid Naksan Provincial Park's stupendous 24km stretch of protected coastline, Naksan-sa is one of Korea's most beautiful Buddhist temples. It's the main attraction of Yangyang, a coastal community offering many gorgeous beaches where you can take surfing lessons or join the experienced surfers riding the waves of the East Sea.

How To

Getting there From Sokcho there are direct buses to Naksan Beach and Naksan-sa. For other beaches further south in Yangyang, you're better off renting a car.

When to go With a wetsuit you can surf year round, with September and October offering the best waves and July and August the warmest waters.

Top tip Naksan-sa offers a templestay program – it's a wonderful way to experience the temple without the daily crowds.

Buddhist Seaside Beauty

With its prime location overlooking the sea, towering effigy of Gwaneum, the Goddess of Mercy, and polychromatic buildings set amid serene, wooded grounds, **Naksan-sa** is a gorgeous temple.

During its long history, the temple has been rebuilt many times, most recently following a devastating forest fire in 2005. The 16m-tall statue of **Gwaneum**, which presides over the East Sea from the temple's highest point, first appeared in 1971. Go to enough Buddhist temples and you'll be as familiar with the Goddess of Mercy as you will be with Buddha. She lends a compassionate ear to those who come needing sympathy. Immediately below the majestic statue's viewing platform is a small shrine, with a window strategically constructed so that a kneeling devotee can look up and gaze upon her kindly face.

SIMON RICHMOND/LONELY PLANET

BIGMARCO/SHUTTERSTOCK

Top Gwaneum statue
Bottom Hajodae Beach

Surfing Hot Spots

The atmosphere along the Yangyang coast is hip and the summer waves are easy for beginners.

Among the popular coastal locations are **Jukdo Beach**, lined with surf shops, bars, cafes and guesthouses; **Seorak Beach**, where you can get surf lessons and hang out at the sandside cafe-bar Meta Beach; and **Hajodae Beach**, home to another lively beach bar, Surfyy Beach, where the motto is 'Surf all day! Party all night!' and it's quite the selfie scene.

At each of these beaches you can rent boards and wetsuits, and usually find English-speaking instructors for surf lessons.

Also don't miss the **Uisangdae Pavilion** and the **Hongnyeonam Hermitage** (one of the temple's oldest buildings dating to 1865), both of which overlook the crashing waves of the sea and are wonderful spots for watching sunrise (the temple opens at 6am). Relax in the arty cafe **Daraeheon**, which also has a gorgeous sea view. Free tea is offered in the Binlru and Botarak pavilions.

Once you're done with the temple, boost your bliss on **Naksan Beach**, one of the east coast's best stretches of sand.

By Simon Richmond
@simonrichmond

Korea's Artisan Coffee Capital

HOW GANGNEUNG GOT ITS CAFFEINE GROOVE ON

The aroma of freshly roasted coffee wafts along Gangneung's Anmok Beach. For some this is where the city's association with coffee began in the 1980s. Then, in the early 2000s, quality artisan brews really took off thanks to pioneering baristas and a bean roaster that has since hit the big time.

Left Coffee Street
Centre Terarosa coffee
Right Terarosa Coffee Factory

KOREA BY BIKE/SHUTTERSTOCK

Anmok Beach's **Coffee Street** is well named – the strip is literally wall-to-wall cafes, each serving barista-brewed coffees and offering vistas of the wind-sculpted pines and rippling waves as tourists pose for selfies beside giant coffee cups sprouting from the sand.

Back in the 1980s there were no fancy coffee shops. Instead, if beachgoers wanted a caffeine fix, they'd get it from a vending machine that would either serve the drink freshly made in little paper cups or preprepared in cans. Koreans lapped up those vending machine coffees and locals recall how radio stations would share tips from listeners on which vending machine coffee tasted best. However, by the turn of the millennium, infinitely tastier brews were just around the corner.

Coffee Pioneers

Across town is Sinami Myeongju, a low-key, historic neighbourhood close by the well-preserved Chilsadang complex of Joseon-era government offices. Here, I sit down with Kim Namkee to chat about Gangneung's rise to become Korea's coffee capital. Kim is an artist who studied at the Slade School of Fine Art in London. In 2011, he set up his cafe **Bonbon Bangatan** in an abandoned flour and chilli pepper mill dating back to the 1940s.

Kim was following in the wake of Pak I-choo, the acknowledged pioneer of gourmet coffee in Gangneung. 'Pak studied hand-drip coffee-making in Japan', Kim tells me. 'When he moved to Gangneung in the early 2000s, he began to teach others the techniques.'

Silver-haired Pak is still roasting his own beans and hand pouring coffees at **Bohemian Park I-Choo Coffee**, 18km north up the coast from the city centre. This rustic

BLOOMBERG/GETTY IMAGES

FOTOGRAFKR/SHUTTERSTOCK

coffee shop is decorated with antique china cups and coffee-making equipment, and only open Thursday to Sunday. It's so popular that customers invariably must sign up on the waiting list for service when they arrive.

Around Kim's Bonbon Bangatan are a fresh crop of convivial coffee spots including **Fine Pine** in a cute two-storey wooden building dating back to the early 20th century and **Oh New World** in a converted *hanok* (traditional wooden building) filled with mid-century modern furniture.

Anmok Beach's Coffee Street is literally wall-to-wall cafes, each serving barista-brewed coffees and offering vistas of the wind-sculpted pines

Enter Terarosa

Kim shares with me a second reason for Gangneung's rise to Korean coffee fame: Terarosa. Founded in 2002 by ex-banker Kim Yong-deok, Terarosa has grown into one of Korea's premier domestic coffee brands with branches across the country. Not only is Terarosa all about premium-quality, expertly made coffee, it has also made part of their brand to serve that coffee in unique, atmospheric and appealing spaces. A case in point is their Gangneung HQ – the **Terarosa Coffee Factory** – a massive brick building on the outskirts of the city. This impressive space houses not only their coffee-roasting facilities but also a cafe, restaurant and museum. Another of the company's Gangneung branches is the library-themed one close by **Gyeongpo Lake** – a choice spot to savour an espresso or cold brew alongside one of their freshly baked sweet treats or bean-to-bar chocolates.

Gangneung Coffee Festival

In 2009, Gangneung became the first Korean municipality to host a **coffee festival** (coffeefestival.net). The event was a hit and has been held yearly since, regularly attracting in the region of half a million visitors to the city. During the opening ceremony, 100 baristas gather to simultaneously brew hand-drip coffee, which festival-goers can then sample for free. The festival, which runs over four days at the end of October and early November, attracts coffee brewers from across Korea with seminars and competitions to find the top baristas for skills such as latte art, pouring hand-drip coffee, and roasting beans.

ART & GARDENS

01

02

03

04

01 Chuncheon National Museum
Be enchanted by this museum's 500 Arhats gallery featuring mini stone-carved monks, each one with a different expression and stance.

02 Les Jardins de Médongaule
Opened in 2025, these beautifully designed gardens include traditional Korean ones featuring wooden viewing pavilions, ornamental ponds and ancient rocks.

03 Museum SAN
Designed by award-winning architect Tadao Ando, this showcase for contemporary sculpture and visual art has a stunning mountain setting near Wonju.

04 Sangdomun
The stone walls of this charming village of *hanok* (traditional wooden buildings) near Sokcho are studded with small paintings of animals and birds.

05

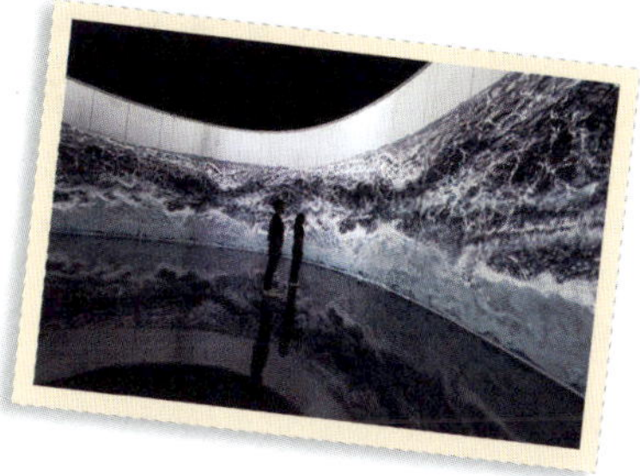

06

07

05 Arte Museum Valley Gangneung
Marvel at the eye-popping digital imagery of some 18 different media art works that reflect the nature and culture of Gangwon-do.

06 Haesindang Park
In the fishing village of Sinnam this quirky park features over 50 phallic sculptures to complement the sweeping sea views.

07 Haslla Art World
Striking artworks designed by Choi Ok Yeung and Park Shing Jung take centre stage at this coastal-located sculpture park, museum and hotel.

01 SAFE DUCK/SHUTTERSTOCK, **02** SIMON RICHMOND/LONELY PLANET, **03** ©KOREA TOURISM ORGANIZATION – PARK EUNKYOUNG, **04** SIMON RICHMOND/LONELY PLANET, **05** ARTE MUSEUM, **06** AMINKOREA/SHUTTERSTOCK, **07** ©KOREA TOURISM ORGANIZATION – KIM HYOSEO.
BACKGROUND QUANG HO/SHUTTERSTOCK

14 HISTORIC Gangneung

HISTORY | ARCHITECTURE | FESTIVAL

A popular seaside getaway, Gangneung is also home to several heritage attractions. These include the Joseon-era buildings of Ojukheon, the birthplace of Shin Saimdang, the paragon of Korean womanhood, and her son, the philosopher and government official Yi Yulgok. Every June the city also celebrates the centuries-old Danoje Festival, inscribed on UNESCO's list for Intangible Cultural Heritage.

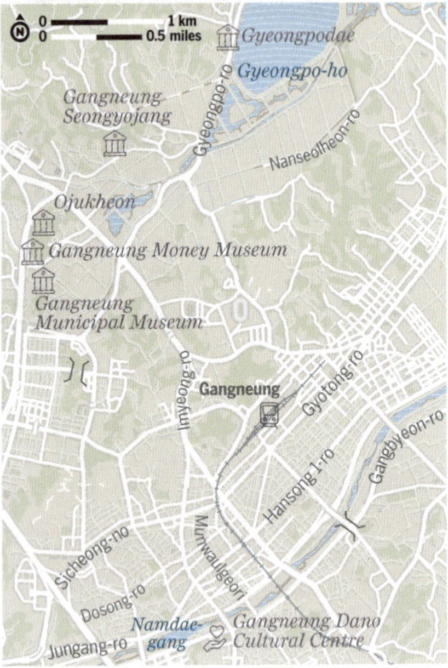

How To

Getting there and around KTX trains take just 90 minutes to reach Gangneung station from Seoul. Around town, several buses go between the city centre and the beaches, or you can catch taxis.

When to go The Danoje Festival usually falls in June. Around Gyeongpo-ho is particularly beautiful in April, when the Gyeongpodae Cherry Blossom Festival is held.

Top tip It's possible to stay overnight in the historic *hanok* complex **Gangneung Seongyojang**.

Shin Saimdang (1504–51), an accomplished poet and artist, is traditionally regarded as a model Korean daughter, wife and mother, according to Confucian ideals. Her paintings feature in the collection of the National Museum of Korea in Seoul (p71) and some are on display at her birthplace **Ojukheon**, including a delicate folding screen with eight studies of flowers and insects.

Ojukheon, one of Korea's oldest surviving Joseon-dynasty homes, sits amid an elegant park, with punctiliously maintained gardens, courtyards, lotus pools and the black-stemmed bamboo groves for which the complex is named. Within the park, and covered by the entry fee, is the **Gangneung Municipal Museum**, with its displays of art, calligraphy and ceramics, and the **Gangneung Money Museum**, celebrating the fact that Shin Saimdang and

AARON CHOI/SHUTTERSTOCK

Yi Yulgok are the world's first mother and son to feature on bank notes.

Nearby is the beautifully preserved **Gangneung Seongyojang**. Dating from late in the Joseon dynasty, this national cultural property was the home of a *yangban* (aristocratic) family for over 300 years. It was built for a descendant of the brother of King Sejong and has been restored in keeping with the original floor plan and architectural style.

Overlooking Gyeongpo-ho is **Gyeongpodae**, a beautifully decorated pavilion built in 1326 and relocated here in 1508. It was traditionally used for moon-viewing parties.

Gangneung Danoje Festival

The Gangneung Danoje Festival is celebrated for one week starting on the fifth day of the fifth lunar month (usually in June). As the climax of a month-long series of shamanist ceremonies for peace, prosperity and bountiful harvests, it's one of the biggest traditional holidays in Korea. On the first day, there's a parade to welcome a mountain deity who unites with his 'wife', a village deity dwelling in Gangneung. To implore their blessings, female shamans perform the *dano gut*, a rite of song, dance and sacrificial offering.

To find out more about the festival, drop by the **Gangneung Dano Cultural Centre**.

Above Ojukheon

15 Glimpses OF THE DMZ

NATURE | LANDSCAPE | HISTORY

The DMZ (p230) runs for 145km along Gangwon-do's northern flank. For a chance to peer into North Korea, head to Cheorwon in the province's northwest and Goseong on the east coast, where you can also encounter the zone's historical sites and natural beauty.

SIMON RICHMOND/LONELY PLANET

How To

Getting there Renting a car or hiring a taxi is the best way to reach and tour both Cheorwon and Goseong.

When to go DMZ tours (p231) and Cheorwon attractions are closed on Tuesday. Between April and November join boat tours along the Hantan River.

Top tip Whenever you pay for an attraction in Cheorwon, you'll be given vouchers that can be used like cash at other attractions and businesses in the town.

SIMON RICHMOND/LONELY PLANET

DMZ Viewpoints

The region around Cheorwon endured some of the fiercest battles of the Korean War – their locations now lie within the Civilian Control Line (CCL), the buffer zone south of the DMZ. To visit the **Second Tunnel**, dug by North Korea and discovered by South Korea in 1975, and the **Cheorwon Peace Observatory**, which offers a panoramic view of the DMZ, you'll need to join the **DMZ Peace Tour**, which departs four times a day from the **Goseokjeong Tourist Information Centre** and lasts around three hours.

Just outside the CCL is **Cheorwan History & Culture Park**, across from which stands the shell of the **Former Labor Party Headquarters** – when Cheorwon was part of North Korea, civilians were imprisoned and tortured here. The park itself evokes an

KOREA BY BIKE/SHUTTERSTOCK

Cranes of the DMZ

For Koreans, cranes are symbols of peace and longevity – there's a crane design on the ₩500 coin. They also stand for hope for reunification of North and South Korea. Over 100 endangered species overwinter at the border, including white-naped and red-crowned cranes, both designated South Korean natural monuments.

Top DMZ observatory **Left** DMZ Museum grounds (p99) **Above** DMZ Peace Town for Migratory Birds (p98)

early-20th-century Cheorwan (long since vanished) and includes a monorail up 362m Soi-san, from which there are panoramic views across the Cheorwon Lava Plateau towards the DMZ.

Over 70 years of limited human interaction with the landscape has made Cheorwon a haven for wildlife. The town is one of Korea's premier birdwatching destinations, a sanctuary for migrating cranes, eagles and other raptors. Partly occupying a former school, **DMZ Peace Town for Migratory Birds** is an educational facility with an exhibition on cranes and other birds native to the area. Cranes can be spotted in the skies between November and February – during these months, birdwatching tours are run out of the facility.

Fortified Coastal Location

A heavy military presence and barbed-wire-lined beaches add a frisson of danger to the

Hantan River Basin

Beautiful scenery is Cheorwan's trump card, with the Hantan River carving through basalt rock gorges. Sculpted by nature 60 million years ago, the area is designated a UNESCO World Geopark.

Look down on the river from the historic pavilion **Goseokjeong**. Follow steps down to the river itself, where you can stand on a sandbank at the foot of a 10m-high rock pillar.

Another memorable perspective over the Hantan is from the asymmetrical **Cheorwon Hantangang Milky Way Bridge**, which offers a prime view into Songdaeso, a basalt canyon. Cross the bridge to climb to the 53m torch-shaped observatory tower.

Left Cheorwon Hantangang Milky Way Bridge **Below** DMZ Museum

gorgeous coastal landscape around Goseong. This was part of North Korea from 1945 to 1953, and today the area around its **Tongil Security Park** is the closest you can get to the border while in South Korea.

From where you fill in the required forms and purchase your admission ticket, it's another 10km to the observatory – there's no shuttle bus, and pedestrians, bicycles and motorbikes are not allowed. If not driving yourself, come here by taxi directly from Sokcho. At the ticket counter, you'll need to present identification, contact information and your (or your taxi driver's) licence-plate number.

Once inside the security area, head straight to the **Unification Observatory** (pausing along the way is strictly forbidden). On a clear day, there are amazing views of Kumgang-san, a celebrated mountain about 20km northwest inside North Korea. The waves breaking along the jagged coast and the empty beaches make for a hauntingly beautiful scene.

Also inside the security area, the **Korean War Exhibition Hall** provides a primer on the war (with some harrowing footage of the conflict), while the **DMZ Museum** covers the history of the demilitarised zone.

FROM LEFT: SEUNG HA KIM/SHUTTERSTOCK, MIRKO KUZMANOVIC/SHUTTERSTOCK

Listings

BEST OF THE REST

Rail Bike Courses

Gangchon Rail Park

From Gimyujeong train station, it's a leisurely 6.5km pedal past farm fields and through tunnels to the Bukhan River. The final 2km to the Gangchon is aboard the 'romantic train'.

Jeongdongjin Railbike

This 3.5km round trip from the popular East Sea sunrise spot lasts around one hour. Jeongdongjin station holds the Guinness World Record for having the closest railway tracks to a beach.

National Parks

Odaesan National Park

Offers splendid hiking and superb views. There's an easy 9km hike between the Buddhist temple Woljeong-sa, which offers templestays, and its sub-temple Sangwon-sa, home to Korea's oldest temple bell.

Taebaeksan National Park

From the park's Danggol entrance follow a 8.4km route up to Janggun-bong (1567m) and down to the Yuilsa entrance. On the way is Cheonjedan, a trio of stone altars associated with Korea's mythical founder, Dangun.

Beaches

Cheongsihaeng Beach

Around 18km north of Gangneung, in Jumunjin. At the beach's northern end is a bus stop created for BTS's *You Never Walk Alone* album cover, which is a popular photo op.

Gyeongpo Beach

This 1.8km strip of golden sand in Gangneung is bordered by wind-twisted pine trees and serene walking paths, winding between benches, picnicking spots and colourful sculptural art works.

Craft Beer

Budnamu Brewery ₩₩

A former *makgeolli* (milky rice wine) factory in Gangneung is the base for this brew pub serving excellent craft beers, pizzas and Mexican dishes. Beer ingredients include local rice, pine and wetland plants.

Gamja Island ₩₩

This Chuncheon brew pub has a breezy seaside and boating theme. Sample their award-winning beers including ones made with potato, corn and tomato, and creative dishes such as *dakgalbi* (spicy chicken) pizza.

Singlefin Aleworks ₩₩

Ales, stouts, *weizen*, IPAs and sour beers are all on tap at this hip craft brew pub at Hajodae where you can also dig into Chicago-style deep dish pizzas.

AARON CHOI/SHUTTERSTOCK

Odaesan National Park

Characterful Cafes

Gallery Cafe ₩

Tucked behind the MBC broadcasting building in Chuncheon, with a good selection of drinks and desserts, and elevated views of Uiam-ho.

SHLTR ₩₩

Desserts and drinks are themed black at this angular dark-grey painted building along Sokcho's waterfront. The floor-to-ceiling windows offer prime views of the Jodo islands.

Yedam the Gallery Cafe ₩

Relax over a cup of Korean fruit tea and traditional rice cake desserts at this charming *hanok*-based cafe in Chuncheon that doubles as an art gallery.

Natural Beauty Spots

Sogeumsan Mountain Grand Valley

Ride the cable car for an easy way up to view this spectacular landscape near Wonju. Also negotiate cliff-hugging walkways and two pedestrian suspension bridges.

Wondae-ri Birch Forest

Standing amid this 25-hectare protected forest of silvery bark trees is an ethereal experience. It's particularly striking in winter when the branches are barren and the ground is covered in snow.

Winter Sports

High1 Ski Resort

Near the town of Gohan, at 1340m, with 18 slopes of varying levels. Offers some of the country's top skiing facilities as well as a ski school for people with disabilities.

Mona Yongpyong

Korea's largest ski and snowboarding resort with 31 slopes and 15 lifts. On clear days you can see as far as the East Sea from the slopes in Pyeongchang.

SUCHART BOONYAVECH/SHUTTERSTOCK

Phoenix Park

Phoenix Park

With 18 slopes, this was the venue for the freestyle skiing and snowboarding events at the 2018 Winter Olympics. It's a great option for intermediate and advanced skiers.

Alpensia Ski Resort

Also used for the 2018 Olympics, this small but well-serviced six-run resort is good for families and beginners.

Unique Stays

The Hanok Heritage ₩₩₩

This luxurious property in Yeongwol county combines traditional wooden architecture on a palatial scale with contemporary amenities and art. The setting is gorgeous and the food alone is worth a trip here.

Romyzian Garden ₩₩₩

Spend time exploring Romyzian's beautifully landscaped grounds by staying overnight either in Mountain House, offering Zen-calm duplexes and suites, or their safari-style glamping tents with proper beds.

Haslla Museum Hotel ₩₩

All rooms are unique at this architectural one-off featuring offbeat design, including big wooden bowl-shaped beds and colourful mosaic bathrooms. There's also discounted access to the museum and sculpture park.

GYEONGSANG-DO

TRADITIONAL HEARTLAND | BUDDHIST SITES | COASTAL CITIES

RESEARCHED BY MARCO FERRARESE

NATHAWAT88/SHUTTERSTOCK

GYEONGSANG-DO
Trip Builder

Straddling South Korea's central-eastern plains, a treasure trove of Korean traditional culture, and the Buddhist shrines of Gyeongju near the southeastern coast, Gyeongsang-do's microcosm thaws into the southern rocky coastlines of technologically chic Busan. This region holds all that's beguiling about Korea.

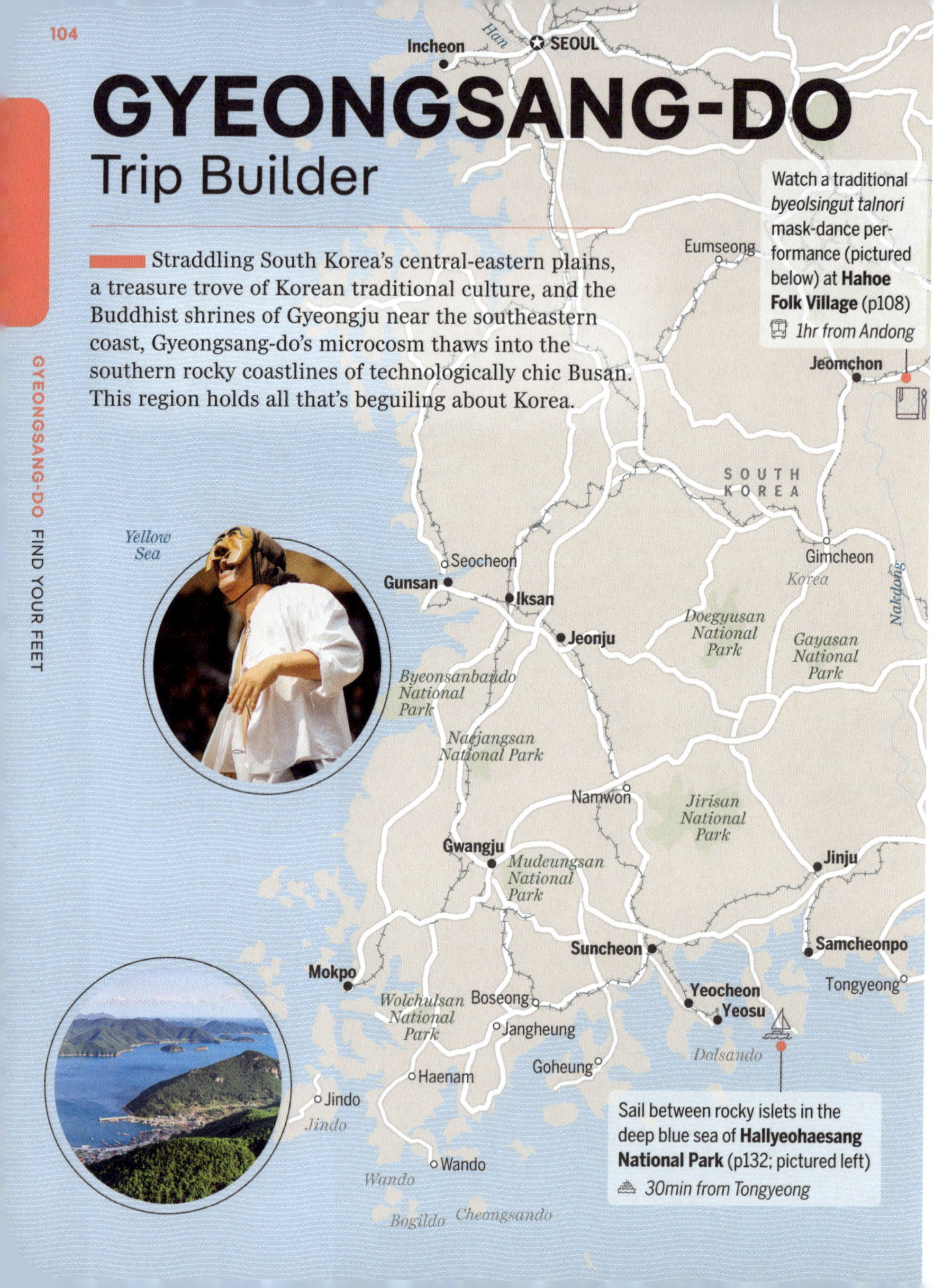

Watch a traditional *byeolsingut talnori* mask-dance performance (pictured below) at **Hahoe Folk Village** (p108)
1hr from Andong

Sail between rocky islets in the deep blue sea of **Hallyeohaesang National Park** (p132; pictured left)
30min from Tongyeong

CLOCKWISE FROM BOTTOM LEFT: NGHIA KHANH/SHUTTERSTOCK, WDLEADER/SHUTTERSTOCK, ASIA IMAGES GROUP LLC/ALAMY, BBEARLYAM/SHUTTERSTOCK

Practicalities

HUN YOUNG LEE/SHUTTERSTOCK

ARRIVING

Gimhae International Airport Gyeongsang-do's main international hub is located about 50 minutes west of Busan's city centre. It's well-connected by taxi, bus and the convenient metro system, which involves a transfer at either Sasang or Daejeo stations.

Train High-speed KTX and slower Mugunghwa train services from Seoul run to Andong (2–3 hours), Gyeongju (2–3 hours), Daegu (2–3 hours) and Busan station (2–5 hours).

HOW MUCH FOR A

Gimbap (rice in seaweed) ₩4000

Black coffee ₩4000

Bibimbap ₩10,000

WHEN TO GO

JAN–MAR
Cold and windy; travel is possible, but stick to cities and indoors. Warmer in March.

APR–JUN
Cherry blossoms galore turn into hot summers.

JUL–SEP
Hot and humid, with the wettest monsoonal rains in July.

OCT–DEC
Pleasantly warm early autumn days turn into freezing winters.

GETTING AROUND

Bus By far the most reliable service to get around the region, buses connect every major city in Gyeongsang-do and most of the countryside. Within cities, and especially in Busan, punctual and frequent bus services (approximately ₩1500 per trip) are ideal for getting around without worrying about parking and also reaching most of the far-flung tourist sights.

Bicycle Gyeongsang-do contains a large chunk of the 633km-long Four Rivers Cycling Path, connecting Incheon to Busan along the Han, Nakdong, Geum and Yeongsan Rivers, considered one of the world's best-maintained cycling paths.

Boat Regular ferries connect Tongyeong with many of the inhabited islands of the Hallyeohaesang National Park and Pohang with the remote Ulleungdo.

EATING & DRINKING

Gyeongsang-do food is bold, spicy and salty. It uses a lot of seafood and fermented pastes. Some of the must-trys are Andong *jjimdak* (braised chicken, vegetables and glass noodles in a sweet-savoury black soy-based sauce; pictured top) and *hoe* (raw fish). Local specialities include *agujjim* (braised anglerfish/monkfish; pictured bottom), *myelchi-jeot* (salted anchovies) and *daege* (snow crab). If that sounds like too much, Busan has all sorts of cuisines – including Central Asian food – and is South Korea's craft beer hotspot. Many bars and breweries serve Western comfort foods.

Must-try beer
Galmegi IPA

Great jjimdak
Solbat Sikdang (솔밭식당), Hahoe Folk Village (p108)

CONNECT & FIND YOUR WAY

Wi-fi Busan offers extensive free public wi-fi through the Free Wi-Fi Busan project at major tourist spots, transportation hubs, parks and libraries. Many public buses also have free high-speed internet. Major attractions around Gyeongju, including Bulguksa temple and its surrounding historic areas, offer free public wi-fi.

Navigation Apps like Naver and Kakao Maps are excellent tools for planning and using public transportation.

WHERE TO STAY

Busan has hundreds of hotels, but every major city in Gyeongsang-do also has a range of well-appointed accommodation to suit all budgets and needs.

Place	Pros/Cons
Busan	Haeundae and Gwangan have the most midrange accommodation, while Nampo-dong is better for hostels.
Tongyeong	Most accommodation is situated around Gangguan Harbour, which is conveniently located near the ferry terminal.
Daegu	Central Dongseong-ro St is within walking distance of the train station and has hostels, midrange hotels, and plenty of nightlife and dining options.
Gyeongju	Plenty of accommodation around the historic centre, where parking is tricky. Get in by train or bus and walk.
Andong	Stick to the hotels near downtown by the old train station.

VISIT BUSAN PASS

This convenient card (visitbusanpass.com) offers 24 (₩55,000) or 48 hours (₩85,000) of free access to over 30 city attractions, as well as discounts at over 200 additional establishments.

MONEY

Credit cards are widely accepted at most establishments, and so are Cashbee and Tmoney cards on public transport and at convenience stores. Remember that foreigners can only reload these with cash, so be sure to carry some.

16 Enter the Soul OF KOREA

VILLAGE | COUNTRYSIDE | MASKS

Set on a looping bend of the Nakdong River that gives it its name, UNESCO-listed Hahoe Folk Village is a living historical community of tiled and thatched-roofed buildings that will almost convince visitors they've stepped back to Joseon times.

WIRESTOCK/GETTY IMAGES

How To

Getting there Bus 210 runs from Andong to the village 12 times daily, with the last departure back to Andong at 7.10pm.

Getting around A shuttle bus included in the ticket price runs the kilometre between Hahoe's ticket office and the village every 10–15 minutes. To move around the village, consider walking or renting a bicycle.

When to go Early mornings and evenings are less crowded. Avoid weekends.

TRABANTOS/SHUTTERSTOCK

A Living Village

South Korea has many refurbished and well-kept 'folk' villages with collections of ancient homes that can often seem artificial. Not **Hahoe Folk Village** (hahoe.or.kr; adult/child ₩5000/2500): set 28km west of Andong, roughly in the centre of the country, this is the historic home of the Pungsan Ryu clan, with over 200 residents today. Clan descendants inhabit century-old dwellings, which are as authentic as possible, reflecting the past of Korea's dynastic kingdoms. Walk by dirt roads, gardens and riverbank escarpments to feel transported back in time. At the centre of the village is Samsindang, a zelkova tree said to be 600 years old, inside of which the Goddess Samsin is believed to live. There's also a Presbyterian church with a brick spire and, outside the main village to the

STOCK FOR YOU/SHUTTERSTOCK

Folk Heartland

Andong is widely known as the 'capital of the Korean spirit' or the 'soul of Korea' due to its focus on preserving traditional culture, Confucian heritage and folk arts, which stand in stark contrast to Seoul's modernity. One of the best times to experience them is in October, when the city hosts the **Andong Mask Dance Festival** (en.maskdance.com).

Top left Hahoe Folk Village
Left *Hanok* (traditional wooden home)
Above Samsindang

east, the 17th-century Confucian academy of **Byeongsan Seowon** is a beautiful spot by the Nakdong River.

Mask Dance Drama

One of the most attractive things to do in Hahoe is witnessing a *byeolsingut talnori*, a traditional mask dance play performance created by ordinary folks, which satirises and criticises the establishment. All characters (p112) wear masks that represent figures such as shady aristocrats, lecherous monks, unsatisfied servants and wanton women, who all speak, sing and dance a set of formulaic stories with a moral. The sounds of a percussion quartet playing *nong-ak*, traditional farmers' music, accompany the dance. From March to December, shows are held daily at 2pm either in the performance hall near the village entrance or at an outdoor area facing the dramatic **Buyongdae Cliff**. During the winter months of January and February, performances are only held on weekends.

Jjimdak & Soju

Most visitors come to Andong to make the diversion west to Hahoe Folk Village, but don't skip the city and try two of its specialities. Andong *jjimdak* is a savoury, soy-sauce-based braised chicken dish cooked with the flavours of braised *galbi* and simmered until thickened after adding glass noodles and various vegetables – downright delicious. It's so good there's a whole street dedicated to this dish, **Andong Market Jjimdak Alley** (안동시장 찜닭골목), with about 30 stores cooking the bird. Wash it all down with Andong soju, a local variety of Korea's national spirit, that also has its dedicated **museum** in town.

Left Jjimdak **Below** Mask, Hahoe World Mask Museum

Masks from Around the World

The **Hahoe World Mask Museum**, located near the ticket office (admission is included with a village ticket), features an intriguing collection of traditional Korean masks on the ground floor. While Andong's variety, carved from alder wood, may be the country's most famous, there are many other regional styles from around the peninsula. Climb to the first floor to check out the museum's international exhibition, which displays masks from around the world, including Southeast Asia, Tibet and Africa.

Rest Your Head

Most travellers base themselves in Andong and commute to Hahoe as a day trip, but staying overnight in one of the many *minbak* and Airbnb-type accommodation options inside the village is the best way to experience the place at its quietest in the evenings and early mornings. After the crowds leave or before they arrive, observe uncluttered local life and adapt to its slow rhythms. There are some restaurants near the parking lot, so if you don't mind walking one kilometre to get there, there's excellent *jjimdak* and *godeungeo gui* (grilled mackerel) to be found.

FROM LEFT: KYTAN/SHUTTERSTOCK, STEVE JANGS/SHUTTERSTOCK

Hahoe Mask Drama's CHARACTERS

01

02

03

04

01 The Fool
Imae *tal* is the mask with no chin, representing a foolish person who is a servant of the Scholar. The downsides of his eyes mean he's free from malice, and he dances with faltering steps.

02 Hasty Scatter-brained Meddler
Choraengi masks represent slaves of the Aristocrat. Twisted, closed mouths indicate discontent, and protruding foreheads symbolise disagreement with their master.

03 The Bride
Long-haired Gakshi is a quiet and calm character. Her tightly closed lips mean she's trying to keep her new marriage and tough life to herself.

04 The Butcher
Baekjeong is an ill-tempered, malicious figure with a crooked forehead and violent tendencies. He has a crazy grin because he feels guilty for killing bulls.

05 The Aristocrat
Yangban *tal* is the best among Hahoe's masks, a mix of gentle and pompous. Connected by

05

06

07

08

09

strings, the chin makes an angry face when drooping the head.

06 The Old Widow
Halmi is an old and impoverished widow, embittered by life's hardships, with an upward gaze symbolising her impending misery.

07 The Scholar
Sonbi's disgruntled expression highlights his reluctance to conform to societal norms. He's a scholar and yet arrogant, and makes long strides when dancing.

08 The Flirtatious Young Lady
A concubine of the Aristocrat and the Scholar, Bune has an oval face, crescent-shaped eyebrows, a high nose, and small mouth – the stereotype of beauty.

09 The Depraved Buddhist Monk
Joong is a wandering, depraved monk with an insidious grin and crescent-shaped eyes that reveal his lecherous behaviour.

01 WDLEADER/SHUTTERSTOCK, **02** SEONTAEK KIM/SHUTTERSTOCK, **03** KEITMA/SHUTTERSTOCK, **04** STEVE JANGS/SHUTTERSTOCK, **05** PHOTO_JEONGH/SHUTTERSTOCK, **06** JULIE FACINE/CC BY-SA 2.0/WIKIMEDIA COMMONS, **07** TIMBER TANK/CC BY-SA 2.0/FLICKR, **08 & 09** STOCK FOR YOU/SHUTTERSTOCK

17

Explore a Museum WITHOUT WALLS

PAGODAS | SILLA HERITAGE | HANOK CHIC

Once the capital of the Silla kingdom for almost a thousand years, the city of Gyeongju is home to more tombs, temples, pagodas, Buddhist statuary and palace ruins than anywhere else in South Korea. And it's also the region's greenest and most walkable city.

Top Ancient Tombs in Noseo-ri and Nodong-ri (p116)
Right Gyeongju National Museum
Far right Cheonmachong (p116)

KOREAKHW/SHUTTERSTOCK

How To

Getting there Gyeongju's **train station** is well-connected to Seoul and other cities, albeit 10km south of the centre. Buses bring you much closer. Once in town, walking and cycling are the best ways to get around.

When to go Gyeongju is very popular. Avoid weekends and holidays, and favour shoulder months like March and October.

Top tip Download the National Museum of Korea's app for an excellent English-language guide to **Gyeongju National Museum.**

TRABANTOS/SHUTTERSTOCK

Plan it Out

The majority of Gyeongju's sights are scattered around the spread-out central **Daereungwon Ancient Tomb Area**, which is peppered with the peculiar, large burial mounds of ancient Silla royalty. The area can be explored on foot, but renting a bicycle (approximately ₩20,000 per day) from a guesthouse or around the historic area allows for quicker exploration and easier access to outlying attractions.

THE MARINER 4291/SHUTTERSTOCK

Museum of Silla Masterpieces

Starting with a few hours at the excellent **Gyeongju National Museum** (gyeongju.museum.go.kr; free; closed Mondays) helps enrich your understanding of the kingdom that unified Korea and prepares you for a city walk. The opulent jewellery, weaponry, impressive artefacts and art gallery dedicated to Buddhist

Gyeongju for Families

Approximately 5km east of central Gyeongju, artificial **Lake Bomun** features a full-fledged tourist district designed for families. **Gyeongju World** amusement park (gjw.co.kr; adult/child/teenager ₩36,000/27,000/32,000) and **Gyeongju World Culture Expo Park** (adult/child ₩12,000/10,000) offer plenty of fun rides, such as **Lumina Night Walk**, a narrated circuit through an illuminated Hwarang forest.

works are great bases for imagining the former wealth of this long-ruling dynasty. Outside the museum, marvel at King Seongdeok's Bell, one of the largest and most beautifully resonant bells ever made in Asia, believed to spread sound up to 3km in radius. Free 90-minute museum tours, conducted in English, are available every Sunday at 10am and 2pm.

Open-Air Mausoleum

The Daereungwon Ancient Tomb Area contains numerous archaeological remains, the most striking of which are the grass-covered, hillock-like burial mounds of the Silla period. Start from the **Ancient Tombs in Noseo-ri and Nodong-ri** at the northern end of the complex, where you'll find the burial mounds of **Seobongchong**, **Geumgwanchong** (adult/child ₩3000/1500) and **Geumnyeongchong**, along with the tree-topped **Bonghwangdae**, the largest tomb at 22m high. The only one that can be entered is **Cheonmachong** (adult/child ₩3000/1000), next to

A Bounty of Buddhist Rock Art

A handful of kilometres south of Gyeongju's centre, **Namsan** mountain (466m) is strewn with temple sites, stone pagodas, stone Buddhas, royal tombs, fortresses and palaces. Numerous well-trodden paths wind uphill; hikers can start at any one of them, then follow the ridge across the mountain. The foothills still hold some of the mountain's most interesting carvings: on the north edge of Namsan, in the upper corner of the hermitage **Ongnyong-am**, are 24 different representations of Buddha carved into boulders. On the southeastern edge of the mountain, **Chilbul-am** features the mountain's largest relics, carved into natural rocks and stone pillars.

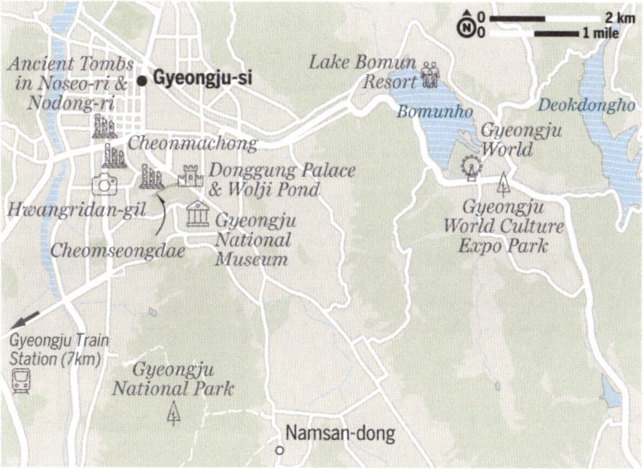

Left Stone Buddha, Namsan
Below Donggung Palace and Wolji Pond

Hwangnamdaechong and the Tomb of King Michu. Soon after exiting at the bottom end of this park, an ancient-looking 9m-high brick tower soars from the well-manicured grass. It's **Cheomseongdae**, the oldest stone astronomical observatory in Asia. Built between 632 and 646 CE, it's made of 365 stones arranged in 30 layers, symbolising the days of the year and the month.

Palace, Bridge & Hangouts

Walk a couple of kilometres east to the grounds of **Donggung Palace and Wolji Pond**, a secondary palace and pond that King Munmu built in the year 674 CE. They are most beautiful after dark, when the water reflects the moonlight – the meaning of *wolji.* Night is also the best time to see the red-and-green 66m-long **Woljeonggyo Bridge**, built in 760 and last restored in 2018, connecting the north and south sides of the Namcheon River. It's lovely in early spring, when frothy cherry blossoms bloom along its sides.

Step back to the present at **Hwangridan-gil** (technically still Poseok-ro), a tourist-centric strip to the west of the Daereungwon Ancient Tomb Complex. Old *hanok* (traditional Korean houses) have been converted into contemporary cafes, restaurants, guesthouses, boutiques, photo studios and more.

18 Buddhist MASTERPIECES

PAGODAS | HISTORY | MOUNTAINS

Korea's most famous temple and a UNESCO World Heritage Site, Bulguksa rises amid pine forest on a series of stone terraces about 16km south of Gyeongju. In the hills above the temple, the mid-8th-century hermitage of Seokguram features a pensive 3.5m-high Buddha statue.

Above Daeungjeon (p120)
Right Cheongungyo and Baegungyo (p120)
Far right Bulguksa

SEUNG HA KIM/SHUTTERSTOCK

How To

Getting there Bus 711 connects Gyeongju's new **train station** to Bulguksa via the city centre in about an hour.

Getting around Once at Bulguksa bus stop, bus 12 (₩1700) leaves for Seokguram every hour from 8.40am to 4.40pm. It returns on the hour between 9am and 5pm.

Top tip From Seokguram, it is possible to walk downhill to Bulguksa by using the easy and scenic 2.2km downhill hiking path through the forest.

DANIEL GAUTHIER/GETTY IMAGES

Meaning 'Buddha Land Temple', **Bulguksa** (bulguksa.or.kr; free) has grounds arranged to represent the Buddha's kingdom, with each hall representing a different world inhabited by Buddha or bodhisattvas. Entering Bulguksa's gate is akin to stepping into a realm of belief and ancestral wisdom, all made more spiritual by the surrounding forest and Zen-like temple architecture.

YEONGSIK IM/SHUTTERSTOCK

Entering the Temple

After stepping off the bus from Gyeongju, make a stop at the information booth by Bulguksa's car park to pick up helpful maps or store your luggage. The temple complex rises on the stone platforms beyond the parking lot.

A beacon of Silla architecture, most of Bulguksa's original structure suffered the ravages of the marauding Mongols and then

Templestay

It's necessary to register in advance to join Bulguksa's popular overnight templestay program (bulguksa@templestay.com), which includes a temple tour, meditation, 108 prostrations and a visit to Seokguram. Due to Bulguksa's designation as a UNESCO World Heritage Site, participants are required to stay in an adjacent house, approximately a five-minute drive away.

Japanese invaders, yet it preserves more national treasures than any other temple in Korea. The first you'll see are two white stone bridges, the two consecutive sections of a national treasure staircase. The lower **Cheongungyo** (Blue Cloud Bridge) has 17 steps and the upper **Baegungyo** (White Cloud Bridge) has 16. Together, their 33 steps represent the 33 stages to enlightenment. To the west, the **Yeonhwagyo** (Lotus Flower Bridge) and **Chilbogyo** (Seven Treasures Bridge) make up another staircase. Visitors cannot climb any of these and must enter from the Bulguksa eastern entrance.

Visiting Bulguksa's Halls

Dating to 1765 – the original was destroyed in the late 16th century – Bulguksa's main hall, **Daeungjeon**, is fronted by a pair of pagodas. On the east side is the intricate **Dabotap** (Pagoda of Many Treasures), and on the west side is the simpler **Seokgatap** (Pagoda of the Historical Buddha), both of which are

Best Time to Visit Bulguksa

Try to arrive by 9am to enjoy the temple grounds in relative quiet and see the stone bridges and pagodas without crowds. Groups start to disperse by late afternoon – consider visiting Seokguram first, and then take the hiking trail down or catch a bus back to Bulguksa. Spring is a good time to photograph trees laden with cherry blossoms, while summer has lush colours but can be very humid. Autumn has the best weather overall and the most photogenic foliage colours, and in winter, you may catch snow blanketing the complex. Weekdays are obviously calmer than weekends year-round.

Left Bulguksa in autumn
Below Buddha statue, Birojeon

designated as national treasures. They are so revered that the Gyeongju National Museum houses replicas of them.

Don't miss two more national treasures inside two other halls. The **Geungnakjeon** (Hall of Supreme Bliss), contains the contemplative 8th- or 9th-century Gilt-Bronze Seated Amitabha Buddha of Bulguksa Temple. And the **Birojeon** (Hall of the Vairocana Buddha) is home to the 9th-century Gilt-Bronze Seated Vairocana Buddha of Bulguksa Temple. The **Stupa of Bulguksa** rises within the Birojeon's courtyard and, legend says, contains the crystallised remains of either a Silla queen turned nun, or eight monks.

Buddha in a Mountain Grotto

Set on the flanks of Toham-san, the 8th-century **Seokguram** (seokguram.org; free) hermitage sits in a spectacular setting at an elevation of 740m. On misty or rainy days, the atmosphere is magical and will make you ponder how it could have been built by quarrying huge granite blocks up narrow mountain paths. Beyond the front gate and a bell pavilion lies the cave itself, where a 3.5m-high Buddha – sealed behind a glass wall – meditates towards the East Sea. Around the statue, more deities, disciples and the 11-faced Goddess of Mercy Gwaneum forever flutter in stone.

19 Shop the Best MARKETS

SEAFOOD | TRADITIONAL MEDICINE | SHOPPING

Gyeongsang-do has some of South Korea's most extensive and most storied markets. One of the reasons was the arrival of about 800,000 displaced Korean War refugees in the early 1950s. They flocked to the temporary capital, Busan, and nearby cities due to the area's strategic ports, distance from the front lines and economic prowess – the legacy continues today.

OSCAR ESPINOSA/SHUTTERSTOCK

How To

Getting around Most markets are located in the centre of cities and are well-connected to bus and metro lines.

When to go Early mornings or evenings are always best for peak action and the best meals.

Shop smart Most vendors these days accept credit cards, but it's a good idea to bring some cash. Unlike other parts of Asia, markets in South Korea have fixed prices and haggling for discounts is not the norm.

Massive fish market
Jagalchi Fish Market in Busan is South Korea's largest fish market, straddling the waterfront in the heart of Old Busan. Many women vendors, called Jagalchi *ajimae*, peddle an incredible variety of fish ranging from flounder to *daege* (snow crabs), oysters, eels and more. Pick your choice and have it cooked fresh in the restaurants upstairs.

Historical refugee market
Busan's **Gukje Market** remains a central commercial hub and grew substantially after the war as refugees established numerous stalls selling a wide array of goods, including imported and often smuggled foreign products – mainly from stationed US troops.

Korea's first night market
Walking distance from Gukje Market, **Bupyeong Kkangtong Market** is Korea's first permanent night market.

It grew as part of Busan's bustling central Nampo-dong area that developed to serve the massive refugee population.

Street filled with books A commemorative and cultural alley packed with second-hand reading material, **Bosu Book Street** was started by a refugee couple who sold used magazines for survival.

Ancient Korean medicine Yangnyeongsi market, on the ground floor of **Daegu Yangnyeongsi Museum of Oriental Medicine**, dates back to 1658. It's Korea's oldest medicine market and still one of its largest, with stores spilling out onto the street and offering fragrant curiosities.

Maze of fish and food **Jukdo Fish Market** in Pohang is the largest permanent market on the eastern coast of Gyeongsangbuk-do. It has fish-tank creatures galore and dozens of simple restaurants; try anything from seafood to rice cakes and other fritters.

Unknown Pohang

Few come to my hometown of Pohang because, from the outside, it's known as the industrial base of the POSCO steel plant – not so attractive for tourists. However, we do have plenty of beaches, water sports, culture and, of course, markets. I live on Songdo, just across the bridge from Jukdo Fish Market. I recommend going in the early morning, when it's quieter and stall operators lay out the fresh catch of the day. Another lesser-known but excellent market is **Yeongildae Bukbu** – it's extremely local and famous for sashimi and mulhoe, a cold, raw-fish soup originating in Pohang.

Park Haneul is the owner and captain of Pohang's Sevenstar Sailing. *@sevenstarsail*

Left Bosu Book Street
Above Jagalchi Fish Market

20 Haeundae's Coastal TRIPPING

OUTDOORS | RAILS | VIEWPOINTS

On the eastern end of Haeundae Beach is Blueline Park, a 4.8km-long coastal walkway along a former section of the East Sea South railway line. Walk, jog or glide on the Green Line train and the romantic Sky Capsule monorail.

F11PHOTO/SHUTTERSTOCK

Three in One

Haeundae Blue Line Park (bluelinepark.com) can be walked along the Green Railway Trail (bikes are not allowed). The **Green Line Beach Train** (adult/child one-way ₩8000/5600, return ₩12,000/8,400) runs parallel at ground level. Above it, there's the nonstop, elevated **Sky Capsule** monorail (2/3/5 people ₩40,000/45,000/50,000; pictured).

How To

Getting there Haeundae is within walking distance of Busan's Haeundae metro station on line 2. Nearby is also the **Haeundae Intercity Bus Terminal**, a direct link to the beach from other cities.

When to go The summer months are hot and rainy. May and October have the best weather and the longest daylight hours.

Save time You can exit midway at Cheongsapo station, where one bus line stops on the way to Jangsan metro station.

01 Before leaving Haeundae Beach, consider taking an elevator ride to the 100th floor of 411m-high Haeundae LCT The Sharp, Korea's second-tallest building (pictured right), to access **BUSAN X the SKY** (adult/child ₩27,000/24,000).

03 The 22m-high **Haewol Observatory** features a 137m-long overwater U-shaped walking path with crescent-shaped pylons positioned directly above the crashing waves below. It's beautiful at night when the LEDs light it up.

05 If you make it to Songjeong Beach, head to **Jukdo Park** near Songjeonghang Port for unbeatable sunset views at **Songiljeong Pavilion** (pictured above). The harbour's white and red lighthouses are a popular photo spot.

04 **Cheongsapo Daritdol Skywalk** is another 20m-high, 72m-long structure, featuring a half-moon-shaped transparent viewing platform at the end that offers a clear view right into the sea.

02 The colourful **Dalmaji Tunnel** is a popular spot for selfies and views, featuring several side staircases for plenty of off-path moseying around the coastal cliffs.

FROM TOP: TULEYHCM/SHUTTERSTOCK, SANGA PARK/SHUTTERSTOCK

21 Busan's Cultural VILLAGES

CAFES | STREET ART | VIEWPOINTS

Maze-like steep alleys, rainbow-tinged houses, cutesy cafes and a fixation with Antoine de Saint-Exupéry's *The Little Prince*. Using art and a touch of glossy chic, Busan's cultural villages transformed formerly dishevelled hillside migrant communities into some of the city's most powerful tourist magnets. Crowds and selfie platforms aside, they offer stunning coastal views and a chance to see painful war history transformed into creativity.

How To

Getting around Busan's excellent bus system can drop you by the villages' entrances; check the constantly updated live schedules and routes on the Naver or Kakao Maps apps.

When to go Every season has its beauty, but May and October have the best weather for walking outdoors.

Top tip To really enjoy the villages, stay overnight at a guesthouse or hotel. Most visitors come on rushed day trips, and almost nobody sticks around after sunset.

Reinvented mountain village Once a mountainside shantytown for the Korean War refugees who settled here in 1955, **Gamcheon Culture Village** is the poster child among all of Busan's cultural villages. It's touristy, but also frankly gorgeous: dozens of rainbow-coloured houses balance on cliffs that tumble into the sea. Many visitors stick to the queues that form behind photo stops, such as the **Little Prince and Desert Fox Statue** in the main village or the **Little Prince** atop the **Gamnae Byeolmaru Sports Centre**, Gamcheon's highest viewpoint. But continue uphill, and you'll soon be hiking on the panoramic and empty trails skirting the top half of Tianma Mountain.

White-washed homes Dubbed the 'Santorini of Korea' for its stark white homes, which hang on a coastal cliff, once serving as shelters for war refugees, **Huinnyeoul Culture Village** is still less crowded than Gamcheon but is rising in popularity. Besides cafes with beautiful ocean views, the village is the starting point of the 3km-long

JAMESTEOHART/GETTY IMAGES

P2N MEDIA/SHUTTERSTOCK

Top Jeoryeong Coastal Trail
Bottom Gamcheon Culture Village

Villages at the Movies

With their colourful hills and art-strewn alleys, both Gamcheon and Huinnyeoul have been featured in several films. Have fun finding some of the locations: Gamcheon was featured in K-Dramas like *L.U.C.A.: The Beginning* (2021) and the heartwarming movie *A Little Princess* (2019). Cafe the Attorney, one of the most creatively furnished in Huinnyeoul Village, was a prime location in the K-Drama *The Attorney* (2013) by Yang Woo-suk. Some poignant quotes from the film are etched on fronting walls. The area was also featured in the action film *Nameless Gangster* (2012) by Yoon Joong-bin, as it retains a 1990s aesthetic.

Jeoryeong Coastal Trail – an exhilarating coastal hike along the southern side of Yeongdo.

Village culture Try **Dakbatgol Mural Village**, perched on a hill west of Nampo-dong, which was established as a residential area in 1953. There's plenty of mural art and it's a favourite photo spot for spring cherry blossoms. The true highlight is the **Somang Stairs Monorail** – a pastel-hued cabin shuttling elder residents (and visitors) above the 192 steps separating two mountain roads.

By Marco Ferrarese
@marcoferrarese

Cinematic Busan

BUSAN WEARS ITS MOVIE INDUSTRY INVOLVEMENT ON ITS SLEEVE

Cinema is one of *hallyu*'s (Korean Wave) most potent forms of soft power. Nowhere else in the peninsula but Busan can you find such a palpable showcase of devotion to the art that helped bring South Korea into the world's spotlight. Learn where to strike on Busan's cinematic trail.

NEXT ENTERTAINMENT WORLD/ REDPETER FILM/ALBUM/ALAMY

Left Still from *Train to Busan* **Centre** Cast of *Parasite* at the 2020 Screen Actors Guild Awards **Right** Handprint, BIFF Square

Even if it just appears at the end of a film that's shot chiefly inside a moving KTX train, Busan's name was finally etched in cinema history when Yeon Sang-ho's zombie action flick *Train to Busan* (2016) became an international hit. This tale of a fraught father-daughter relationship, set against the backdrop of a zombie apocalypse, was shot creatively on a train and became South Korea's highest-grossing film of that year. It topped box offices across Asia (Malaysia, Hong Kong, Singapore), broke records in the US and Canada, and earned global acclaim for its nonstop action and profound social commentary. *Train to Busan* also helped pave the way for the international recognition of South Korean cinema, which gained momentum soon after when Bong Joon-ho's masterpiece, *Parasite* (2019), the highest-grossing Korean film internationally, became the first non-English language film to win Best Picture at the 92nd Academy Awards in 2020.

Yet Busan's cinematic rise was no accident. Long before Korean films conquered global box offices, the port city had quietly laid the groundwork for international production: an openness to foreign influences, a visual landscape distinct from Seoul's bureaucratic sprawl, and a pragmatic approach to filmmakers. With its hills tumbling toward the sea, traditional neighbourhoods layered with vertical skylines and the lap of the ocean that infuses an ever-present sense of movement, Busan offers directors a ready-made canvas that feels like both past and present.

The truth is, Busan has been involved in upholding and celebrating Korean and international cinema for over a century. The roots hark back to a much more remote past: between 1895 and 1915, Busan's Haengjwa Theatre was

ROBERT GAUTHIER/LOS ANGELES TIMES/GETTY IMAGES

TUPUNGATO/SHUTTERSTOCK

one of the first places to ever screen a film in Korea. The city also maintained nearly two dozen theatres during the Japanese colonial era, which ended with Korea's liberation in 1945.

Celebrating Cinema

The **Busan International Film Festival** (BIFF) began in September 1996 as the country's first international film festival. The primary focus was and still is to promote new films and up-and-coming directors, especially from Korea and Asia, particularly trying to attract young spectators and new talent. From humble beginnings, BIFF has become one of Asia's most important film festivals: the latest editions have attracted audiences of over 70,000 people and since 2025, BIFF has also introduced a brand-new competition section dedicated only to Asian cinema. The festival's growing popularity helped Busan become the first UNESCO Creative City of Film in Asia in 2014.

> Busan offers directors a ready-made canvas that feels like both past and present.

It all started in Nampo-Dong's **BIFF Square** – a central pedestrian alley set between the Daeyeong Cinema and Megabox Busan and within walking distance to the Jagalchi Fish Market – which earned the official BIFF name in 1996 in anticipation of the festival's first edition. Even if at first sight it looks like a random shopping street lined with *pojangmacha* (food carts) spilling over from the nearby Gukje Market, BIFF Street offers a year-round tribute to cinema with its bronzed handprints and signatures of screen idols from Korea and

Watch Before You Go

Ode to My Father (2014) Spanning decades of Korean history, this family drama features memorable scenes filmed in Busan markets and cliffside parks.

Steel Flower (2015) A quietly powerful indie about a young woman's struggles to find work in Busan.

Friend (2001) A neo-noir drama about four childhood friends in Busan, notable for its local dialect and authentic hometown setting.

The Thieves (2012) Hit Korean heist film that was partly filmed in Busan alongside other locations such as Seoul, Hong Kong and Macau.

Haeundae (Tidal Wave) (2009) A hit-or-miss disaster film that saves itself thanks to striking computer-generated images of a giant tsunami hitting Busan's beaches.

beyond – new names pop up every year after each festival edition. Look out for the imprints of silver-screen greats such as Takeshi Kitano, Dario Argento, Wim Wenders, Tsui Hark, Jeremy Irons and more.

Since 2011, the BIFF has had a new permanent home at **Busan Cinema Centre** in Centum City. Besides being a magnificent building that features the world's longest cantilevered structure, Busan Cinema Centre also has a free cinema library on the fourth floor of the Double Cone building. Movie lovers can spend days browsing a collection of over 44,000 cinema-related items, including magazines and rare vintage movie soundtracks on vinyl, which can be played on freely available analogue stereo systems.

What makes Busan so attractive on screen is not just recognisable landmarks, but how the city develops horizontally between sea and mountains.

Museum of Movies

Not far away from BIFF Square and near the leafy park of Yongdusan, **Busan Museum of Movies** (busanbom.kr; adult/child ₩14000/11000; closed Mondays) provides hours of entertainment and a deep dive into Busan's – and Korea's – cinematic origins. The exhibits cover local cinema's history from the Japanese colonial occupation to the consolidation of the modern movie industry that, together with K-Pop music, cemented South Korea as a global entertainment powerhouse. The visit is super hands-on in different aspects of moviemaking: you can have fun recording voiceovers, trying a green screen, editing and even play a movie trivia game – but only in Korean.

Popular Filming Locations in Busan

Fans of Marvel superhero movies may have first unknowingly seen Busan from the neon-basked car-chase scene shot in the narrow lanes around Jagalchi Market and Gwangalli Beach as featured in Ryan Coogler's *Black Panther* (2018) – but many other local film crews have shot in the port city before.

What makes Busan so attractive on screen is not just recognisable landmarks, but how the city develops horizontally between sea and mountains. Steep staircases, cliff-hugging roads, foggy hills and container ports intersect with space-age modernity and blasts of powerful nature. At the same time, the constant proximity of water adds a feeling

NOINA/SHUTTERSTOCK

STEFANGDE/SHUTTERSTOCK

of nature's unpredictability. Directors often exploit the city's compressed geography, where working-class neighbourhoods, beaches and glass towers sit within minutes of each other, allowing Busan to double as multiple cities or moods within a single film.

Among the most famous are *Train to Busan* (2016) and its sequel *Peninsula* (2020), which showed the city as a post-apocalyptic playground for flesh-eating romps. Park Chan-wook's *Decision to Leave* (2022) works viscerally well thanks to its atmospheric scenes set with Busan's foggy hills and dramatic coastline. His earlier international chiller, *Oldboy* (2003), featured maniacal depictions of the *mandu* dumplings from Busan's Jangsunghyang restaurant in Chinatown that the protagonist, Oh, must eat for 15 years. The film won the Grand Prix at the Cannes Film Festival in 2004, introducing the pull-no-punches intensity of Korean cinema to the world.

Tourist magnet Gamcheon Culture Village could not be left out. It has been featured in multiple films and series, such as *L.U.C.A.: The Beginning* (2021) and *A Little Princess* (2019). Another lesser-known sibling, the coast-hugging Huinnyeoul Culture Village, was also used as a central location for Yang Woo-seok's *The Attorney* (2013), a legal thriller rooted in Busan's political history, which also features scenes shot at the nearby Taejongdae Park. More recent movies, such as the supernatural horror *Exhuma* (2024), have also used Busan's unique old-meets-new streetscapes and skyscraper-sheltered beaches as unforgettable backdrops. Take a look and try to find them on your next visit.

Far left Gamcheon Culture Village **Left** Jagalchi Market **Top left** Busan Cinema Centre **Top right** Busan Museum of Movies

South Korean Cinema Today

The industry is steadily recovering despite post-COVID-19 setbacks, with new releases thriving at home and attracting regional attention. In 2024, South Korea sold over 123 million movie tickets, showing robust domestic demand. The horror film *Exhuma* (2024) drew nearly 12 million domestic viewers, while only a few foreign blockbusters managed to break through. By mid-2025, K-Dramas, such as the three series of Netflix's *Squid Game*, had totalled almost 600 million views internationally, keeping the world's attention on Korean content. While no film has matched *Parasite*'s worldwide acclaim yet, the global success of American-made and Korea-inspired animated film *K-Pop Demon Hunters* (2025) only helped keep up the momentum.

22 SAILING Hallyeohaesang

ISLANDS | BOATS | HIKING

The balmy coastal city of Tongyeong is often considered the centrepiece of the 535-sq-km Hallyeohaesang National Park, Korea's first marine park. There are more than 100 islands surrounding this sapphire sea, many of which are easily reachable from Tongyeong's various ferry terminals. Striking out on a private sailing boat tour makes things even more adventurous and beautiful.

ICEDAMERICANO/SHUTTERSTOCK

How To

Getting there Tongyeong has multiple ferry terminals to the offshore islands. The main one near Gangguan Harbour has departures to Hansando (30 minutes), Bijindo (one hour) and Somaemuldo (1½ hours). You'll need your passport to buy tickets.

When to go Weekends, and May to September, get very busy and have steeper accommodation prices.

Budget tip Pack enough food and a portable stove to save money. You can also free camp as most locals do.

PHOTO_JEONGH/SHUTTERSTOCK

Popular getaway **Bijindo** must be the marine park's most popular island – in fact, it's two, connected by a sandbank. There are plenty of boats from **Tongyeong Ferry Terminal** that drop visitors at the main port. A 550m-long, soft beach attracts visitors for a swim and a nice picnic.

Hiking paradise To the west of Tongyeong, the archipelago of **Saryangdo** comprises more than 30 islands, of which only three are inhabited. A 530m-long bridge connects the northern and southern islands. The main attraction is the thrilling five-hour-long **Jirisan** trail above a six-peaked ridge, starting with 368m-high Jirisan to the west and ending with 263m-high Oknyeobong in the east. Suspended bridges hang between some of the peaks, offering vertigo-inducing views over the bay.

Historical site **Hansando** is an important naval battle site of the Imjin War's Great Battle of Hansan, when national hero Admiral Yi Sun-sin defeated the Japanese. A shrine commemorates the site of the 16th-century naval headquarters.

Finding peace Only about an hour from Tongyeong, **Haklimdo** features a seawater pool hemmed by rock and a short hiking platform to the top of the only central hillock. Take a shellfish-digging and village experience with Mr Song Geun-hyeong (WhatsApp 010 44333450). **Yeonhwado** features a peaceful Buddhist hermitage and bridges that connect the island to Banhado and Udo.

Top left Bijindo
Bottom left Tongyeong Ferry

Sailing Matters

Korea's southern coast is the prettiest, with multiple bays and islands backed by tall mountains. Weather-wise, spring and fall are probably the best for sailing. That's when events like the Busan Super Cup Yacht Race and Tongyeong's Yisunsin International Cup take place. Sometimes boats look for experienced crews – ask around at the marinas in Haeundae Beach, Busan or Tongyeong. The Korea Sailing Association Federation website (ksaf.org) is also a good starting point. These days, yacht tours are popular, but many are just an hour-long catamaran sightseeing trip. More extended sailing tours to the islands are less common.

Adam Tacey is a Busan-based sailor and English teacher.

Listings

BEST OF THE REST

Traditional Food

Solbat Sikdang (솔밭식당) ₩

One of the best choices among restaurants outside Hahoe Folk Village, it serves excellent *jjimdak* (braised chicken and vegetables in dark soy sauce) and *godeungeo gui* (grilled mackerel).

Hongsi Hanjeongsik ₩₩

Traditional *hanjeongsik* (banquet) style family restaurant in a stunningly decorated *hanok* house on the western side of Gyeongju, with large portions and a curated, ever-changing menu of dozens of side dishes.

Gaejeung ₩₩

In business since 1978, this spot in Daegu serves bibimbap, pork bulgogi, *naengmyeon* (cold noodles) and more. This is the main branch; others are located around the city.

Ddungbo Halmae Gimbap Jip ₩

This simple restaurant is a long-time favourite and serves just *chungmu kimbap*, Tongyeong's local specialty of mini rice rolls wrapped in dried seaweed, with spicy squid and radish.

Craft Beer

Galmegi Brewing

Busan's first American-style brewery has two main branches, located in Haeundae and Nampo. Try their signature beer, Galmegi IPA, or sample the flavourful Yuja Gose if you prefer a sour option.

Hugus Beer Pub

Set on the southern side of Busan's Gangwalli Beach, this pub uses local produce, including honey, carrots, mushrooms and perilla leaves, in its beers. They frequently change their taps and offer specials.

The Beer Shop

Jeonpo's best place to drink features an outdoor patio, offering a large selection of beers sourced from the Gorilla Beer brewery. Don't skimp on the food: try the house's pastrami burgers.

Mireuk Mireuk Beer Hostel

Unique Buddhist-cum-beer concept and hip hostel in an old sauna in Tongyeong, with rooms up above and a bar on the ground level where the congenial owner serves craft beer.

Rein Deutsch Brewery

Tongyeong's own 'Pure German' brewery recreates Bavarian-type malts in a seaside locale. It's also a pub-type restaurant, serving fried pork cutlets, burgers and other greasy grub to complement the drinks.

Hikes & Trails

Taejongdae Park

On the southernmost tip of the island of Yeongdo in Busan, experience the city's rugged

TERIMMA/SHUTTERSTOCK

Taejongdae Park

coastline along a well-groomed 4.5km walking path that follows a circular road.

Igidae

A part of Busan's 23-section, 278km-long Galmaetgil Trail, Igidae's 4.7km coastal route, paved with staircases and platforms, goes through forests and over bedrocks and is possibly Busan's most popular hike.

Tongyeong Undersea Tunnel

Built in the early 1930s, the 483m-long Undersea Tunnel is a short but very atmospheric walk across Seoho Bay. From the north end, take the cement corridor and see historical photographs of its construction.

Namsan Samneunggol Valley Loop

One of Gyeongju's best hikes goes past royal tombs, rock-carved Buddhas, stone pagodas and mountain shrines to 468m-high Geumobong Peak, the reserve's second-highest, across Namsan's relic-richest valley.

Spiritual Temples & Shrines

Haedong Yonggung-sa

One of the country's few temples situated right on the coast, Haedong Yonggung-sa in Busan's northeastern Gijang-gun district offers spectacular views of the temple grounds and the surrounding ocean.

Donghwa-sa

Set on the foothills of Palgongsan National Park, north of Daegu, this temple was built in 493 CE and features buildings dating back to the 18th century. Don't miss the 33m-high Tongil Yaksa Buddha statue, one of the world's largest stone medicine Buddhas.

Haein-sa

West of Daegu is one of Korea's most stunning and important temples, containing the Tripitaka Koreana – a historic and priceless collection of 81,258 carved woodblock

EVA MONT/SHUTTERSTOCK

Songdo Marine Cable Car

Buddhist scriptures that took 16 years to complete.

Bongjeong-sa

The largest temple in Andong features a main hall, the Geungnakjeon, presumed to be the oldest wooden building in Korea, dating back to the early 1200s, during the Goryeo dynasty.

Cable Cars

Palgongsan Cable Car

A 1.2km, seven-minute ride to the top of the sacred Sinnimbong Peak of Palgongsan. Hike to the east peak, Dongbong, or eat at one of the restaurants with panoramic views.

Songdo Marine Cable Car

Initially launched in 1964 in Busan as Korea's first cable car, Songdo Beach's main attraction reopened in 2017 as Busan Air Cruise and traverses emerald waters for 1.62km.

Tongyeong Cable Car

This 1975m-long cable car takes nine minutes to reach near the top of Mireuk-san (461m). Walk the rest of the way for bird's-eye views of the surrounding islands of Hallyeohaesang National Park.

JEOLLA-DO

CULTURE | MYSTIC PEAKS | INFINITE ISLANDS

RESEARCHED BY MARCO FERRARESE

TRABANTOS/SHUTTERSTOCK

JEOLLA-DO
Trip Builder

Once stereotyped by Koreans as a rural backwater and famous for the pro-democracy Gwangju Uprising of 18 May 1980, in truth, the southwestern part of Korea is a treasure trove of beguiling cities, wild nature and more islands than one can see in a lifetime.

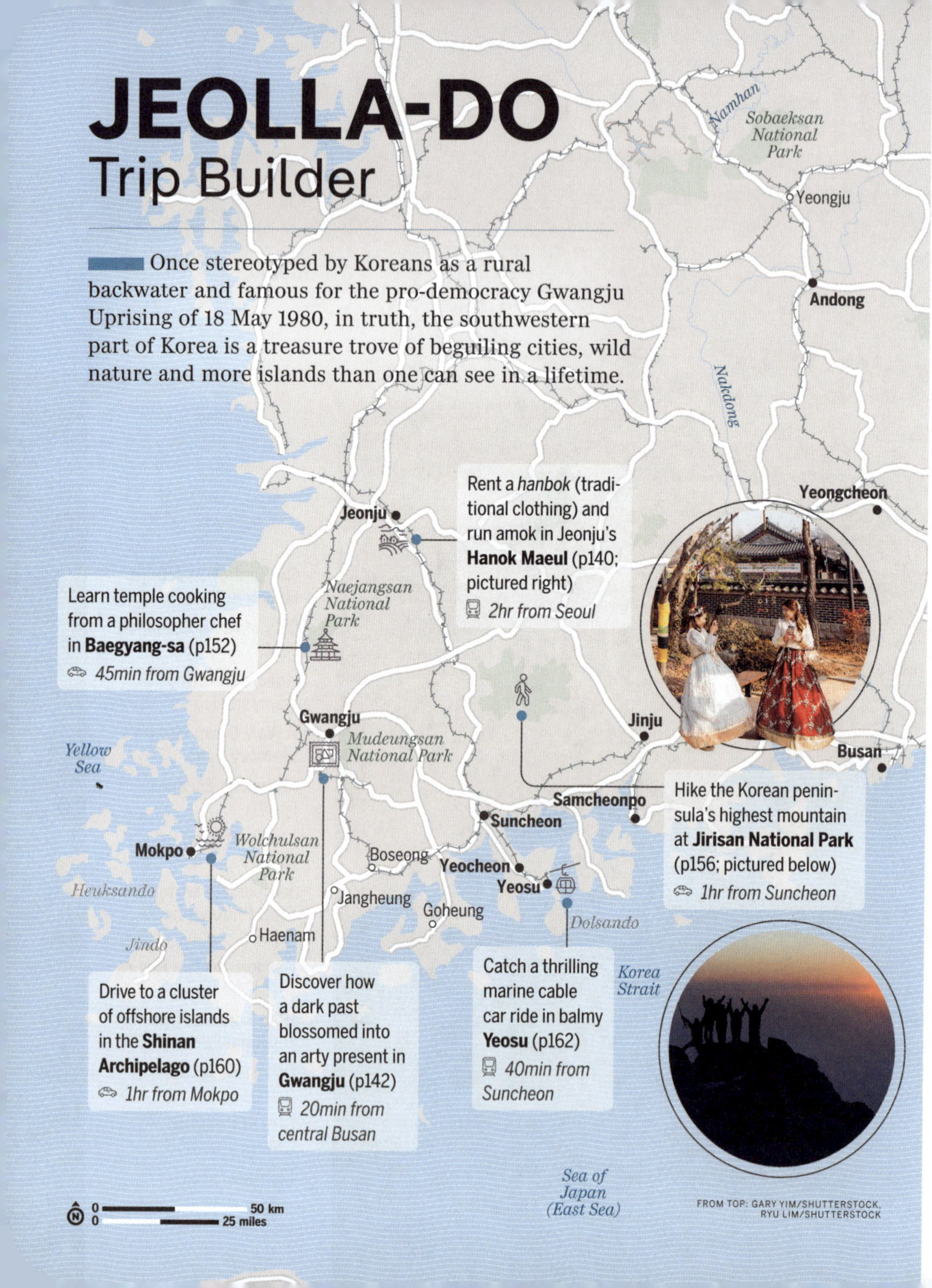

Rent a *hanbok* (traditional clothing) and run amok in Jeonju's **Hanok Maeul** (p140; pictured right)
2hr from Seoul

Learn temple cooking from a philosopher chef in **Baegyang-sa** (p152)
45min from Gwangju

Hike the Korean peninsula's highest mountain at **Jirisan National Park** (p156; pictured below)
1hr from Suncheon

Drive to a cluster of offshore islands in the **Shinan Archipelago** (p160)
1hr from Mokpo

Discover how a dark past blossomed into an arty present in **Gwangju** (p142)
20min from central Busan

Catch a thrilling marine cable car ride in balmy **Yeosu** (p162)
40min from Suncheon

FROM TOP: GARY YIM/SHUTTERSTOCK, RYU LIM/SHUTTERSTOCK

Practicalities

ARRIVING

Gwangju Airport has flights to Jeju-do and Seoul's Gimpo Airport.

Gwangju Songjeong station in the west of the city is well connected by KTX trains and Gwangju's metro line 1.

CONNECT

Free wi-fi is not always reliable. Check if your provider's roaming plans include South Korea as they can be cheaper than local SIM cards.

MONEY

Credit cards are widely accepted, though some businesses on the islands may still prefer cash.

WHERE TO STAY

Place	Pros/Cons
Jeonju	Jeonju Hanok Village has atmospheric accommodation, but can get crowded.
Gwangju	The area around the Asia Culture Centre is close to most sights.
Suncheon	Stay near the train station for good food and walking to the gardens.
Yeosu	Yi Sun-sin Square is smack central, even though exploring Dolsan Island will need wheels.

GETTING AROUND

Bus Jeolla-do's scattered countryside is best travelled by bus, even though the smaller destinations still have few daily services. Cities have bus services to most outlying sights and hikes.

Train Jeonju, Gwangju and Mokpo are well-connected to Seoul via the Honam line, while the Jeolla line links Iksan to Suncheon and Yeosu. For Busan, it's necessary to change trains at Mulgeum station in Gyeongsangnam-do.

EATING & DRINKING

Jeolla-do is considered Korea's best food region, known for its abundance of *banchan* (side dishes) and Joseon dynasty fermentation techniques. Jeonju is the birthplace of bibimbap (pictured top), a simple mixed rice dish served with many toppings, while Mokpo and the coastal areas are paradise for seafood lovers. The region is also famous for its strong, savoury *makgeolli* (rice wine; pictured bottom).

Must-try coffee with traveller vibes
Voyagers Cafe (p164)

Best cooking class
Philosopher chef Jeong Kwan (p152)

JAN–MAR
Frosty temperatures but the best season to ski in Muju.

APR–JUN
Spring brings pleasant sunny days that slowly turn into summer.

JUL–SEP
Summer means rainy season, particularly in the coastal areas.

OCT–DEC
Autumn has dry, pleasant weather with clear skies, perfect for travelling.

23 Go Hanbok in Jeonju HANOK VILLAGE

TRADITION | CITY WALK | PHOTOGRAPHY

Step into the heart of Jeollabuk-do's provincial capital, Jeonju, where the touristy yet picture-perfect *maeul* (village) features more than 700 restored *hanok* (traditional wooden homes). A visit to Jeonju Hanok Village is not just for pretty pictures: between cafes and boutiques, the vestiges of Jeonju's history are hidden in plain sight.

YEONGSIK IM/SHUTTERSTOCK

How To

When to go Every season has its own perks but early spring, when cherry blossoms dot the surrounding hills, makes for great pictures.

Getting there The *hanok maeul* is a short bus or taxi ride from Jeonju's Intercity and Express Bus stations, which are only 100m apart.

Local snack Try the choco-pies by Jeonju's oldest bakery, Poong Nyeon JeGwa (**PNB**), a cocoa cake sandwich with a dollop of jam.

DEKWEAGWANG/SHUTTERSTOCK

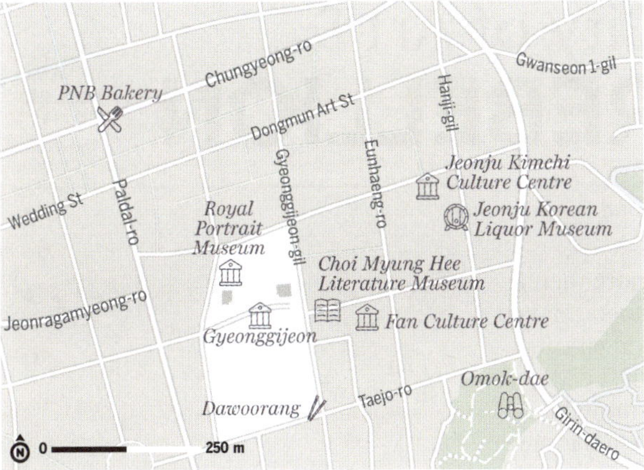

Top left Gyeonggijeon
Bottom left View from Omok-dae

Rent a Hanbok

Many shops have *hanbok* costumes for rent for about ₩20,000–30,000 for three hours. Some offer photo packages with a crew ushering you around the village's most photogenic spots.

Dynastic Past

The village's centrepiece palace, the **Gyeonggijeon** (adult/child/teenager ₩3000/1000/2000) dates back to 1410 and is a preferred backdrop for photo sessions. The large compound beyond the temple-like doorway is filled with shrines, storehouses and guardrooms related to the Confucian rituals once held here. At the back is the **Royal Portrait Museum**, with a replica portrait of the Joseon dynasty's (1392–1910) founder Yi Seong-gye – free guided tours of the complex in English start at 11am and 2pm.

Interesting Museums

Some of the *hanok* contain museums. The **Fan Culture Centre** (jeonjufan.kr; free) promotes the heritage of traditional fans made in Jeonju, while the **Choi Myung Hee Literature Museum** (free) celebrates the work of the author of the epic novel *Honbul*, about three generations of women during Japanese colonial rule. **Jeonju Korean Liquor Museum** (free) provides a look into Gayang-ju spirit-making, and you'll learn kimchi-nomics at **Jeonju Kimchi Culture Centre** (free).

Perfect Viewpoint

Set on the southeastern side of the village, **Omok-dae** hill is one of the best spots for a panoramic view of over a hundred slanted roofs. A pavilion commemorates General Yi Seonggye's 1380 victory over Japanese pirates.

Must-Try Jeonju Hanok Village Snacks

Choco-pie: An old-school snack made of two discs of cocoa cake around a filling of cream and strawberry jam, all dunked in chocolate. PNB is a popular brand with a shop that attracts queues.

Strawberry red bean mochi: Whole strawberries and sweetened red bean paste wrapped in a layer of mochi.

Meatball skewer: Marinated, juicy meatballs on a stick are very popular.

Grilled cheese skewer: A block of grilled golden-brown mildly flavoured cheese, served with a yoghurt dip.

Shrimp dumplings: There are long queues for those made by **Dawoorang** (다우랑).

24 City of Art & REBELLION

MUSEUMS | ART GALLERIES | DARK HISTORY

Gwangju is much more than a modern city of tall skyscrapers. Hailed as the country's most liberal city, its rebellious fame stems from the May 18 Democratic Uprising that brought havoc here in 1980. Gwangju has since rebranded as a centre for arts and culture, hosting the Gwangju Biennale and Design Biennale, and funding many cutting-edge art galleries.

How To

Getting there KTX train services from Seoul and the rest of Jeolla-do arrive at **Gwangju Songjeong station** in the west of town, connected to the **Asia Culture Centre** by metro line 1. Buses from the rest of the province and beyond arrive at the central **U-Square**.

When to go Mid-October is a good time to catch the week-long oldie music and culture festival, **Chungjang Street Festival of Recollection**.

Traces of the uprising The **May 18 National Cemetery** (free) in the city's northeast is the final burial place of the victims – primarily students – who protested against military dictator Chun Doo-hwan's seizure of power in May 1980. Official numbers estimate 228 dead, but the toll is believed to be higher.

Democracy ground zero The battleground is remembered with **May 18 Democracy Square**, set in the old downtown to the city's southeast. Cross the road and enter the **Jeonil Building 245** (free), whose 10th floor features an exhibit on the events, including the empty room with traces of 245 shots fired by a military helicopter during the crack-downs. Get to the terrace on the 12th floor for dramatic views of the city and the surrounding amphitheatre of wild mountains.

Art museums and centres Amid the cluster of museums in the city's northern suburbs don't miss

ED JONES/GETTY IMAGES

Gwangju Follies

A little-known aspect of my artistic and progressive city is the Gwangju Folly Movement (gwangjufolly.org) – an urban regeneration project initiated as part of the Gwangju Design Biennale, which has already held five editions. This is not just about pretty museum-like showpieces: Korean and foreign artists and architects have used small, functional architecture as installations, thus revitalising Gwangju's downtown area in ways that integrate seamlessly with the urban landscape – think of art used to improve children's playgrounds and to beautify with a useful scope, rather than eye candy. Spend a day seeking them out as you walk around downtown.

■ **Pedro Kim** is the owner of Voyagers Cafe and Pedro House Hostel. *@voyagers_cafe*

Gwangju Museum of Art (artmuse.gwangju.go.kr; free), **Gwangju Culture & Art Centre** (free) and the **Gwangju Biennale Exhibition Hall** (gwangjubiennale.org; adult/child/teenager ₩16,000/5000/8000), the festival's primary location, which all sit near each other and showcase work from established and up-and-coming Korean artists.

Art by Democracy Square

Back in May 18 Democracy Square, don't miss the **Asia Culture Centre** (free), a cluster of buildings hosting rotating exhibits, performance spaces, a library, free coworking space and plazas to relax. It's a five-minute walk north to **Gwangju Art Street**, packed with cafes, art galleries and studios.

Above May 18 National Cemetery

25 Nature Getaways IN DAMYANG

NATURE | GARDENS | WALKS

It doesn't take long to leave Gwangju's urban sprawl and find yourself surrounded by soothing nature. The town of Damyang, only about 20km to the northeast of the city, is possibly the most popular among Gwangju's satellite green getaways. A central meandering river dotted with food stalls, walking and cycling paths sets the stage for Juknokwon, the country's most famous bamboo forest.

JO HAKHWAN/SHUTTERSTOCK

How To

Getting there Buses 311 and 311-2 leave the bus stop in front of Gwangju's U-Square and take about 20 minutes to reach Juknokwon.

Getting around Walking along the riverside paths connecting the sights is very enjoyable, but rental bicycles will get you further.

Signature bamboo dishes Try *daetong-bap*, rice often cooked with black beans, chestnuts and jujubes inside a bamboo stalk. Other dishes use *juksun* (bamboo shoots) for preparation.

SANGA PARK/SHUTTERSTOCK

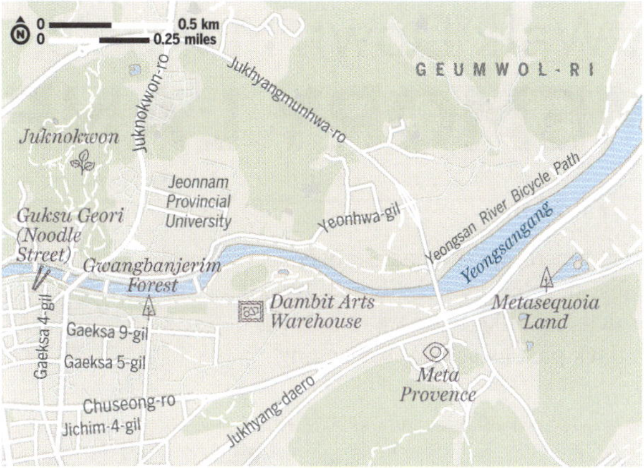

Enter the bamboo forest Atop a temple-like entry staircase, **Juknokwon** (adult/child/student ₩3000/1000/2000) is Damyang's prime tourist magnet and South Korea's most popular bamboo grove. Eight different sandy trails lead visitors into tunnel-like paths where bamboo stalks soar overhead, past pavilions, photo spots and film locations used in multiple Korean dramas. The forest can get crowded on weekends, so try to pick a quiet weekday to enjoy the atmosphere best.

Riverside stroll The Yeongsangang River splits Damyang in half. Start walking right across the road from Juknokwon and enter the protected **Gwangbanjerim Forest**. A 1.6km walking trail on the southern bend of the river features over 170 protected trees, including muku, zelkova, hackberries and cherry trees over 300 years old, whose foliage changes colour with the seasons. Less than a kilometre into the walk, pay attention to the **Dambit Arts Warehouse**, a literary cafe and art gallery set inside a former rice storage. There's a century-old bamboo pipe organ, the only one found in Korea, preserved under glass.

Sequoia road Planted in the 1970s beside National Road 24, Damyang's **Metasequoia Land** (adult/child/teenager ₩2000/700/1000) trees today are so high they block out the sun. A walk here is a different experience in every season – spring and autumn being the most striking – and an excellent spot for photography.

Top left Metasequoia Land
Bottom left Juknokwon in winter

Foodie Diversions

Many come to Damyang not just for bamboo and trails, but also to wolf down some delicious food.

The handiest, simplest and cheapest is found at **Guksu Geori (Noodle Street)**, a collection of riverside stalls across the road from the start of the Gwangbanjerim Forest.

Another local speciality is *tteok-galbi* (grilled short-rib patties), found all over town.

An interesting place for more cafe-style options is **Meta Provence**, a quirky European-themed walking area next to the entrance to **Metasequoia Land**, featuring French- and German-looking squares and buildings. It's a good spot for a date or finding Damyang's best coffee shops.

26 A Walk Down Mokpo's MEMORY LANE

HISTORY | ARCHITECTURE | DESIGN

The southwestern port city of Mokpo has changed very little compared to its fast-developing neighbours. A walk through its low-rise downtown feels like taking a trip down memory lane from Korea's dark past as a Japanese colony to its turbulent modernity.

YLLYSO/SHUTTERSTOCK

How To

Getting there **Mokpo train station** is within walking distance of most historical buildings. It's connected to most parts of Korea by frequent KTX and Mugunghwa services via Gwangju Songjeong station.

Getting around Mokpo's downtown is compact and very much walkable. Bicycles make it possible to strike further out along the coastline with little effort.

Evergreen snack Fuel up with a shrimp or cream cheese baguette from the historical **Colombang Bakery**.

Tears of Mokpo

This *trot* song (the oldest type of Korean pop music), released in 1935 and first sung by Lee Nan-young, is strongly associated with the city of Mokpo and Japanese colonial rule. Seemingly evoking images of longing for love, some interpreted the lyrics as an expression of Korean nationalism – one line specifically resents the first Japanese attacks during the Imjin War 300 years earlier.

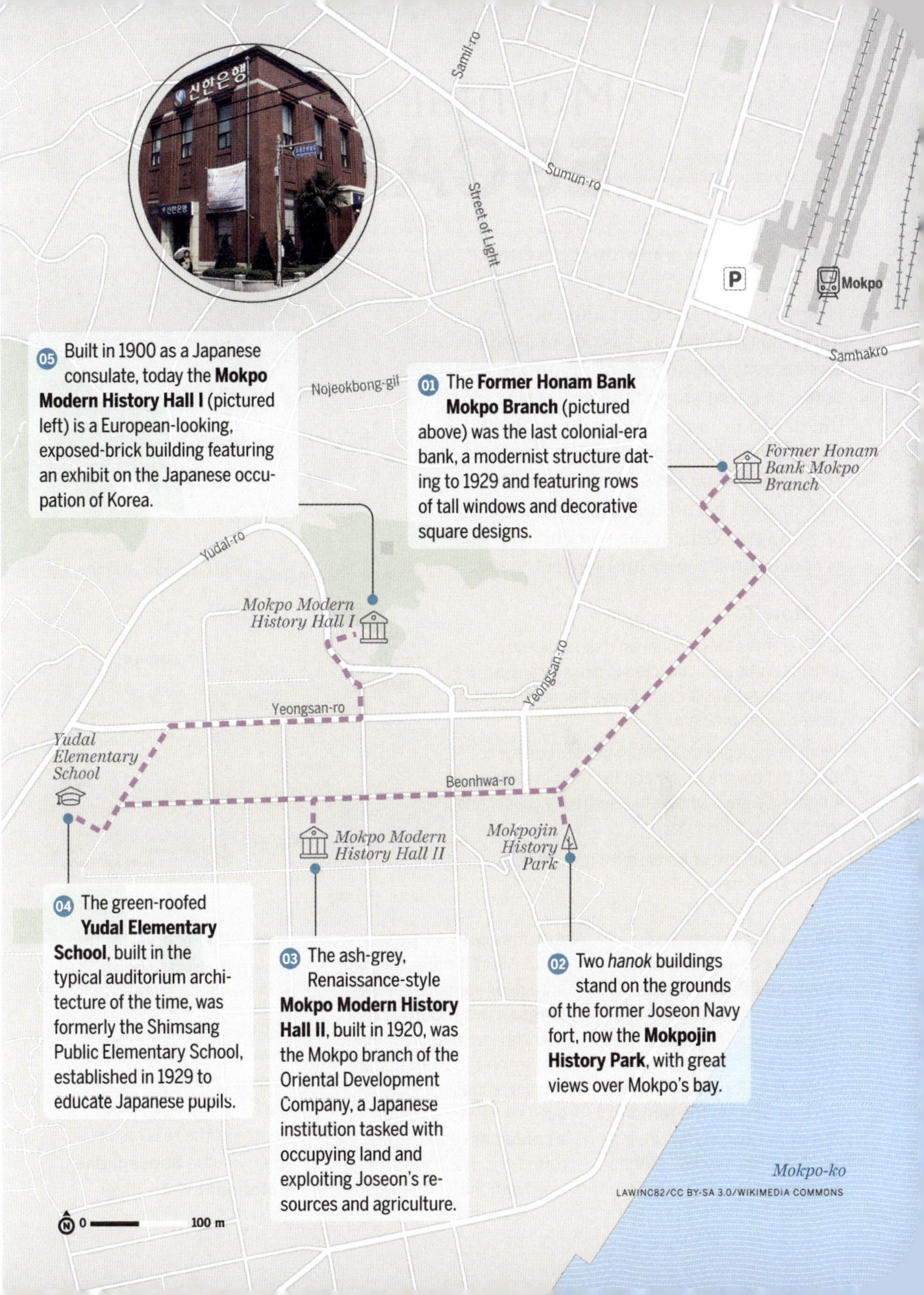

01 The **Former Honam Bank Mokpo Branch** (pictured above) was the last colonial-era bank, a modernist structure dating to 1929 and featuring rows of tall windows and decorative square designs.

02 Two *hanok* buildings stand on the grounds of the former Joseon Navy fort, now the **Mokpojin History Park**, with great views over Mokpo's bay.

03 The ash-grey, Renaissance-style **Mokpo Modern History Hall II**, built in 1920, was the Mokpo branch of the Oriental Development Company, a Japanese institution tasked with occupying land and exploiting Joseon's resources and agriculture.

04 The green-roofed **Yudal Elementary School**, built in the typical auditorium architecture of the time, was formerly the Shimsang Public Elementary School, established in 1929 to educate Japanese pupils.

05 Built in 1900 as a Japanese consulate, today the **Mokpo Modern History Hall I** (pictured left) is a European-looking, exposed-brick building featuring an exhibit on the Japanese occupation of Korea.

27 Mountain ESCAPES

HIKING | NATURE | BUDDHIST SHRINES

Step off the coast and the hundreds of offshore islands to Jeolla-do's tapestry of dozens of mountains. Some rise like stone fans protecting the flanks of mega-cities while others stand alone inside national parks criss-crossed by perfect hiking trails and draped with Buddhist temples and hermitages. Whichever you choose, prepare for serenity and perfect views.

How To

Getting there Most mountain trailheads and national parks are connected to cities by bus, although departures are not always frequent. A rental car solves the problem.

When to go Jeolla-do's mountains are open year-round, but beware of snow on the trails in winter. Autumn is a great season to see striking copper and orange hues in the foliage.

Cost Like the rest of Korea, most mountains in Jeolla-do are free to hike.

Twin peaks Located east of Jeonju, beautiful **Maisan Provincial Park** features twin mountains shaped like donkey ears. Only 685m-high Ammai-san can be climbed via a 1.7km-long boardwalk starting beyond the temple of **Tap-sa**, whose sculpture garden features over 80 stones and pinnacles.

Autumn colours poster child A well-known hiking area near Jeongeup, **Naejangsan** is famous for its autumn leaf displays. Hike the amphitheatre-shaped rim via a challenging trek over six peaks, or catch a **cable car** (adult/child round-trip ₩8000/5000). Use Namchang, the western side of the reserve, for the 4.5km **Ibamsanseong Trail** to 641m-high Gatbawi.

Natural protection Gwangju's guardian mountain rises on the eastern flanks of the city. At the centre of the reserve is the majestic **Seoseokdae Colonnade**, with sheer

SEUNG-IL RYU/NURPHOTO/GETTY IMAGES

Practical Trail Wisdom

Jeolla-do's hiking trails are well marked but rarely explained in English, so a Korean map app like Naver, along with the offline GPS Maps.me, is very useful. Most of the trailheads are reachable by local buses, though services thin out in the afternoons – start early and check return times before setting off, to avoid being stranded. Carry cash for village shops, trail snacks or a last-minute taxi ride back to town. Weather changes fast, especially up in the hills, and fog can roll in without warning. If in doubt, follow the friendly *ajeosshi* and *ajumma* (local middle-aged male or female hikers).

boulders up to 30m-high and 2m-wide, spread horizontally like a folding screen. Nearby is **Cheonwanbong**, the highest peak at 1187m.

City heights Coastal mountain Yudal-san soars above Mokpo's city centre, offering fantastic views of the Dadohae Sea and a power hike across its three rocky peaks. The **Mokpo Marine Cable Car** (mmcablecar.com; adult/child round-trip ₩24,000/18,000) also stops near the peak.

Korea's smallest national park **Wolchulsan National Park** has crags, spires and unusually shaped rocks around every corner, as well as an 8m Buddha rock carving, steel stairways and a 52m steel bridge spanning two ridges.

Above Tap-sa

By Marco Ferrarese
@marcoferrarese

The Best Food in Korea?

KOREANS OFTEN RAVE ABOUT THE QUALITY OF JEOLLA-DO'S CUISINE

Jeolla-do has long been framed as Korea's rural corner, a hotbed of rebellion and left-leaning politics. The question is whether some of that unease isn't rooted in something simpler: jealousy. Spend any time eating in the region, and you'll understand how Jeolla's food is generous, grounded and among Korea's most delicious.

JOHNATHAN21/SHUTTERSTOCK

Left *Hongeo-hoe* **Centre** Crab, Yeosu **Right** *Tteok-galbi*

South Korea's Surprising Breadbasket

Mention Jeolla-do to any Korean person, and you may be met either with a stern look hinting at the province's reputation as a hotbed of progressive politics, or with a dreamy, wide-eyed acknowledgement that yes, that's where 'Korea's best food comes from'.

Korea's so-called breadbasket owes its status to favourable geography. In the north, Jeollabuk-do has vast, fertile plains that have long produced reliable rice harvests, largely uninterrupted by the mountain ranges that fragment farmland elsewhere on the peninsula. In the south, Jeollanam-do's endless coastlines and scattering of islands have always made it easy to put fish on the table quickly and efficiently.

At its simplest, Jeolla-do is often credited with gifting Korea with one of its quintessential dishes: bibimbap, the rice-based medley of vegetables and meat commonly associated with Jeonju, the provincial capital of Jeollabuk-do. Yet a single well-known dish should not take the spotlight away from the region's southern half, Jeollanam-do. This is where local cuisine becomes more layered yet delicate, shaped by the umami of seafood hauled fresh (oftentimes still wriggling, like the seasoned, chopped-but-writhing octopus tentacles of Mokpo's *san-nakji*) from the long western and southern coasts.

Jeolla-do's flavours are also shaped by a deep fermentation culture centred on *jang*, Korea's fermented sauces recognised by UNESCO in 2024 as Intangible Cultural Heritage. Traditionally stored in earthenware jars known as *onggi*, these sauces underpin much of the region's cooking. Travellers can explore this tradition firsthand at

COCA COCO/SHUTTERSTOCK

SUNGSU HAN/SHUTTERSTOCK

Ki Soon-do's Fermentation School in Damyang or at the **Gochujang Village** in Sunchang, both to the northeast of Gwangju.

A Cuisine of Abundance

Some argue that Jeolla-do's food culture diverges from the typical kimchi and barbecued meat-heavy menus found elsewhere in Korea because of the province's past role as a regional centre during the Joseon dynasty. The Geumseonggwan Hall in Naju, once a state guesthouse for dignitaries, stands as a reminder of the 16th century, when refined tastes were cultivated here to satisfy the picky palates of political exiles sent from the north. Others prefer to think that it was because of the province's relative isolation – even tourism arrived in Jeolla-do only recently, despite the region's quick two-to-three-hour railway access from Seoul – that allowed local culinary traditions to develop.

> Jeolla-do is often credited with gifting Korea with one of its quintessential dishes: bibimbap

The most logical explanation, however, is abundance. Jeolla-do's fertile land and fish-rich seas explain the generous food portions, accompanied by some of Korea's most prolific *banchan* (side dishes) that support even the most modest meals, often featuring seafood and fermented specialities such as *hongeo-hoe*, a pungent fermented skate. A traditional *hanjeongsik* (full-course meal) can then arrive as a bewildering spread of small plates, not as spectacle but as routine. It reflects a region long accustomed to feeding itself well, and confronts travellers with flavours and preparations they may have never experienced before.

Local Delights

Jeolla-do's cuisine thrived thanks to the mild climate and vast plains where rice and a variety of vegetables can grow, plus the plentiful seafood coming from the west and south coasts. Deep, rich flavours characterise our culinary culture and the region's warm hospitality is evident from the generous portions and the number of side dishes served, no matter which restaurant you visit. I recommend you try duck soup in Gwangju, bamboo rice and *tteok-galbi* in Damyang, live octopus in Muan, *hongeo-hoe* (fermented skate) in Mokpo and the cockle set menu in Boseong. Go for crab in Yeosu: both seasoned marinated or soy sauce–marinated are delicious.

Park Jehyeon is a Gwangju-based travel content creator. @jehyeon_park

28 Templestay with a Chef PHILOSOPHER

BUDDHISM | COOKING CLASS | SPIRITUALISM

South Korea is filled with templestays, but nowhere else can one pair a spiritual stay with a cooking class from a revered celebrity philosopher chef, as at the Chunjinam hermitage of Baegyang-sa on the southern side of Naejangsan National Park. Meet Jeong Kwan, a Buddhist nun who gained global attention for her philosophical approach to vegan temple cuisine in season three of Netflix's *Chef's Table.*

IMAGEBROKER.COM/ALAMY

How To

Getting there The easiest way to reach Baegyang-sa is to catch a KTX train from Seoul's Yongsan station to Jung Eub station. The bus terminal is a 10-minute walk away, from where buses take roughly 40 minutes to reach the temple. It's another 20 minutes on foot to the templestay office.

What to bring Comfortable slip-on footwear for the temple grounds and some layers, as it can get chilly at night, even in summer.

CHEONGHAE/SHUTTERSTOCK

ST_TRAVEL/SHUTTERSTOCK

Far left top Jeong Kwan
Far left bottom Baegyang-sa
Left Naejangsan National Park in autumn

Templestay programs Baegyang-sa offers two options: the first is the resting program, which provides the opportunity to make a 108-bead necklace and experience a tea ceremony and temple culture. You'll want to book the other, monthly **Cooking with Jeong Kwan Program** (adult/child over 10/teenager ₩200,000/100,000/160,000) which includes a four-hour class with the revered nun, an overnight stay in a comfortable templestay room, and meals (breakfast and either lunch or dinner, depending on which meal you'll be cooking with Jeong Kwan). Contact baekyangsa@templestay.com or WhatsApp +82 10 9037 0434.

What to expect Jeong Kwan's class is entirely in Korean, with one interpreter at hand to help foreign guests navigate her explanations. The class starts with an informal chat with the guests and personal introductions that help the philosopher chef choose the recipes to teach. Classes usually start around 4pm and end before 8pm, when guests are directed to a dining room to enjoy what they have prepared, along with additional dishes to try.

Jeong Kwan's food The recipes are strictly vegan and follow the common practice in some Mahayana Buddhism schools of excluding onion and garlic. Each class is absolutely unique, with no recipe taught twice, since produce varies by season. Remember that her recipes are somewhat vague, as the chef's emphasis is on the philosophical aspect of temple food, rather than replicating the same taste all the time.

Hikes around Baegyang-sa

Jeong Kwang's mother temple is also the starting point for some interesting hikes in the southern part of Naejangsan National Park. The two main options are the 8km hike to 741m-high **Sangwangbong**, first reaching 651m-high **Baekhakbong**, then descending a mostly paved road back to the temple. A second trail goes directly to Baekhakbong and then to **Yaksaam Heritage**: while the hike is only 3.8km, the first 2.6km are pretty steep. It's also possible to move west along the 5.9km-long **Monggyepokpo Trail** towards the southwestern **Namchang entrance** of the park, where the 4.5km **Ibamsanseong Trail** climbs to 641m-high Gatbawi.

29 Gardens by the RIVER

WALKS | GARDENS | BIRDWATCHING

The city of Suncheon in Jeollanam-do doesn't figure on many first-time Korea itineraries, but that's a mistake. Nature lovers will immediately realise that no greener city exists in Korea. After hosting the Suncheon-man International Garden Expo in 2013, Suncheon's downtown area transformed into a green patch of flawless manicured gardens, water pools and open lawns where locals enjoy spring and summer nights.

PANWASIN SEEMALA/SHUTTERSTOCK

How To

Getting there **Suncheon train station** is a southern hub serving both the Jeolla line to Seoul and the transversal Gyeongjeon line between Busan and Mokpo. It's also a key stop for KTX trains going south to Yeosu.

Getting around The National Gardens are made for walking. On the west riverbank, catch the **Suncheon-man Sky Cube** (skycube.co.kr; adult/child round-trip ₩8000/6000, oneway ₩6000/5000) for sunset at Suncheon-man Bay Wetlands.

Top tip Entry to the National Gardens is half-price after 5pm.

PANWASIN SEEMALA/SHUTTERSTOCK

Beautiful public gardens Set on the western side of the Dongcheong River, **Ocheon Green Square** is a perfectly manicured patch of freely accessible gardens and a good introduction to Suncheon's green central heart. The grassy meadow features a lagoon on its northeastern side, connected to the Dongcheong's riverbed by bridges and platforms. The square's southwestern corner has two panoramic mounds topped respectively by a geodesic dome and a futuristic steel-rod sculpture.

Korea's first national gardens **Suncheon Bay National Garden** (adult/child/teenager ₩10,000/5000/7000) is a sprawling area planted with 790,000 trees of over 500 different types, a staggering 3.15 million flowers that change colour with the seasons and canola fields that fire up in bloom around mid-May. The Dongcheong River splits the garden into two banks connected by the technological Bridge of Dreams, which lights up after sunset. On the eastern bank are interesting country-themed gardens, from France to the Netherlands, China and more.

Where the river meets the sea Seven kilometres south of the Gardens – either a short but very scenic hop on the **Suncheon-man Sky Cube** monorail or about 45 minutes cycling – the **Suncheon-man Bay Wetlands** offer a chance to walk on platforms above a coastal estuary inscribed on the Ramsar list. Birdwatchers can expect to see rare migratory birds such as hooded cranes, black-faced spoonbills, yellow-billed egrets and swans that stop here during their transcontinental flights.

Top left Suncheon Bay National Garden **Bottom left** Netherlands themed garden

Time-Travel Village

To the southwest of Suncheon is the village of Nagan and its **Naganeup-seong** (suncheon.go.kr/nagan; adult/child/teenager ₩4000/1500/2500), a unique folk village surrounded by 1400m of Joseon-period fortress walls built to protect the dwellings from Japanese pirates. Dating back to the 10th century and the Goryeo dynasty, they're up to 5m wide – perfect to walk on the ramparts for a timeless peek (and much-coveted photo opportunity) above narrow alleys, little vegetable gardens, green thickets and adobe homes with thatched roofs, some of which are still inhabited and offer simple minbak-type accommodation.

30 Hike Korea's First NATIONAL PARK

MOUNTAINS | SUNRISES | ADVENTURE

Established in 1967, Jirisan is Korea's first and largest national park. Spanning three provinces, it's famous for its rich biodiversity and extensive hiking trails leading to peaks like Cheonwang-bong – the hardest set is on a multi-day west-to-east park traverse.

YEONGSIK IM/SHUTTERSTOCK

How To

Getting there Buses from most Korean cities travel directly to Gurye's bus terminal, where sporadic buses (9am and 2.20pm Mon-Thu; 8.40am, 10.20am, 2.20pm and 4.20pm Fri-Sun) travel to the trailhead at the Seongsamjae Service Area.

Day trip Most visitors only hike for 2.2km from Seongsamjae through Jongseokdae peak to the Nogodan Shelter at 1540m and then back down.

Stock up There's an Emart at Seongsamjae, but we'd recommend buying food before you arrive, to prepare for a multi-day trek.

VOLODYMYR BURDIAK/SHUTTERSTOCK

Summit Planning

The traverse of Jirisan's main ridge is 33km and typically takes three days and two nights to complete, with overnight stays at official shelters along the way. It's necessary to book them in advance through the Korea National Park Service at reservation.knps.or.kr.

It's best to make an early departure (trails open at 3am from April to October) to be able to reach the midrange shelters before their 2pm cut-off times, after which you won't be allowed to hike further east for the day. Accommodation is of the simple mat-on-the-floor type, with *ondol* (underfloor) heating and basic kitchen facilities provided – bring a camping stove and enough provisions. Water is sold at the shelters, so don't stress too much about it. Filters are also a good idea.

HEEGAB/IMAZINS/GETTY IMAGES

Asiatic Bear Country

About 86 Asiatic black bears, including cubs, live inside Jirisan National Park. Even though the bears tend to avoid humans, mothers with cubs can be more dangerous. There's no need to worry – as long as you stick to the trails, there's minimal risk of bumping into one.

Top left Hikers, Jirisan **Left** Sunrise, Cheonwang-bong **Above** Asiatic black bear

Going Up

The real traverse begins from the **Nogodan Shelter** at 1540m, from where it's 3.6km to the **Imgeollyeong Spring** and then 1.3km ascending to **Nolumog**, where the trail swerves north to proceed 900m to 1734m-high **Banya-bong**, the reserve's second-highest peak. Less than a kilometre away is 1499m-high **Samdo-bong**, where the three provinces of Jeollanam-do, Jeollabuk-do and Gyeongsangnam-do meet. There's another 4.7km of trail across 1534m-high **Ttoki-bong** and 1586 m-high **Myeongseong-bong** peaks to the **Yeonhacheon Shelter**, where hikers can overnight. The total distance to this point is 17km, which takes between seven and eight hours from Seongsamjae.

Second Day

The second day starts with a 2km descent to 1178m-high **Hyeongje-bong**. It's another 1.2 km to the **Byeoksoryeong Shelter**, a crossroads of multiple hiking routes. The trail

What to Pack

Assuming you're hiking Jirisan in the warmer months between April and October, there's not much to worry about. As it's necessary to book into a shelter, and free camping is prohibited, you won't have to carry your own bedding, but an extra inflatable mat or pillow can provide additional comfort. Also, bring extra toilet paper. It's possible to cook inside the shelters using your own camping stoves and gas, and water – including hot for instant meals and drinks – can be bought from the shelters.

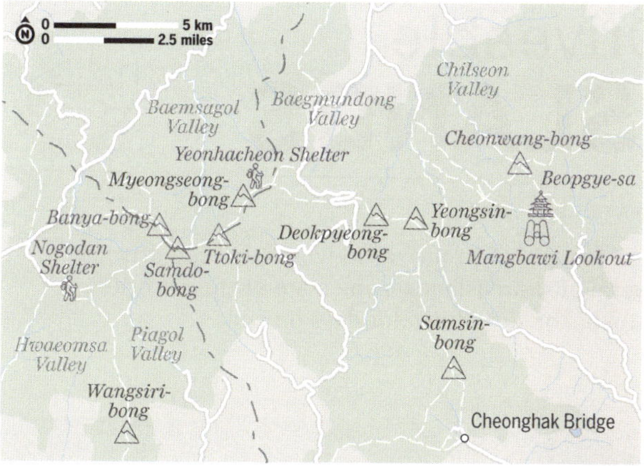

ascends towards 1522m-high **Deokpyeong-bong**, where there's a small eternal spring called Seon-bisem, where it's possible to stock up on water and wash. **Chilseon-bong** is 1.8km away; it boasts seven rocks that, legend says, are the petrified remains of seven angels who came to rest here. It's another 1.5km to **Yeongsin-bong**, a 10-minute downhill walk from Seseoksam, where many stay on the second night. If you want to try to catch the stunning but hard-to-see sunrise, you have to proceed for another 3km to the **Jangteomok Shelter**.

Sunrise & Descent

Sunrise seekers should get going by 5am to walk an hour to 1915m-high **Cheonwang-bong**, mainland Korea's highest peak. Afterwards, the descent to Junsang-ri town starts with an hour to cover 1.5km to the **Beopgye-sa** temple. The large rock formations of the **Mangbawi Lookout** are 1km further down, and 870m later is **Kalbawi**, with even more impressive rocks. One last 2km stretch takes you down to Jungsan-ri village, where there's a car park from where buses depart to Jinju's bus terminal. From there it's easy to either overnight and enjoy the town's fortress **Jinjuseong**, or catch one of the many intercity buses serving Seoul, Gwangju, Busan, Suncheon and many other locations.

Left Hikers, Jirisan **Below** Stone carving, Jinjuseong

FROM LEFT: STOCK FOR YOU/SHUTTERSTOCK, DEA/G WRIGHT/GETTY IMAGES

31 Driveable ISLANDS

COASTAL SCENERY | MUDFLATS | BEACHES

Jeolla-do is one of the few places in the world where you can drive or cycle over the ocean to several offshore islands using state-of-the-art bridges. Make it a day trip out of Mokpo, or slow down for days on end.

REDCR/SHUTTERSTOCK

How To

Getting there The spectacular 7.2km-long Cheonsa Bridge connects Aphaedo and Amtaedo islands and gets you to the centre of Shinan.

Getting around Mokpo is the closest city, but you can also rent a vehicle in Gwangju, which offers more options. Consider spending at least a half-day.

When to go Spring, summer and October have the best weather and visibility; fog often clouds up the views during the rest of the year.

Trip extension To continue exploring, go to **Amtaenamgang Harbour** and catch a car-capable ferry to any of the archipelago's southern islands.

Adventurous Shinan

Driving from Mokpo takes you to the central and northern parts of Shinan, but for a real adventure, take a ferry from **Amtaenamgang Harbour** and explore less-known islands. I suggest **Gijom-soakdo** (Pilgrim's Island), the starting point of an incredible religious-themed hike across five islands and footbridges that disappear with the tides.

Keunha Kim is a Shinan archipelago travel expert.

01 Leave Mokpo and drive along the suspended **Cheonsa Bridge** (pictured below) watching a cluster of islets emerge from the ocean below you.

02 Drive south on Amtaedo's main road to the **Gidong Samgeori Perm Hair Mural**, a wall portrait of an elderly couple with real treetops for hair.

03 The **100th Anniversary Exhibition Hall of the Stem Farming Struggle** is an art museum inside a warehouse, featuring mixed-media works by the celebrated painter Suh Yongsun.

04 Once on Anjwado, check out **Kim Whanki's Birthplace**, the childhood home of the famous Korean painter, who migrated to the US and died in New York.

05 The end of the road is at the **Purple Bridge** (pictured far left), which leads to the footbridges to cither of the popular Purple Islands, **Banwoldo** (pictured right) and **Bakjido**.

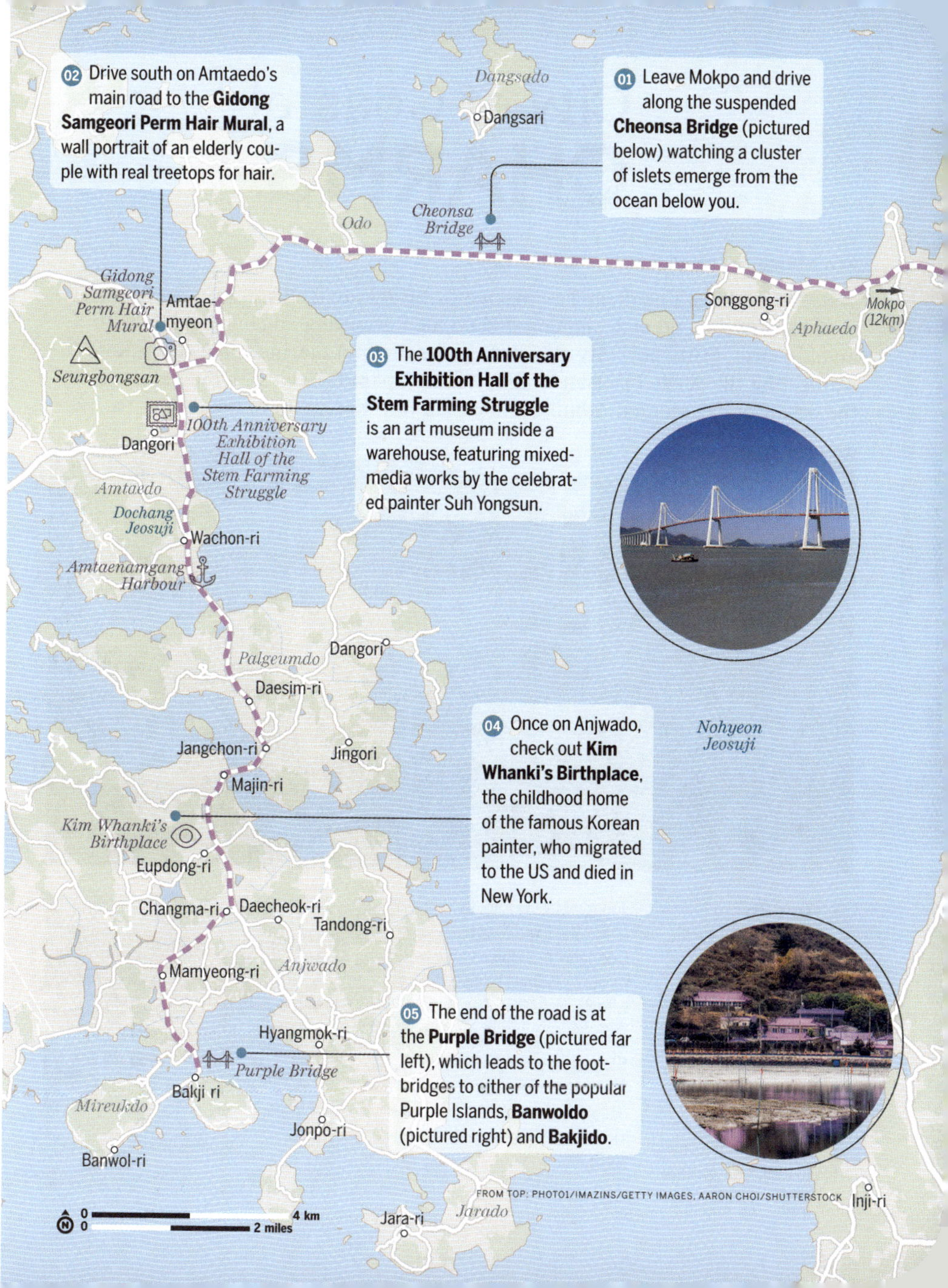

FROM TOP: PHOTO1/IMAZINS/GETTY IMAGES, AARON CHOI/SHUTTERSTOCK

32 City of Coastal CHARMS

SEA VIEWS | ISLAND CRUISING | HISTORY

Straddling a peninsula connected by bridges to a cluster of large islands, Yeosu sits at the end of Jeollanam-do and blends cutting-edge modernity with an old-world, gritty port city vibe. It features the first marine cable car in Korea, connecting the rugged Dolsan Island (a hiking paradise) with the mainland over the ocean that cemented Admiral Yi Sun-sin into Korea's hero-hood.

PANWASIN SEEMALA/SHUTTERSTOCK

How To

Getting there Yeosu Expo station marks the end of the Jeolla line, easily reached by KTX, ITX and Mugunghwa trains from Seoul via Suncheon, which is close enough for day trips.

Getting around It's possible to walk from central Jongpo Marine Park to either the Expo area or Odongdo, but Dolsan and its surroundings need wheels.

Evergreen snack **Yeosu Strawberry Mochi** (삼대옥) has been making delicious rice cakes in Yi Sun-sin Square since 1968.

SANGA PARK/SHUTTERSTOCK

Top left Yeosu Marine Cable Car
Bottom left Aqua Planet

Bird's-eye ocean views Opened in 2014 as the first over-ocean cable car in Korea, **Yeosu Marine Cable Car** (yeosucablecar.com/en; adult/child round-trip ₩17,000/12,000, one-way ₩14,000/9000) starts in **Jasan station** near Odongdo and soars for 1.5km over the waves to the northern side of Dolsan Island. Stunning coastal views aside, it's a beautiful journey to take after dark, when Yeosu's city lights flicker below like thousands of fireflies in flight across tumbling hills and sinuous beaches.

Walk to a craggy island The crests and spikes of Odongdo float 750m off the mainland and are connected by a footbridge that can be walked, cycled or crossed aboard a small tourist train. Paths lead to the Cave of Dragon, a dramatic coastal hollow you can walk almost into before climbing the staircase and platforms back up and across a bamboo forest to **Odongdo Lighthouse**. An elevator takes you to the top deck, from where views encompass far-flung islands such as Geomundo, Beakdo and Geumodo.

Expo area Yeosu's been on the map since hosting the Expo in 2012 on the northwestern side of town. The area today still hosts a branch of the **Arte Museum** (artemuseum.com; adult/child/teenager ₩19,000/12,000/15,000), which celebrates the ocean theme intertwined with the city through 16 striking multimedia art exhibitions that reflect the local sea and coastal landscapes. Within walking distance, **Aqua Planet** (adult/child/teenager ₩35,000/29,000/32,000) features 300 species, including rare beluga whales and Baikal seals.

Cliff-Hanging Shrine

Set on the southern end of Dolsan Island, halfway up a mountain facing the sea, the Buddhist hermitage of **Hyangir-am**, of the Jogye Order of Korean Buddhism, is one of South Korea's most beautiful and storied sites, harking back 1350 years. From the parking lot at the bottom of the hill, where buses and cars stop, it's a 10-minute uphill walk to the beginning of the staircase leading to the temple's lower platform. Reaching the main shrine involves squeezing through tight rock passages to the temple's first pagoda, from where the coastal views are dramatic – a very early climb offers magical sunrises.

Listings

BEST OF THE REST

Must-See Historic Sites

Gochang Dolmen Site

Northwest of Gwangju, the hills around Gochang are scattered with 440 ancient dolmens – prehistoric tombs from the Bronze and Iron ages – also found in other clusters near the towns of Hwasun and Ganghwa.

Naju

Jeolla-do's former royal capital is less-known but features an important cluster of historical sights around the Geumseonggwan Hall, a large guesthouse and magistrate's office rebuilt in 1617 after the Japanese invasion.

Waeseong Japanese Fortress

The ruins of this 16th-century Japanese fortress rise on a hillock amid unspoilt countryside southeast of Suncheon. It was staged as the final battleground in the historical K-Drama *The Admiral: Roaring Currents* (2014).

Unique Cafes

Kko-ji-tta-ppong Cafe (꼬지따뽕) ₩

Bright pink walls, a lovely terrace and a mania for pop culture manifesting in Barbie dolls and a life-sized ET figure seated at a table make this Jeonju Jaman Mural Village's most characteristic cafe.

Voyagers Cafe ₩

Gwangju's beautifully bohemian spot blends travel memorabilia, books and vibes from all over the world. The drip coffee is as great as the backdoor veranda for kicking back.

Youth Store ₩

Set inside a loft-like space with stadium-style tiered seating, this collection of hip cafes, bakeries and homegrown restaurants in Suncheon keeps changing and showcases the passion of young entrepreneurs.

Beautiful Gardens

Boseong Tea Gardens

Since 1939, the Daehan Dawon Tea Plantation has produced Korea's most famed green tea on a cluster of hills that blend manicured tea gardens with metasequoia forests.

Gwanghallu Garden

In the town of Namwon, walk amid a collection of Joseon-era pavilions, manicured lawns and water ponds celebrating Lee Mong-ryong and Lady Chunhyang's love from a classic Korean folk story.

Deokjin Park

One of Jeonju's most popular parks has *hanok* architecture galore, including a lakeside library and shady walking paths surrounding a central lake that fills with lotus flowers in July.

Wansan Chilbong

Hidden on a hill above the centre of Jeonju, photographers love this garden for its

CSTRIKE/SHUTTERSTOCK

Gochang Dolmen Site

deep-pink double cherry blossoms and red azaleas in spring, and for a cascade of red maple leaves in autumn.

Art-Rejuvenated Districts

Jaman Mural Village

Walk across the blue bridge from Jeonju's Omok-dae Hill to a hillside community on Seungamsan Mountain. Dozens of murals range from Edward Scissorhands to portraits of John Lennon and anime characters.

Penguin Village

Gwangju's bohemian Penguin Village in the historic Yangnim-Dong area is plastered with junk art, old frames, wall clocks and plenty of penguin-themed artworks and installations. Cafes and handcraft boutiques also abound.

Seosan-dong

This sea-facing hillside community in Mokpo revived after artists spruced up its walls with 1970s and '80s-themed vintage artworks, including a 'poetry road' decorated with verses etched on the walls.

Off-the-Beaten-Track Islands

Seonyudo

Sunbathe, swim, and hike on four islands (Sinsido, Munyeodo, Bangchukdo, and Maldo), connected by bridges to the west of Jeonju. They are tethered to the 33.9km-long Saemangeum Sea Wall, the longest in the world.

Wando & Shinjido

Another driveable island, home to the 76m-high Wando Tower observatory, is set at the top of Dongmangsan Mountain. Neighbouring Shinjido features a 4km-long Myeongsasim-ni, one of Korea's most beautiful beaches on the southern coast.

Jindo

Korea's third-largest island is famous for its unusual spring tides that expose Jindo

AMANKGUPTA/SHUTTERSTOCK

Penguin Village

Miracle Sea Road – a 2.8km-long causeway to the tiny island of Modo-ri. Some 300,000 people cross each year.

Gijomsoakdo (Pilgrim's Island)

Starting point of a religious-themed hike across five islands, touching chapels named after the Twelve Apostles. The 'sea road' connecting them only emerges twice a day based on shifting tides.

Hauido

The birthplace of former President Kim Dae-jung, winner of the Nobel Peace Prize, has incredible coastal scenery – an islet shaped like a human face makes for fun photos.

Chairlifts & Cable Cars

Muju Deogyusan Resort

Jeolla-do's prime winter ski destination features the highest altitude and longest slope (6.1km) gondola in the country, ferrying passengers up 1520m-high Seolcheon-bong.

Mokpo Marine Cable Car

At 3.23km long and 155m high, the Mokpo Marine Cable Car is among Korea's longest and highest. It connects the North Port Terminal via the summit of Yudalsan Mountain to Gohado across the Dadohae Sea.

JEJU-DO

VOLCANIC | TRAILS | SEA

RESEARCHED BY ANN BABE

JIPEN/SHUTTERSTOCK

JEJU-DO
Trip Builder

Korea's island of volcanic stone, meandering trails, aquamarine bays and super-sweet citrus reminds us to slow down and truly savour life. Swim with fierce freediving women, bathe in rocky-terrain forests – whether in water or on land, just enjoy being alive.

CLOCKWISE FROM LEFT: KIM WONKOOK/SHUTTERSTOCK, SOOHYUN KIM/SHUTTERSTOCK, SUNGMOON HAN/SHUTTERSTOCK

Practicalities

JOHNATHAN21/SHUTTERSTOCK

ARRIVING

Jeju International Airport As Jeju-do's main point of entry, all commercial flights from the mainland arrive here. It's only a few kilometres west of central Jeju-si, and connected by many transit routes, including the 101 and 102 express buses. To get to Seogwipo, catch bus 600 or 181.

Jeju International Ferry Terminal Travellers who've opted to take the ferry from Mokpo, Wando and elsewhere on the mainland will arrive in Jeju-si just east of downtown.

HOW MUCH FOR A

***Heukdwaeji* (black pork) barbecue ₩25,000**

***Gogi-guksu* (pork noodle soup) ₩10,000**

Basket of *hallabong* ₩10,000

GETTING AROUND

Car Driving on Jeju-do is fairly easy, with English signs on roads and English-language GPS systems in rental cars.

Bus Transit services will get you lots of places. Several routes circle the island, circumnavigate Halla-san, and run between Jeju-si and Seogwipo.

Walking The Jeju Olle Trail (p184), which spans 437km along 27 routes, is the premier way to walk the island (along with some outer islands).

WHEN TO GO

MAR–MAY
Mild, balmy springs, with temperatures reaching around 20°C in May.

JUN–AUG
Scorching hot and incredibly humid, particularly in August. Typhoon season.

SEP–NOV
Still hot in September, cools to comfortable temperatures by November.

DEC–FEB
Chilly, occasional snow. Strong winds make it feel colder than it is.

EATING & DRINKING

Famed for its richly marbled black pork (pictured top), the island features *heukdwaeji* in everything from barbecue and burgers to stews and soups. *Gogi-guksu* is a pork noodle soup that's a Jeju speciality.

Freshly caught seafood shines both raw and cooked up in dishes like *jeonbok juk* (abalone porridge; pictured bottom), braised or grilled *galchi* (hairtail) and *momguk*, a Jeju soup of gulfweed and pork.

Look out for *hallabong*, a mandarin-orange hybrid local to Jeju that's found in orchards, at markets and on dessert menus everywhere.

Best food market
Seogwipo Maeil Olle Market (p187)

Must-try makgeolli
Nakwhagokju (p195)

TOP: KIM YJ/SHUTTERSTOCK
BOTTOM: LIU YU SHAN/SHUTTERSTOCK

CONNECT & FIND YOUR WAY

Wi-fi There's free wi-fi at the airport, on public transportation and other public areas. Consider a SIM card or portable wi-fi egg; buy at mobile counters in the airport, or online in advance to pick up on-site.

Navigation Use Korean apps Naver and Kakao Maps, which are better integrated than foreign apps with local transit. Driving and walking routes are more accurate, particularly in rural areas.

WHERE TO STAY

There is no shortage of lodging options on Jeju-do, ranging from luxury to budget. Instead of international chains, consider choosing independent B&Bs, pensions and Korean-style *minbak* (private homes with rooms for rent).

Place	Pros/Cons
Jeju-si	Jeju-do's capital, home to the airport and lots of hotels. Downtown is the island's biggest nightlife district. Good transit links, with close proximity to Halla-san's Gwaneum-sa trailhead.
Seogwipo	Jeju-do's second-largest city, with a high concentration of resorts, plus a wide range of other options, too. At your doorstep: prime surfing and diving, and some of the most scenic Olle routes.
Western Jeju-do	Plenty of pensions, particularly in the northwest area of Aewol and Hyeopjae, where there are beautiful beaches for snorkelling.
Eastern Jeju-do	Gateway to Seongsan Ilchul-bong and Udo. Not as well connected to transit.

JEJU PASSES

Check out the Jeju Tour Pass or Jeju All Pass for discounts at museums, cafes and more.

MONEY

Carry some won as some small shops won't be too happy about swiping your card.

33 WATERY Wonderland

ADVENTURE | WAVES | LEISURE

It's no surprise Jeju-do is a water lover's paradise. It has both calm and strong waves, both white- and black-sand beaches, crystal-clear waters, spectacular wildlife, dramatic rock formations – plus plenty of rentals and operators around to make enjoying it all a breeze. Truly, there's something for everyone, from casual boaters and novice surfers to serious certified divers.

SIMON SHIN KWANGSIG/SHUTTERSTOCK

How To

Getting around There are several buses that edge the island, such as the 101, 102, 201 and 202. It's more convenient to rent a car.

When to go July and August are not only the island's hottest months, but also prime time for typhoons. Keep an eye on weather conditions, and heed government and operator advisories.

Booking Make reservations with operators in advance, at least two weeks for popular courses like diving and surfing.

PTERA/SHUTTERSTOCK

Snorkelling Good snorkelling is all around Jeju-do, with gentle and clear waters in which to spot beautiful small fish and, on the island's south side, colourful soft corals. On the west coast, **Hyeopjae** and **Geumneung** are some of the best beaches for snorkelling; northeast, head to **Woljeong**, **Sehwa** or **Hado**.

Diving Jeju-do's southern shore, in the area around Seogwipo, is Korea's premier diving destination. Near the islands of Seopseom, Munseom and Beomseom, you can take uncertified or full certification courses that range from a couple of hours to a few days. Sign up with English-speaking operators like **MJ Jeju Diving Club** (mjjejudivingclub.co.kr) or **Big Blue 33** (bigblue33.com).

Surfing **Jungmun Beach**, west of Seogwipo, has the best intermediate and advanced waves, but also many surf schools that teach beginner lessons, along with surf bars and surf hostels for those surfer community vibes. Check out **Jeju Surfing School** (blog.naver.com/jesurf). On the north coast, Woljeong Beach is particularly recommended for beginner surfers because of its extra calm waves. There are lots of surfing operators here as well.

Boating From luxury yachts to traditional *tewoo* (wooden raft), Jeju-do offers boating experiences of all types. Kayak at Woljeong Beach, hop on a *tewoo* at **Soesokkak Estuary**, ride a boat around Moseulpo in hopes of spotting dolphins or go yachting off the coast of **Jusangjeolli-dae** to see the volcanic rock formations up close.

Top left Diving, Jeju-do
Bottom left Jusangjeolli-dae

Marine Protected Area

Jeju-do is a marine protected area, with the entirety of the island, plus the surrounding waters 5.5km from its shoreline, designated since 2002 as a UNESCO Biosphere Reserve. Despite its protected status, however, development projects and tourism (which saw a 17.5% increase in international visitors following the hit Netflix series set on Jeju, *When Life Gives You Tangerines*), along with global climate change, continue to put the island at risk of ocean desertification. Rising sea temperatures and coastal pollution have led to habitat loss, endangering wildlife and decreasing biodiversity. Soft corals and kelp, for example, are declining, and seaweed production has dropped by more than 95%.

34 Volcanic VOYAGES

GEOLOGY | PEAKS | FANTASTICAL

Formed by four stages of volcanic activity over a span of 1.2 million years, Jeju-do's landscape is like a study in volcanic geology – from its 1950m-high Halla-san and the dormant volcano's 368 parasitic cones, to tuff cone Seongsan Ilchul-bong and record-breaking lava tubes.

PICHIT TONGMA/SHUTTERSTOCK

How To

Navigating You can get to Halla-san trailheads or Seongsan Ilchul-bong by bus, but in the early morning it's better to go by car. Halla-san trail maps are available at the main entrances, where there's usually also parking.

When to go Halla-san can be climbed year-round, though trails are limited to daytime use only.

Halla-san tip Make your wake-up easier by staying overnight at the campground at the Gwaneum-sa entrance, then hitting the trail right when it opens.

BUDDHI44/SHUTTERSTOCK

Hike up Halla-san

To the top! Of the seven trails up and around Halla-san, only two go to the summit, where **Baengnokdam** ('white deer lake') awaits, its pool of water reflecting the changing seasons. The popular route of **Seongpanak Trail** (9.6km, 4½ hours) has a gradual ascent, with a side trail to the **Sara Oreum** observatory deck. **Gwaneum-sa Trail** (8.7km, five hours) is much more challenging because of its steepness. While it's most common to take Seongpanak up and Gwaneum-sa down, consider what your knees can handle.

Midway up There are three trails that go midway up Halla-san, meeting at Witse Oreum Shelter. The **Yeongsil Trail** (5.8km, 2½ hours), covered with boardwalks much of the way, is a short, easy course that offers grand scenery – you'll hike through mixed deciduous

DONGBAO/SHUTTERSTOCK

Wildlife at Halla-san

While hiking Halla-san, you might glimpse wild boar, falcons, feral dogs and, most famously, Jeju roe deer. These medium-sized deer are a subspecies of Eastern roe deer, different from European roe deer, and they are native to the island. Once listed as a local endangered species, their population has recovered in recent years.

Top left Yeongsil Trail **Left** Baengnokdam **Above** Jeju roe deer and evergreen forests and dwarf firs, before coming to panoramas of green *oreum* (volcanic cones) and pinnacle rocks atop sheer cliffs. The **Eorimok Trail** (6.8km, three hours) begins with a steep climb through thick woodland. Halfway up, the dense trees give way to an open, subalpine moorland of bamboo, grass and dwarf firs. The **Donnaeko Trail** (7km, 3½ hours) starts from the Donnaeko Visitor Information Centre, providing coastal vistas of Seogwipo and running through a red pine forest. For the best views, it's recommended to climb up Yeongsil or Eorimok, then down Donnaeko.

Short and sweet One of the shortest mountain trails, **Seokgul-am** (1.5km, 50 minutes) starts at Cheonwang-sa and terminates at the female hermitage Seokgul-am. There is the occasional stretch of steep steps, but the end is worth it. Even shorter is **Eoseungsaengak** (1.3km, 30 minutes), an easy hike beginning at the **Hallasan National Park Visitor**

Halla-san Practicalities

Trails open at 5am in summer, 5.30am in spring and autumn, and 6am in winter, and they close at sunset. Park rangers will stop you from climbing higher if you don't reach the uppermost shelters by certain cut-off times – 1pm in summer, 12.30pm in spring and autumn, and noon in winter.

The two trails that reach the summit require free online reservations (which open the first day of every month for registration up until the end of the following month), as Seongpanak is limited to 1000 hikers per day, and Gwaneum-sa to 500. (Whichever one you choose, you're free to descend the other.) The rest of the trails don't require advance registration.

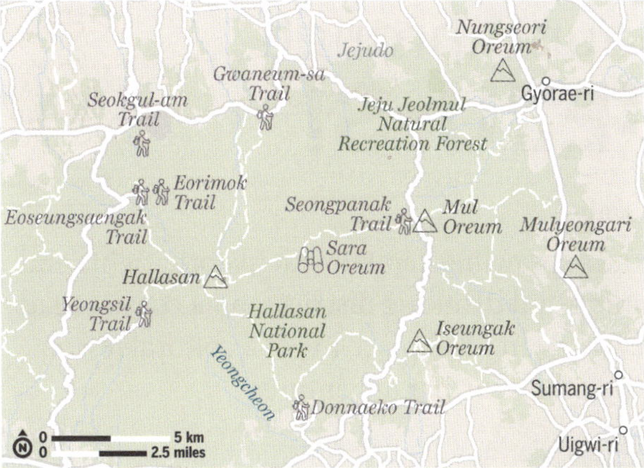

Left Shelter, Halla-san
Below Manjang-gul

Centre and finishing atop Eoseungsaeng Oreum, with views of the Jeju plains and Halla-san's summit.

Oh the Oreum!

Halla-san's eruptions created 368 parasitic cones (called *oreum* in Jeju dialect), the most from a single volcano. Many *oreum* have walking paths for enjoying panoramic views from the top, and come autumn, are covered by a sea of silver grass.

See the Sunrise at Seongsan Ilchul-bong

Spend the night in Seongsan-ri to wake up the next morning in time for a sunrise hike up the 182m-high extinct tuff volcano **Seongsan Ilchul-bong** – the World Heritage Site is called 'sunrise peak' after all. The steep ascent up a set of stairs only takes about 20 minutes, and the view at the top of the forested crater ringed by jagged rocks is well worth it.

Meander through Manjang-gul

Up to 18m wide and 25m high, **Manjang-gul**, east of Jeju-si, is part of the Geomunoreum Lava Tube system, the world's largest cave created from flowing lava. Most of the 7.4km length is closed off, but visitors can walk inside a 1km stretch of it to reach a 7.6m-high lava pillar.

35 Jaunt through JEJU-SI

MYTH | HISTORY | DRAGON & PIG

Jeju-si is the island's sprawling capital with historic sights and museums; a vibrant dining and drinking district; and a coastal road of splendid seaside views. It's an ideal place to get a cultural lesson on Jeju-do before setting off on further adventures.

TRABANTOS/SHUTTERSTOCK

How To

Getting there From Jeju International Airport, catch a bus into the city, about 25 minutes. Or hail a taxi, about 15 minutes.

Getting around This part of Jeju-si is pleasantly walkable, albeit hot in the height of summer. Keep an eye out for giant umbrella awnings stationed at crosswalks for shade.

When to go Jeju Folklore & Natural History Museum is closed Mondays. On other days it's open 9am-6pm.

Celebrating Tamna Culture

If you're in Jeju-si in October, check to see if the **Tamna Cultural Festival** overlaps with your dates. Since 1962, the island's flagship festival has been celebrating the history and heritage of Tamna – the ancient kingdom of Jeju-do – along with its mythical demigod founders at Samseonghyeol and venues across Jeju-si.

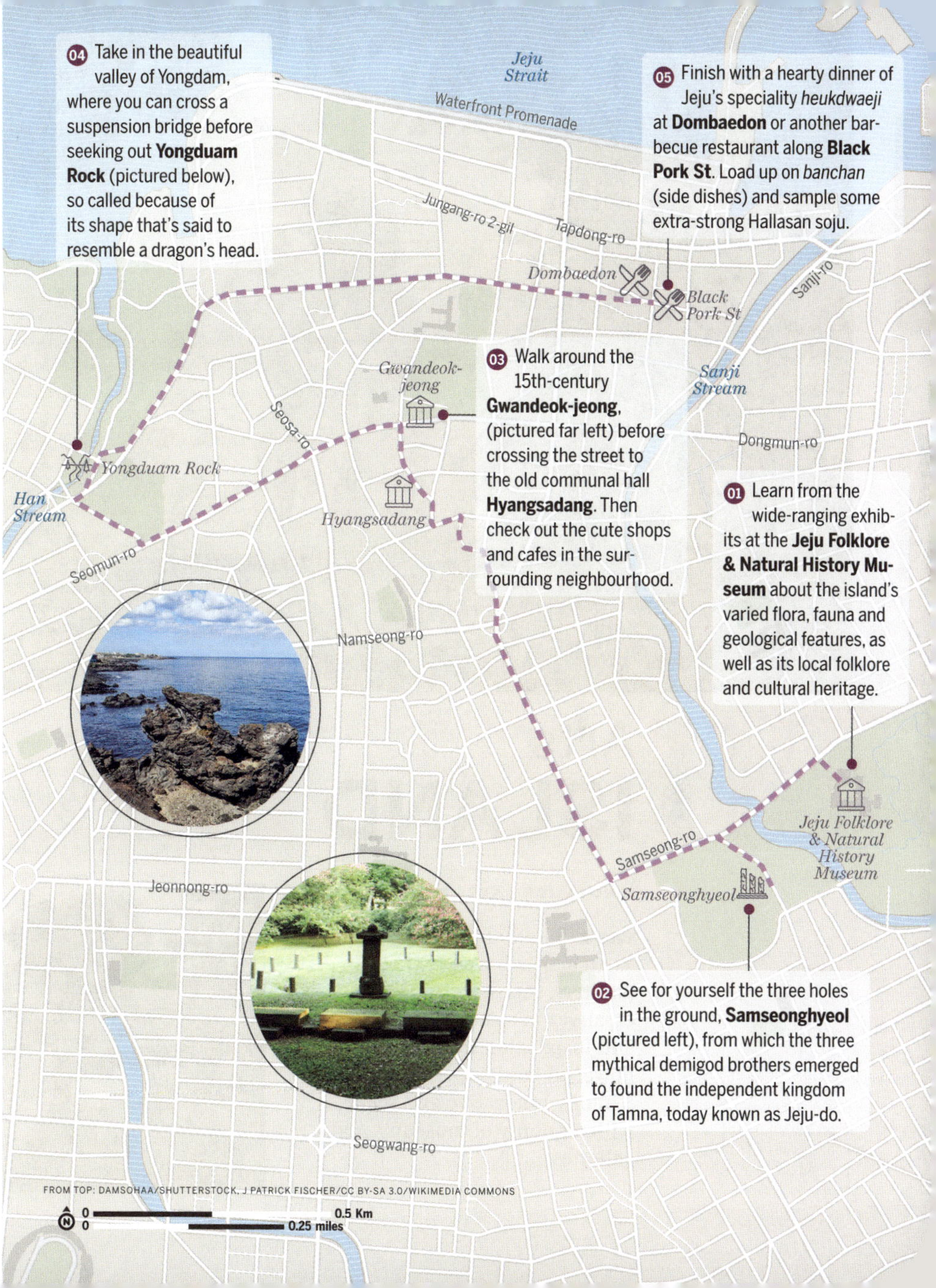

01 Learn from the wide-ranging exhibits at the **Jeju Folklore & Natural History Museum** about the island's varied flora, fauna and geological features, as well as its local folklore and cultural heritage.

02 See for yourself the three holes in the ground, **Samseonghyeol** (pictured left), from which the three mythical demigod brothers emerged to found the independent kingdom of Tamna, today known as Jeju-do.

03 Walk around the 15th-century **Gwandeok-jeong**, (pictured far left) before crossing the street to the old communal hall **Hyangsadang**. Then check out the cute shops and cafes in the surrounding neighbourhood.

04 Take in the beautiful valley of Yongdam, where you can cross a suspension bridge before seeking out **Yongduam Rock** (pictured below), so called because of its shape that's said to resemble a dragon's head.

05 Finish with a hearty dinner of Jeju's speciality *heukdwaeji* at **Dombaedon** or another barbecue restaurant along **Black Pork St**. Load up on *banchan* (side dishes) and sample some extra-strong Hallasan soju.

FROM TOP: DAMSOHAA/SHUTTERSTOCK, J PATRICK FISCHER/CC BY-SA 3.0/WIKIMEDIA COMMONS

36 Arts ISLAND

INNOVATION | ART | BOLD

Jeju-do has become known as an artists haven, attracting painters, sculptors and other creatives in search of quiet retreat and inspiration from the island's powerful landscapes. It's led to a highly innovative arts scene, with a bounty of museums and galleries.

Above Kim Young Gap Gallery Dumoak (p182)
Right Jeju Museum of Contemporary Art (p182)
Far right Lee Jung-seop house

©KOREA TOURISM ORGANIZATION – KTO_KIM JIHO

How To

Getting around While museums in Jeju-si and Seogwipo can easily be reached by bus, the others, including Bonte, are better accessed by car.

Admission Entrance fees vary widely, with digital arts exhibitions and private collections like the Arario and Bonte being on the pricier side. Small galleries and the Jeju Museum of Art and Museum of Contemporary Art range from free to ₩10,000.

When to go As is the case with mainland Korea, most museums on Jeju-do are closed Mondays.

SANGA PARK/ALAMY

©KOREA TOURISM ORGANIZATION – KIM JIHO

Contemporary Art in Jeju-si

Split over three locations, the **Arario Museum** (arariomuseum.org) showcases pieces from the outstanding contemporary-art collection of business magnate Kim Chang-il. The former Tapdong Cinema is the largest facility, covering five floors with works that include pieces by Gilbert & George, Damien Hirst and Anselm Kiefer. Dongmun Motel I features art by Antony Gormley, Tracey Emin and Isaac Julien, and Dongmun Motel II is devoted to a solo exhibition of sculptures and installations by Gu Bonju.

Seogwipo's Artistic Icons

Lee Jung-seop (1916–56) lived in Seogwipo for only a year, but his legacy is stoutly celebrated, with his distinctive, Fauvist-influenced images reproduced on walls around town, particularly along the street that's named after

Inside Lee's Art

Peering inside Lee's modest 4.6-sq-metre traditional thatched house, see where he created foil drawings and conceived his iconic 'Bull' paintings. And at Jaguri Coast, gazing at the island of Seopseom, take in the scenery that inspired his major work *Landscape with Seopseom Island*.

Stella Choi is an author whose bookshop and studio overlooks Lee Jung-seop's home. *@sayiseoga*

him. Here you'll find a **museum** (set to reopen in early 2027) displaying some of Lee's art and the traditional thatched house in which he and his family lived.

Lee Wal-chong has been creating art in Seogwipo for more than 30 years. Check out his colourful and charming paintings, ceramics and painted wood carvings in his self-designed **Walart Museum** (walartmuseum.or.kr), a distinctive circular building close by the entrance to **Jeongbang Pokpo**.

Photographing the Island's Beauty

The countryside **Kim Young Gap Gallery Dumoak** (dumoak.co.kr) showcases the work of Kim Young Gap (1957–2005), a self-taught photographer whose panoramic landscapes capture the island's wild beauty. Diagnosed with Lou Gehrig's disease, Kim devoted the last year of his life to creating the gallery from an abandoned school. It's surrounded by a lush garden dotted with whimsical sculptures.

Artists Villages on Jeju-do

Jeju-do has several artists and mural villages. **Jeoji-ri** in southwest Jeju is an artists village dotted with engaging pieces of modern and traditional architecture. It's home to the **Jeju Museum of Contemporary Art** (jeju.go.kr/jejumuseum/index.htm) and the **Kim Tschang-Yeul Museum of Art** (kimtschang-yeul.jeju.go.kr), two excellent galleries. The latter, which features Kim's iconic water droplet art, was designed by Tadao Ando.

In southeastern Jeju is the **Sincheon-ri Mural Village**, where there are around 100 paintings of *haenyeo* (p190), as well as sea- and landscapes. Meanwhile, northward, the **Gimnyeong Craft Metal Mural Village** uses discarded metals to decorate the sides of buildings and walls.

Left Kim Young Gap Gallery Dumoak
Below Lee Jung-seop street

Digital Arts in Reimagined Spaces

In eastern Jeju, the **Bunker des Lumières** (deslumieres.co.kr/bunker) is an immersive art exhibition housed in a 3000-sq-metre bunker once used to manage a submarine optical cable system. The concrete walls, floors and ceilings are now projection screens for imaginative, colour-drenched digital art shows featuring works by the likes of Monet, Renoir and Chagall.

Over on the west side, **Arte Museum** (kr.artemuseum.com) is Korea's largest immersive media art exhibition, created by d'strict, a digital design company, in a former speaker factory.

Admiring Architectural Art

For lovers of art and architecture, the inland **Bonte Museum** (bontemuseum.com) is a must-see. Designed by Tadao Ando and incorporating Korean traditional features, it showcases an amazing private collection of historic Korean arts and crafts, as well as contemporary art by Paik Nam-june and others. (If you enjoy Ando's style, **Phoenix Island** is home to two more of his buildings.)

Northward, outside of Jeju-si, the **Jeju Museum of Art** (jeju.go.kr/jmoa) occupies a beautifully designed building that appears to float on a pool of water. Inside are permanent and temporary exhibits of contemporary visual art.

37 Hiking OLLE!

TRAILS | UNHURRIED | SCENIC

Spanning 437km across 135 villages, the Jeju Olle Trail is slow, local tourism at its best. Choose from 27 routes, ranging between 4.2km and 20.9km, that meander mainly along the coast (with some inland diversions, too) and three outer islands.

JONGHOLEE/SHUTTERSTOCK

How To

When to go Spring and autumn have the best weather. Avoid July and August when it's very hot. The Jeju Olle Walking Festival (₩30,000) takes place in November.

Finding your way Navigate by following arrows on poles, walls and the ground, and ribbons dangling from trees. Orange is for going counterclockwise around the island; blue, clockwise.

More information There are 14 information centres around Jeju-do, including the **headquarters** in Seogwipo, with friendly staff to help.

YLLYSO/SHUTTERSTOCK

Launched by former journalist and Jeju native Suh Myeong-sook in 2007, the Jeju Olle Trail (jejuolle.org) is one of the great success stories of local tourism. *Olle* is the local word for a pathway that connects a house to a main street, signifying one of the project's aims – to open up Jeju's unique culture and scenery to visitors. There's truly no better antidote to Korea's stressful *ppalli ppalli* (hurry up) culture than joyfully plodding along like a *ganse*, the trail's pony-shaped logo (named after *gansedari*, Jeju dialect for 'slow idler'). Along the way, slow idlers will go past farm plots worked by grandmothers, ascend grassy *oreum* (volcanic cones) where horses and cows graze freely, and take in sweeping vistas over crashing blue seas. Here are some of the best routes.

Wheelchair Accessibility

Ten sections of the Jeju Olle are wheelchair accessible, so those with limited mobility can also experience the transformative power of the trail. A good example is **Route 10-1** – the shortest trail at just 4.2km – on Gapado. Even at its highest point, this compact island is barely 20m above sea level.

JIPEN/SHUTTERSTOCK

Top left Gwangchigi Beach (p186)
Left Route 10 trail (p187)
Above Navigation ribbons

Scenic Routes

Route 1 (15.1km) The trail from Siheung Elementary School on Jeju's east coast down to rocky **Gwangchigi Beach**, where black and white sands swirl together in undulating patterns, is a beautiful introduction to the Olle experience. The landscape along the way is classic Jeju-do: verdant fields grazed by cows and fringed by black basalt stone walls, sleepy fishing villages beside azure seas and salt flats. The highlight is spectacular Seongsan Ilchul-bong, a giant moss-green-coated tuff volcano rising out of the sea.

Route 7 (12.9km) Starting from the **Jeju Olle Tourist Centre** in Seogwipo, this course hugs the coast with a view onto the 'lonely rock' Oedolgae, before going along Subong-ro, an ecology trail created by former Olle ranger Kim Subong who followed a goat path, and coming to the restaurant and cafe-lined port of Beophwanpogu. The route finishes at Seogwipo Bus Terminal.

Jeju Olle Passport

Get a Jeju Olle Passport (₩20,000) to record and remember your time walking on the trails. It's fun to collect the unique beginning, middle and ending stamps of each route, and a fully stamped passport also entitles you to receive a certificate and medal of completion, as well as induction into the Jeju Olle hall of fame. The passport also comes with benefits such as discounts on various accommodation, restaurants and attractions along the routes, as well as on some transportation, like ferries and rental cars. Purchase a passport at any Jeju Olle information centre.

Left Jeju Olle Passport
Below Jusangjeolli-dae

FROM LEFT: © JEJU OLLE FOUNDATION, WISDOM32/SHUTTERSTOCK

Route 8 (20km) In addition to **Yakcheon Temple** and Daepo Port, this route goes past the spectacular **Jusangjeolli-dae**, basalt hexagonal columns formed by lava meeting the ocean. It then cuts inland to climb Beritnae Oreum, before returning to the coast to Jungmun Beach. It ends in the small village of Daepyeong-ri.

Route 10 (15.6km) One of the network's most stunning trails, this fantastic section takes you along the **Yongmeori Coast**, around Songsak-san and past Gapado and Marado.

Urban Routes

Route 6 (10.1km) A relatively easy course that climbs the 95m Jejigi Oreum, before going through Seogwipo, where you'll walk up Lee Jung-seop St, admiring the art of this celebrated mid-20th-century Korean artist (p181), and have a chance to explore **Seogwipo Maeil Olle Market**, a great place to indulge in traditional local eats. It finishes at the main Jeju Olle Tourist Centre downtown.

Route 18 (17.1km) Starting in the old downtown of Jeju-si, near bustling **Dongmun Market**, this trail takes you to the 149m summit of Sara-bong for sweeping vistas of the city.

Gems of **JEJU**

02

01

03

04

01 Halla-san
South Korea's highest mountain, a 1950m-high dormant volcano, rises out of Jeju-do's core. It's a UNESCO Biosphere Reserve, a World Heritage Site, a national park and the prized jewel of the island.

02 Hallabong
Named after Halla-san for their shape – like an orange but with a bump on top – this mandarin orange hybrid introduced to Korea from Japan is known for its candy-like sweetness.

03 Wind
There is a saying that Jeju has three abundances, or *samda*: wind, women and stone. The goddess of wind is prayed to each year to bring the winds necessary for good fishing and farming.

04 Stone
From the stone walls that enclose Jeju houses and fields to the island's unique *gotjawal* ecosystem (p193) where forests grow from rocky terrain, the basalt remnants of volcanic activity are everywhere.

05 Black Pigs
The black pork eaten at restaurants is a cross-bred black pig, but Jeju's

native purebred black pigs are so endangered they're a protected national treasure.

06 Horses
Short and stocky, Jeju horses are a cross between those native to the island and the Mongol breed that were brought over in the 13th-century invasion.

07 Haenyeo
A living heritage, Jeju's fierce freediving women have been harvesting seafood for their families and communities for centuries, but today fewer than 2900 remain.

08 Orange & Blue
Almost anywhere you go along the coast, you're sure to spot the orange and blue arrows and ribbons of the Jeju Olle Trail, ready to lead you on a slow walking journey.

09 Dol Hareubang
Another stone icon, Jeju's 'stone grandfather' statues, carved out of basalt, stand sentinel all across the island. They are said to ward off evil spirits and bring good fortune, including fertility.

01 & 04 W3007/SHUTTERSTOCK, **03** MIMIN DOODLE/SHUTTERSTOCK, **02, 05, 06, 07 & 09** BLUEHOUSESTUDIO/SHUTTERSTOCK, **08** GWEN COTTER/LONELY PLANET

38 Women of THE SEA

FIERCE | FREEDIVING | RESILIENCE

For centuries, women on Jeju-do known as *haenyeo* have freedived to gather seafood. *Haenyeo*, in Korean 'sea women', are able to hold their breath underwater for up to three minutes and reach a depth of 20m. As of 2024, there are only 2839 active *haenyeo* remaining, 90% of whom are aged 60 or older. *Haenyeo* are a living heritage who are working hard to keep their culture alive.

SHANAE ENNIS-MELHADO/SHUTTERSTOCK

How To

Getting around It's possible to travel by bus, with the 201 stopping (from clockwise) at Hado-ri, Gwangchigi Beach, the Jungmun Resort Complex and Gwideok-ri. A car, as always, offers maximum flexibility.

When to go *Haenyeo* work year-round, adjusting their dives according to weather conditions. July and August is the hottest time on the island, and it's also typhoon season. Spring and autumn have ideal temperatures, but winter is when many fish are at their peak.

FEBRI BORNEO/SHUTTERSTOCK

Haenyeo haunts Observing *haenyeo*, you'll marvel at their endurance and skill. At the eastern base of Seongsan Ilchulbong, a long staircase leads down to **Umutgae Beach**, a crescent-shaped cove where you can witness *haenyeo* at work most days around 2pm. Another place to spot the women freedivers is **Gwangchigi Beach**, a strip between Seongsan-ri and Seopji-koji featuring mossy-green seaweed-coated rocks and black sand.

Jeonbok, galchi and more Perhaps there's no better way to appreciate *haenyeo*'s hard work than to actually taste the delicious salty fruits of their labours. Be sure to lunch at one of the island's many *haenyeo jip* (houses), small restaurants that serve foods like sea cucumbers, mackerel and *galchi* (hairtail). One must-try is *jeonbok* (abalone), either raw or cooked in a *juk* (porridge). *Haenyeo jip* can be found all around the island, including by Umutgae Beach, Jungmun Beach and on the smaller island of Udo, too.

Haenyeo as teachers You can learn freediving skills from *haenyeo* at centres such as **Hansupul Haenyeo School** in Gwideok-ri.

Learn about haenyeo The village of Hado-ri, a small attractive beach along the northeastern coast punctuated by basalt outcrops, is where the excellent **Haenyeo Museum** (jeju.go.kr/haenyeo) explains the history and culture of the amazing women divers. Browse exhibitions about their traditional homes, boats, tools and dress.

Top left *Haenyeo*
Bottom left *Jeonbok*

Read & Watch

Learn more about *haenyeo* with these excellent resources.

Jeju Island's Haenyeo: A User's Manual (Joey Rositano; 2019) Documenting the lives of *haenyeo* then and now, amid Jeju's tourism, pollution and other challenges.

Moon Tides: Jeju Island Grannies of the Sea (Brenda Paik Sunoo; 2011) A photojournalist's account of Jeju's *haenyeo*, told through interviews.

My Mother, the Mermaid (Park Heung-sik; 2004) Fantasy film about a young woman who travels back in time to witness the love story between her father and *haenyeo* mother.

The Ocean Calls: A Haenyeo Mermaid Story (Tina M Cho; 2020) Children's picture book about a girl who overcomes her fear of the sea with the help of her *haenyeo* grandmother.

39 Healing FORESTS

THERAPY | ESCAPE | VERDANT

For burned-out professionals on Korea's fast-paced mainland, Jeju-do has become a popular escape, its azure waters, fresh winds and forest-green landscapes providing a dose of nature's medicine. From meditative walking to forest bathing, therapeutic activities feature prominently at 'healing' woodlands throughout the island, which encourage visitors to get off their devices and connect with nature.

CAT CLOUD/SHUTTERSTOCK

How To

Getting around Save a lot of time by renting a car or hailing a taxi to reach Jeju's healing forests.

When to go While beautiful in every season, shaded woodlands are an extra-welcome reprieve from Jeju-do's extreme heat and humidity in the summer.

Top tip Where it's safe, try removing your shoes and walking barefoot, to better stimulate circulation, absorb the environment's therapeutic properties and encourage slower, more mindful steps.

AARON CHOI/SHUTTERSTOCK

Top left Jeolmul Recreational Forest
Bottom left Bijarim Forest

Forest therapy South of Halla-san, **Seogwipo Healing Forest** is a mixed subtropical, temperate and boreal woodland that features cypress trees. Choose from various circuits, some along boardwalks; rest in a forest bathing chair; and head to the observatory for views over the city.

Stay the night With a variety of trails winding through cedar, pine and other evergreen forests, **Jeolmul Recreational Forest** also has several *oreum* that visitors can climb, as well as a woodcraft centre, playground, pond and forest bathing area. Rent a forest cabin to stay overnight.

Spotting wildlife A much-frequented weekend walking spot on the eastern border of Hallasan National Park, **Saryeoni Forest** is close to Jeolmul Recreational Forest. Shaded by maples, oaks and cedars, it has 15km of forest paths and the occasional roaming deer.

Medicinal woodland With some 2800 *bija* (ancient yew) trees, some more than 800 years old, **Bijarim Forest** in northeastern Jeju is protected as a natural monument and a popular place to go forest bathing. It's said that being amid *bija* trees helps rejuvenate the body and mind, and in traditional medicine *bija* berries were used to kill parasites.

Volcanic biome Part of the Hangyeong-Andeok Gotjawal Zone, **Jeju Gotjawal Provincial Park** is a great place to learn about this unique type of forest. The park has an information centre, ecological experience school, exhibition space and rest areas.

Jeju-do's Gotjawal Ecology

Unique to Jeju-do are *gotjawal*, a local-dialect word for forest biomes where trees, brush, moss and other plants naturally intertwine as they grow from the island's rocky volcanic terrain. The *gotjawal* ecosystem maintains a relatively stable temperature year-round of about 10–15°C, so diverse species of tropical northern and southern plants are able to coexist. Around 224 sq km of the island is covered by *gotjawal*, areas that are under threat from tourism-related construction. Jeju's four main *gotjawal* zones are Hangyeong–Andeok Gotjawal and Aewol Gotjawal in the west, and Jocheon–Hamdeok Gotjawal and Gujawa–Seongsan Gotjawal in the east.

40 Off to UDO

PEANUTS | BEACHES | CYCLING

The largest of 62 islets surrounding Jeju-do, Udo is also sometimes referred to as Soseom, or Cow Island, because its shape resembles a sprawled-out cow. Just 3.8km off the coast, it's a lovely, windswept place.

EMMET LEE/SHUTTERSTOCK

How To

Getting there Catch a ferry; they depart frequently from Seongsan terminal and arrive at either Haumokdong or Cheonjin terminals. Bring your passport.

Getting around It takes four to five hours to walk around the whole island. Bicycle rental operators are clustered near the ports. Also available are motorbikes and enclosed three-wheel scooters, which require an international driver's permit (type B). Alternatively, there's a bus that circles Udo, going clockwise on even-numbered days and counter-clockwise on odd-numbered days.

Land of Peanuts

Udo is known for its high-quality peanuts, in Korean *ddangkong*, which feature on lots of local menus, flavouring everything from ice cream to *makgeolli* (milky rice wine) to baked goods, burgers and beyond. When trying peanut *makgeolli*, make sure it's Nakwhagokju, the brand that's brewed on Udo, as there's another that's actually brewed in Cheongju on the mainland.

Splashy Sights

njiyeon Pokpo

opular 22m-high waterfall, most ssive following a heavy rain, is reached a 10-minute walk through a beautifully ed, steep gorge along Olle Route 6 in vipo.

bang Pokpo

urite among photographers, this igh waterfall is notable because it's y one in Asia that falls directly into the A 15-minute walk east of Seogwipo entre.

ng Beach

beach east along Hwy 1132 from his one is jet black when wet. In sum- the locals and bury yourself in the sand for its therapeutic effects.

een Gardens & Tea Fields

Garden

g a collection of over 2000 *bunjae* an style of bonsai), this botanical artfully contorted miniature trees s is a portal into a fantasy world.

k

tre of Hallim, this is Jeju's best garden, which includes a *bunjae* garden, a water garden, an aviary, houses of subtropical plants and hrough lava-tube caves.

Museum

ctively landscaped grounds over- lant tea fields, this complex is a p for tea-based souvenirs, and to eat and drink products made from the fresh green leaves.

Historical Highlights

Jeju National Museum

Get a wide-ranging overview of the island's history, beginning with its formation by volcanic activity 1.8 million years ago, through to the Goryeo and Joseon dynasties.

Jeju April 3 Peace Park

Thirteen kilometres southeast of downtown Jeju-si, this thoughtful and evocative museum chronicles the events that led up to and followed the April 3 Incident, an island uprising in the late 1940s and early 1950s that resulted in a large-scale massacre of Jeju civilians.

Seongeup Folk Village

A former provincial capital, Seongeup has benefitted from government assistance in preserving and renovating its traditional rock-walled, thatch-roofed houses, and unlike other touristy villages, is the real deal, with people living and working here still.

HEVOLKZZ/SHUTTERSTOCK

Cheonjiyeon Pokpo

01 Begin on Udo's west coast at the island's largest and most popular beach, **Sanho Beach** (pictured right), its brilliant white coral sand stretching out in a crescent-moon shape between the two ports.

02 Stop for lunch at the friendly burger joint **HahaHoho**. Order the peanut black pork burger, pair it with a *hallabong* lemonade or peanut shake, and enjoy with a window view onto the emerald-blue ocean.

03 Cro... rea... where... restau... black... do Li...

05 Finish with a bottle of the island's famous *ddangkong makgeolli* at **Nakwhagokju**. You'll know it's the local stuff because Nakwhagokju is where the peanut rice wine is brewed.

FROM TOP: SUNGMOON HAN/SHUTTERSTOCK, TSUGULIEV/SHUTTERSTOCK

L...

BE...

Che...
This impr... after... fores... Seog...

Jeon...
A favo... 23m-... the or... ocean... town c...

Samya...
The fir... Jeju-si... mer, jo... iron-ric...

G...

Spirited...
Displayi... (the Kor... garden c... and shru...

Hallim P...
In the ce... botanical... and stone... large gree... passages...

Osulloc Te...
Set in attr... looking ve... place to sh...

Jeju's Favourite Foods

Seogwipo Maeil Olle Market ₩

An essential stop to browse stalls of delicious fruit, live seafood and souvenirs. Seek out Negeori Olle, specialising in fat deep-fried cabbage rolls of black pork, seafood and kimchi, and Jeseong Bakery for savoury bread buns.

Dongmun Market ₩

This bustling market, covering several city blocks of Jeju-si, is well worth a wander to peek at local seafood and stock up on island citrus. Also be sure to sample the street food at its lively night market (5.30-10pm) by Gate 8.

Sukseongdo ₩₩₩

Have your orders delivered to your table by a robot at this premium K-BBQ restaurant with several locations around the island, including near Jungmun Resort.

Dasoni ₩₩

Sit cross-legged at rustic wooden tables at this superb meat-free restaurant in Jeju-si. Dishes such as bibimbap use local Jeju produce.

Haejin Seafood Restaurant ₩₩₩

A popular place to try cuttlefish, eel, squid, octopus, sea cucumber, abalone and other seafood specialities while looking over Jeju-si harbour.

Negeori ₩₩

In Seogwipo on Arang Joeul Food Street, Negeori is rightly beloved for its mouthwatering renditions of *galchiguk* (hairtail fish soup) and grilled fish dishes.

Yetnal Patjuk ₩

This restaurant inside Seongeup Folk Village serves hearty red-bean porridge, along with other varieties like pumpkin. Pair it with *sikhye*, a traditional rice punch.

CHERISH GONZALES/SHUTTERSTOCK

Dongmun Market

Seaside Drinks

Rose Marine (로즈마린)

Order *makgeolli* (milky rice wine) and *jeon* (savoury pancakes) at this tumbledown shack pub (which featured as a location in the K-Drama *Extraordinary Attorney Woo*) and enjoy with a view of Seogwipo's sun-kissed harbour.

Bluebird by Magpie

Sample an excellent range of craft beers brewed on the island and poured at this industrial space in Jeju-si overlooking the coast. Also serves tasty pizzas and fried chicken.

Floyeast Bakery Cafe

Having a latte or Americano inside Tadao Ando's Glass House on Phoenix Island is a delight, best enjoyed during the day to fully appreciate the views through the floor-to-ceiling windows.

Cafe Hallasan

In Hado-ri, potted plants and vintage odds and ends, including an old rocking horse, add charm to this sea-view cafe serving coffee and carrot cake.

CHUNGCHEONG-DO

UNEXPLORED COAST | FORTRESSES | LAKE ADVENTURE

RESEARCHED BY PHILLIP TANG

TERA/SHUTTERSTOCK

CHUNGCHEONG-DO
Trip Builder

Savour Korea's unsung heartland, where ancient Baekje capitals and the origins of printing meet a rugged coastline. Hike through national parks that are studded with temples or go slow by Chungju-ho. This is a place to discover the country's most overlooked treasures.

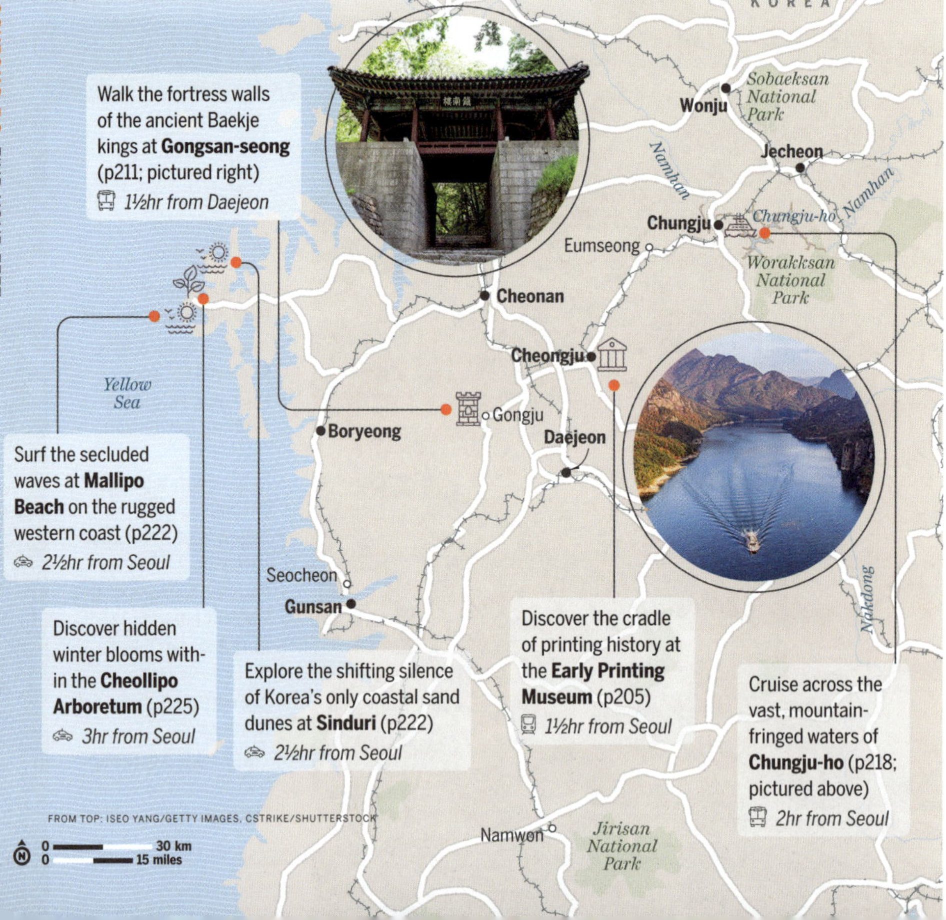

Walk the fortress walls of the ancient Baekje kings at **Gongsan-seong** (p211; pictured right)
1½hr from Daejeon

Surf the secluded waves at **Mallipo Beach** on the rugged western coast (p222)
2½hr from Seoul

Discover hidden winter blooms within the **Cheollipo Arboretum** (p225)
3hr from Seoul

Explore the shifting silence of Korea's only coastal sand dunes at **Sinduri** (p222)
2½hr from Seoul

Discover the cradle of printing history at the **Early Printing Museum** (p205)
1½hr from Seoul

Cruise across the vast, mountain-fringed waters of **Chungju-ho** (p218; pictured above)
2hr from Seoul

FROM TOP: ISEO YANG/GETTY IMAGES, CSTRIKE/SHUTTERSTOCK

Practicalities

ARRIVING

Cheongju International Airport Flights from Jeju and Asian countries. A 25-minute taxi ride to central Cheongju; one-hour bus to Daejeon.

Daejeon station or **Osong station** KTX station hubs for high-speed trains from Seoul, Gangneung, Cheongju and Busan.

Intercity Bus Terminal Direct buses from Seoul, Daejeon, Gongju and Buyeo.

FIND YOUR WAY

Download apps Naver or Kakao Maps for routing; Kakao T is in English and accepts foreign bank cards for ordering taxis.

MONEY

Choose the slower Mugunghwa train over KTX to halve transport costs and enjoy hinterland views to Cheongju or Daejeon.

WHERE TO STAY

Place	Pros/Cons
Cheongju	Ample spacious budget hotels. Downtown is less grungy than around the bus terminals.
Chungju-ho	Wide-ranging camping and glamping sites with lake views. Car needed.
Taeanhaean National Park's coast	Hotels and campsites backed by pine forests near beaches. Car needed.

GETTING AROUND

Bus The local bus systems in the cities of Chungcheong-do are easy to understand and route using the English version of the Naver Maps app. Rides are comfortable and charged as a flat fare, not by distance; tap on and off with Tmoney card only.

Car Driving required for Taeanhaean National Park's coast, including Mallipo Beach and Cheollipo Arboretum. Tours are the recommended way to reach Chungju-ho from Seoul.

TOP: PHOTOHWAN/SHUTTERSTOCK
BOTTOM: THEERAWAN/SHUTTERSTOCK

EATING & DRINKING

Cheongju, Gongju and Buyeo offer diverse dining hubs near their historical cores, with stylish cuisine available at the likes of SORORI (p228) in Cheongju. If you're camping or glamping near Chungju-ho or Taeanhaean, large Hanaro or Lotte marts are available in the city centres.

Must-try seafood
Korea's Best Seafood Hotpot (p228)

Must-try pork belly
Samgyeopsal Alley (p206)

JAN–MAR
Crisp, snowy peaks and ice festivals; clear winter skies.

APR–JUN
Cherry blossoms line Chungju-ho; mild, perfect hiking weather.

JUL–SEP
Peak beach season in Taeanhaean; mud festival and humidity.

OCT–DEC
Autumn foliage blankets Songni-san; cool, dry days for sightseeing.

41 The West Coast MIRACLE CIRCUIT

COAST DRIVE | BEACH CAMPING | PINE FORESTS

Escape to the Taean Peninsula's resilient shores, where desert-like dunes meet ancient red pine forests. Made for coastal hikers and K-Drama fans, this drive pairs isolated, sunset-rich beaches with the inspiring history of Korea's most successful ecological recovery.

STOCK FOR YOU/SHUTTERSTOCK

The Muddy Miracle

In the early 1990s, the closure of local coal mines prompted Mayor Park Sang-don to rekindle the economy by developing cosmetics from Boryeong's mud. Believed to have anti-ageing and healing properties, this mineral-rich mud has been popularised by the Mud Festival for over 20 years. Today, Boryeong mud masks are worldwide favourites.

How To

Getting there and around Buses run from Seoul Nambu to Taean-gun. Local services reach Sinduri and Mallipo, but a rental car is essential for hopscotching Anmyeondo and crossing the Boryeong Undersea Tunnel.

When to go Late spring offers blooming gardens at Cheollipo, while September provides crisp, fog-free views of Kkotji's sunsets. Winter is serene but requires heavy layers.

Driving highlight Take the 6.9km Boryeong Undersea Tunnel, Korea's longest, linking Anmyeondo directly to the mud-festival hub of Daecheon.

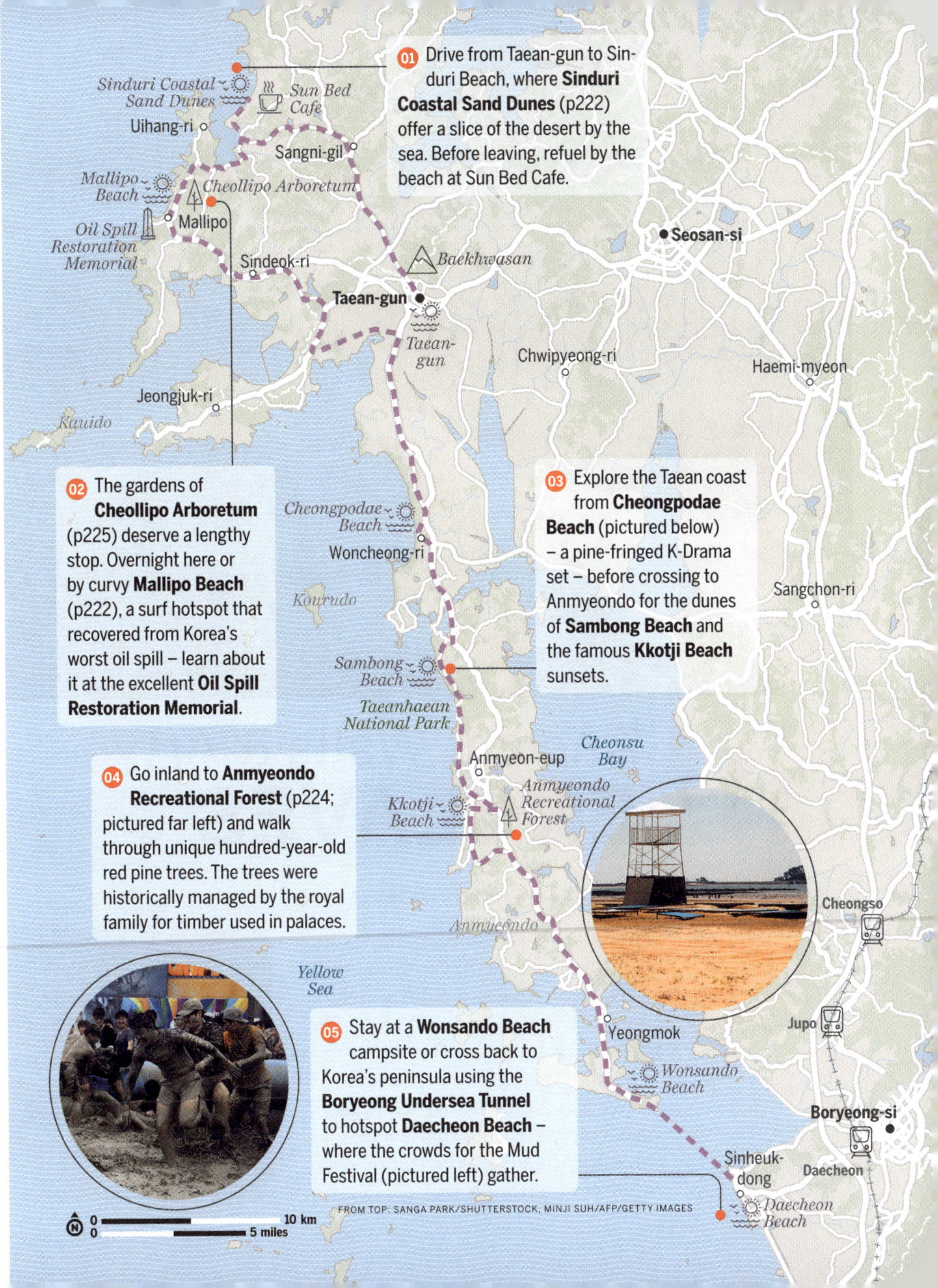

01 Drive from Taean-gun to Sinduri Beach, where **Sinduri Coastal Sand Dunes** (p222) offer a slice of the desert by the sea. Before leaving, refuel by the beach at Sun Bed Cafe.

02 The gardens of **Cheollipo Arboretum** (p225) deserve a lengthy stop. Overnight here or by curvy **Mallipo Beach** (p222), a surf hotspot that recovered from Korea's worst oil spill – learn about it at the excellent **Oil Spill Restoration Memorial**.

03 Explore the Taean coast from **Cheongpodae Beach** (pictured below) – a pine-fringed K-Drama set – before crossing to Anmyeondo for the dunes of **Sambong Beach** and the famous **Kkotji Beach** sunsets.

04 Go inland to **Anmyeondo Recreational Forest** (p224; pictured far left) and walk through unique hundred-year-old red pine trees. The trees were historically managed by the royal family for timber used in palaces.

05 Stay at a **Wonsando Beach** campsite or cross back to Korea's peninsula using the **Boryeong Undersea Tunnel** to hotspot **Daecheon Beach** – where the crowds for the Mud Festival (pictured left) gather.

FROM TOP: SANGA PARK/SHUTTERSTOCK, MINJI SUH/AFP/GETTY IMAGES

42 Ancient Walls & Arty ENCLAVES

CRAFTS | PRINTING | FORTRESS HIKE

A city that successfully pairs a printing legacy with youthful energy, Cheongju remains a culture-rich hub with a distinct small-town vibe. Beyond its historic mountain fortress and unique pork belly tradition, it offers a sophisticated scene and immersive artistic experiences, all blissfully free from the frantic pace of larger metropolises.

Above Sangdang-sanseong (p207) **Right** Early Printing Museum **Far right** Replica Jikji

TMPRTMPR/GETTY IMAGES

How To

Getting there and around Catch the KTX to Osong (45 minutes from Seoul), then a 20-minute taxi or bus to the centre. Within the city, use efficient buses or walk pedestrian-friendly Seongan-gil downtown.

When to go In spring (April to June) cherry blossoms frame streams. Autumn (October to November) offers crisp air and golden ginkgo trees, ideal for hiking the Sangdang-sanseong.

Secret sunset Suamgol Village has exceptional city views as the lights flicker on.

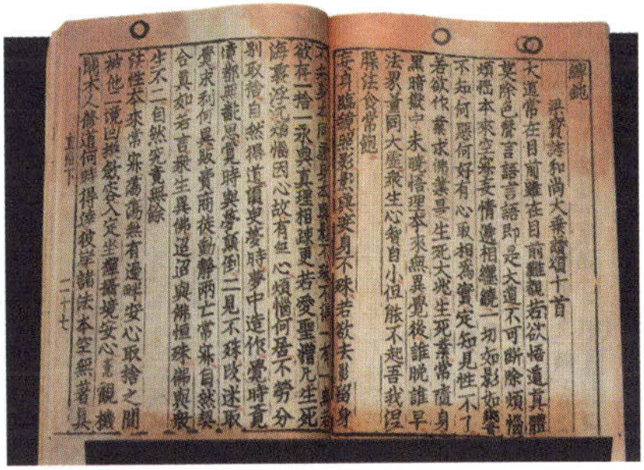

DADEROT/CC0 1.0/WIKIMEDIA COMMONS

An Ancient Book

While the Gutenberg Bible needs no introduction, the **Jikji** (p208) languished for many years in relative obscurity, even though it is the oldest book in the world printed with movable metal type. It was printed in 1377 (78 years before the Gutenberg) at the temple of Heungdeok-sa in modern-day Cheongju. Today, the small Cheongju **Early Printing Museum** (cheongju.go.kr/jikjiworld/index.do; free) tells you everything about the Jikji, which was admitted to UNESCO's Memory of the World Register in 2001. Sadly the original is not here – it's in the National Library of France – and in its place there's a copy.

The Jikji itself is small: 38 sheets of thin mulberry paper, each one measuring 24.6cm by 17cm. Its full title is *Baegun hwasang chorok buljo jikji simche yojeol* – that is, an

SOBEAUTIFUL/SHUTTERSTOCK

Hidden Heart of Cheongju

East of Seongan-gil's shopping throng, there's a cosmopolitan energy emerging within the **Jungang-dong** district of leafy narrow lanes, characterful cafes such as **Hyper Market**, and vintage boutiques. In the evening, laughter spills onto the streets from eclectic bars, fusion Japanese bistros and soju-soaked restaurants. Get a glimpse of Cheongju's youthful, hip enclave being born.

anthology of the monk Baegun Gyeonghan's teachings on Seon Buddhism (Zen Buddhism), though of the two-volume set, only the second volume remains.

Culture Factories

Cheongju has successfully transformed its industrial and historical remnants into a sophisticated network of creative spaces you can visit in one afternoon. The journey begins at the **Culture Factory**, a vast former tobacco plant that now serves as a vibrant cultural hub. It houses diverse restaurants, boutiques and an open library, while also acting as the prestigious home of the Cheongju Craft Biennale.

Nearby, the **MMCA Cheongju** offers a groundbreaking experience for art lovers, featuring South Korea's first 'open storage' system where the public can view contemporary masterpieces in their archival setting.

Cheongju-Style Barbecued Pork

Tucked inside Seomun Market, **Samgyeopsal Alley** is the birthplace of Cheongju-style pork belly. Unlike the standard salted barbecue found elsewhere, locals here practice the 'dip and grill' method. Diners receive a bowl of *ganjang* (soy sauce) infused with ginger and traditional herbs. Each slice of meat is briefly submerged in this savoury bath just seconds before hitting the heat. This quick soak tenderises the pork and creates a deep, caramelised glaze as it sizzles. Historically used to ensure the meat's freshness, the tradition now defines the city's most authentic culinary experience. Grab a seat at one of many restaurants to try this sweet-salty Cheongju icon.

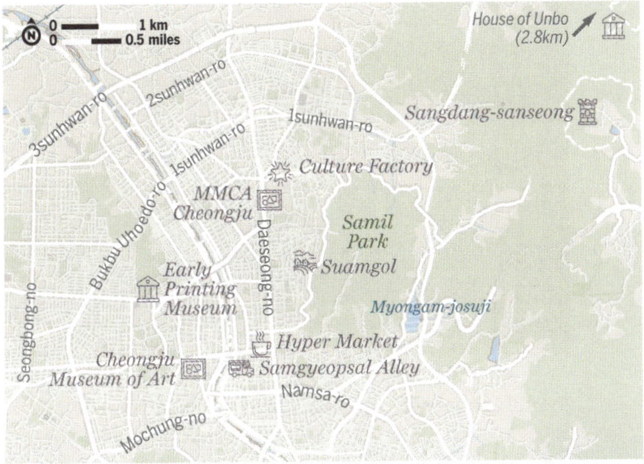

Left Cheongju-style barbecued pork
Below House of Unbo

For a change of pace, the **Cheongju Museum of Art** provides a cultural playground for modern works, while the **House of Unbo** allows visitors to explore the private galleries and workshops of the famous, albeit controversial, artist. Finally, the hills of **Suamgol** – once a Korean War refugee camp – now host a small mural village. While the murals have faded, the area remains a trendy filming location famous for its lofty rooftop cafes.

Mountain Fortress Day Out

On the slopes of the mountain Uam-san, the sprawling fortress **Sangdang-sanseong** (free), 4km northeast of the city, was originally constructed in the 1590s and renovated in the 18th century. With walls up to 4m in height that stretch 4.2km around wooded hillsides, Sangdang-sanseong's size makes it easy to imagine that it once housed three temples and several thousand soldiers and monks. Today, it offers superb views of farms, mountains and the city, and is a popular place for Korean families to picnic on the fields outside the ornate south gate. A hike around the wall takes about 1½ hours, the easier direction to follow being counter-clockwise. Once you're finished, stop at a restaurant near the bus stop for *jeon* (savoury pancake) and *makgeolli* (milky rice wine).

FROM LEFT: JREIKA/SHUTTERSTOCK, SOBEAUTIFUL/SHUTTERSTOCK

By Phillip Tang
@mrtangtangtang

History's Forgotten Printing Revolution

THE BUDDHIST ORIGINS OF MOVABLE TYPE

Long before Gutenberg's Bible transformed Europe, a quiet revolution was forged in the hills of Cheongju. In 1377, Buddhist monks at Heungdeok-sa printed the Jikji, which stands as the world's oldest book made with movable metal type. It represents a pinnacle of Goryeo dynasty innovation, predating the West's typographic revolution by 78 years.

Left Jikji detail **Centre** Jikji, National Library of France **Right** Jikji printing plates

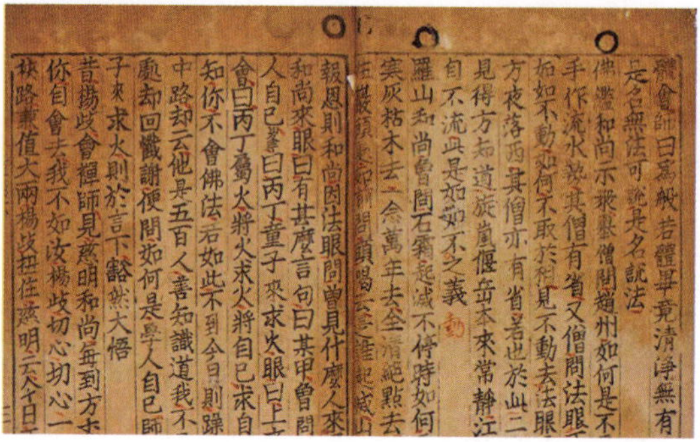

UNIVERSAL HISTORY ARCHIVE/GETTY IMAGES

In 1455, Johannes Gutenberg printed his famous 42-line Bible in Mainz, Germany – an event widely heralded as the dawn of the modern world. Yet nearly eight decades earlier, a small temple in the Korean hinterland had already mastered the art of the bronze press. The Jikji Simche Yojeol, a collection of Zen Buddhist teachings, was not merely a book; it was a technological leap.

Groundbreaking Type Technique

While Chinese artisans had experimented with fragile baked clay and the Goryeo dynasty had used static woodblocks, the monks of Cheongju refined the painstaking process of casting individual, reusable metal characters from bronze. This enabled the production of diverse texts with a single set of type, a development that predated the European Renaissance by generations.

The technical brilliance of the Jikji lay in its beeswax method. Monks would engrave characters into wax, cover them in clay to create a mould, and then pour molten bronze into the cavity. This allowed for a level of durability and precision that wood could never achieve.

Forgotten in the Vaults

Despite this unprecedented technological feat, the world assumed the printing press was a purely European invention and the Jikji was largely ignored by global historians for centuries. Its journey to the West began in the late 19th century when Collin de Plancy, the first French consul to Korea, 'acquired' the second volume of the text. When he returned to Europe, the Jikji travelled with him, eventually being donated to the National Library of France (BnF) in 1950.

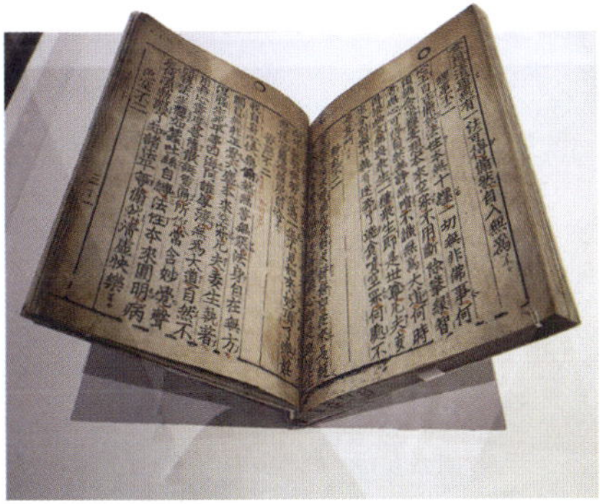

ANNE-CHRISTINE POUJOULAT/GETTY IMAGES

TORSTEN SILZ/GETTY IMAGES

For decades, the book sat in the library's Manuscrits Orientaux division, effectively forgotten. It was classified as a mere curiosity, tucked away in a basement vault where it remained unrecognised by the French staff.

The Librarian Detective

The silence was finally broken in the late 1960s by Dr Park Byeong-seon, a Korean scholar working as a librarian at the BnF. Tasked with cataloguing the collection, she spent years of solitary archival detective work trying to prove the book's true age. She even reportedly experimented with metal-casting in her own kitchen to understand how the ink interacted with the bronze type.

> The Jikji sent shockwaves through the academic world

In 1972, which was named International Book Year by the United Nations, Dr Park finally introduced the Jikji to the world at an exhibition in Paris. Her meticulous research proved that the book was printed in 1377: 78 years before the Gutenberg Bible. This discovery sent shockwaves through the academic world, effectively dismantling the myth that movable type was a German invention.

While the original volume remains in Paris today, its legacy has been restored to the global stage, finally repositioning Cheongju as the true cradle of the world's typographic history and cementing Korea's legacy as a pioneer of information technology.

The Missing Masterpiece

The original Jikji remains in the National Library of France, protected by laws regarding the 'inalienability' of French public property. This has sparked the 'Bring Jikji to the World' campaign, spearheaded by the cyber-diplomacy group VANK. The movement seeks not only the book's physical return or a long-term loan but also its 'globalisation' – ensuring international textbooks and museums recognise Cheongju, not Mainz, as the birthplace of movable metal type. While the book has only returned to Korean soil once (on a temporary 2023 loan), for many, it remains a 'hidden hero' awaiting its final journey home.

43 In the Footsteps OF KINGS

HISTORY | CULTURE | HIKING

In Gongju, the Baekje (two of ancient Korea's Three Kingdoms) ruled over a settlement that lasted two centuries from 475 CE. Trace this Baekje history on easy fortress wall hikes and by ducking inside the burial mounds of kings.

TRABANTOS/SHUTTERSTOCK

How To

Getting there and around Gongju has direct buses from Seoul Nambu and Cheongju, and a KTX Honam Line train station outside the town centre.

When to go Time your visit for the Baekje Cultural Festival for traditional parades, light shows and mild weather in September and October.

Eat local Chestnuts are a local speciality and chestnut bread, pies and snacks abound in the cafes outside these sites.

©KOREA TOURISM ORGANIZATION – JEON HYEONGJUN

Great Wall of Baekje

Slung like a dormant dragon on a hill overlooking the Geum River, stunning **Gongsan-seong** reminds us of the time when Gongju was Ungjin, the capital of the Baekje kingdom between 475 and 538 CE. The 2.6km-long fortress walls enclose a large area whose notable structures include **Imnyu-gak**, a banquet hall built initially in 500 CE (the building seen today is a replica); the **Manharu Pavilion** overlooking Gongju's central river Geum-gang, a building that once served twin purposes of defence and recreation; the pavilion **Ssangsu-jeong**, named for a pair of trees that King Injo used to lean against while contemplating the fate of his kingdom; and **Yeongeun-sa**, a temple first constructed in the 15th century that once served as a boarding house for warrior monks.

KOREA BY BIKE/SHUTTERSTOCK

Baekje History

Roughly halfway along Gwangwangdanji-gil, the **Gongju National Museum** (free) provides a comprehensive overview of Baekje's history – including most of the artefacts found in the tombs – among a staggering 41,000 other relics from the Neolithic age to the Joseon dynasty.

Top left Gongsan-seong
Left Geumseoru West Gate (p212)
Above Manharu Pavilion

After entering through the grand stone **Geumseoru West Gate**, you can walk along the perimeter and on the old walls, passing numerous pavilions, including **Gongbung-nu** and **Gwangbongnu**, rebuilt according to archaeological evidence of their original structures. For the most dramatic views over the river and the rest of the 'new city' that extends beyond its northern shore, hike to the northwest section of the wall. In the evening, the whole fortress is lit up with floodlights.

King's Tombs

A 20-minute walk south of the stone arch in front of Gongsan-seong in Songsan-ri is a group of six UNESCO-protected Baekje-era tombs, the most important of which belongs to **King Muryeong**, the 25th Baekje king, discovered miraculously intact and completely by accident in 1971.

The tomb is inside a huge earth mound with a rectangular burial chamber opening

The Cultural Third Kingdom

The Baekje Kingdom (18 BCE–660 CE) flourished as a vibrant, outward-looking state that defined the era's artistic standards from its capitals in Gongju and Buyeo. During the Three Kingdoms period, Korea was divided among distinct regional powers: the Goguryeo (modern-day North Korea and Manchuria) forged a rugged identity through mountain warfare, while the Silla (modern Gyeongju) remained relatively isolated.

In contrast, Baekje leveraged its southwestern coastline to dominate regional trade. It functioned as the primary channel for advanced civilisation, introducing Buddhism, sophisticated pottery and urban planning to Japan. Rather than focusing solely on military expansion, Baekje artisans prioritised an understated elegance that avoided excessive flashiness.

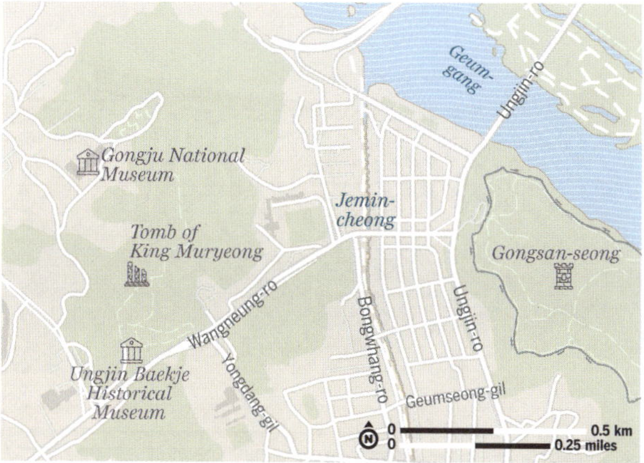

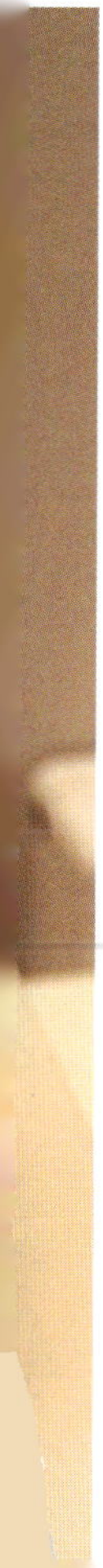

Left Baekje Kingdom pottery
Below King Muryeong's tomb museum and replica

into a semi-circular vault with hundreds of moulded bricks decorated with Buddhist lotus-flower motifs and geometric designs. The original tombs aren't open to the public but an on-site museum has models of two that visitors can enter, as well as English-language information about the history of the Baekje dynasty.

King Muryeong ascended the throne (501–523 CE) during a vital Baekje recovery, leveraging a century-long alliance with Silla to secure Baekje's borders. During his 22 years in power, Muryeong centralised state control and expanded the empire, annexing the Jeju island-based state of Tamna and territories of the Gaya Kingdom.

The treasures from his intact tomb testify to this golden age: besides arboreal gilt-bronze crowns, the chamber contained gold jewellery and two silver bracelets decorated with intricate dragons. Together, these exquisite artefacts reflect the peak of the kingdom's diplomacy, wealth, and mastery of metallurgy.

The **Ungjin Baekje Historical Museum** has more exhibits, augmented reality videos and a tourist office near the entrance.

44 Legends of the Forest FORTRESS

HIKING | TEMPLES | HISTORY

Explore a sprawling mountain fortress where pine-scented paths lead to cliffside temples with legendary stories and panoramic river views. Combining royal burial mounds with a bustling cultural heart, Buyeo is an easygoing walk through living history.

LINEGOLD/SHUTTERSTOCK

How To

Getting there and around Express buses from Seoul Nambu Terminal take roughly two hours. Buyeo's centre is highly walkable, but a taxi is best for reaching the Love Tree or royal tombs.

When to go Late spring offers lush greenery, but icy mid-winter has crowd-free hiking.

Local sips Reward your hike with Buyeo chestnut *makgeolli*. The region's famous chestnuts give this milky rice wine a unique, nutty sweetness.

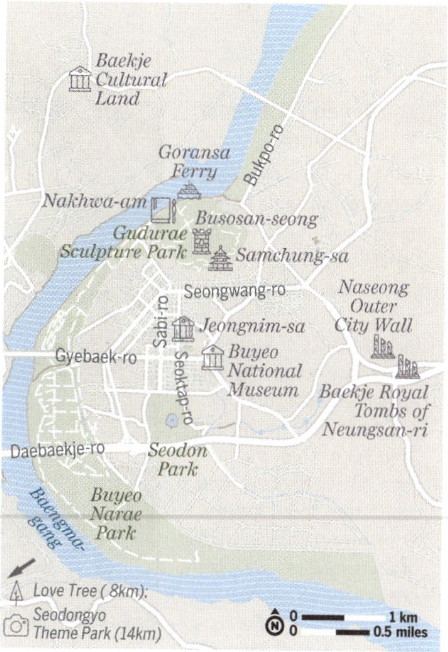

TRABANTOS/SHUTTERSTOCK

Hiking the Walls of the Last Capital

Reconstructed in 605 CE, the walls of the mountain fortress **Busosan-seong** to the north of Buyeo's compact city centre once sheltered the Baekje capital of Sabi on 106m-high Buso-san. Today, paved and sandy paths and stairs weave through pine forests past pavilions and temples. On the northern part of the enclosure, the **Nakhwa-am** cliff ('falling flowers rock') and its ornate pavilion commemorate the spot where 3000 court ladies flung themselves into the waters of Baekma-gang rather than submit to the conquering Silla and Chinese armies in 660 CE. One temple, **Samchung-sa**, is dedicated to three loyal Baekje court officials, including General Gyebaek, who led the last stand against the invaders even though he was outnumbered 10 to one.

Top left Busosan-seong **Left** Nakhwa-am

The fortress is officially open until 6pm, but gates stay open 24 hours and access is free after 6pm. Come prepared – it takes hours to see it all (short visits are also possible), temperatures drop quickly and there are no stores inside, just water bubblers.

Downtown Baekje Heritage

Like Gongju, Buyeo is part of the UNESCO-protected Baekje Areas and has a cluster of other important historical sights. Right in the centre of town, an austere 8.3m-high five-storey stone pagoda is all that remains of the original structure of the **Jeongnim-sa** (jeongnimsaji.or.kr; free). A new temple lies next to it at the centre of extensive and well-manicured gardens.

Buyeo National Museum (buyeo.museum.go.kr; free), an exhibition of some of the best collections of Baekje artefacts, is a short walk away. A highlight is an incense burner from the era weighing 12kg and covered with

Buyeo's K-Drama Locations

Step into a living film set at **Seodongyo Theme Park**, an expansive *hanok* (traditional Korean house) village perched beside the Deogyong Reservoir. Originally built for *Ballad of Seodong*, it has since hosted period epics like *Moonlight Drawn by Clouds* and *Scarlet Heart Ryeo*. For a more romantic vista, hike to the **Love Tree** atop Garim-seong fortress. The sweeping canopy of this 400-year-old zelkova – famously featured in *Alchemy of Souls* and *Hotel Del Luna* – forms a perfect half-heart silhouette against the sky. It remains one of Korea's most iconic sunset spots, offering panoramic views of the Geum-gang river valley below.

Scenic Ferry

The traditional **Goransa Ferry** (one-way/return adult ₩5000/7000, child ₩2500/3500; 9am to 6pm) glides on the Baekma-gang between two piers at **Gudurae Sculpture Park** (free) and **Goran-sa**, a temple set at the bottom of a steep path leading to the Nakhwa-am cliff. The 20-minute ride passes nice stretches of the coastal landscape.

BERNHARD SCHMID/ALAMY

intricate metalwork, crested with the legendary *bonghwang* bird. There is also a sculptural representation outside at the entrance.

Hillside History

Set on a hillside 3km out of town are seven **Baekje Royal Tombs of Neungsan-ri** (baekje-heritage.or.kr; adult/child ₩1000/400) dating from 538 to 660 CE. The grass-covered tumuli (earthen burial mounds for royalty) are reminiscent of the larger ones in Gyeongju. They are sealed for protection, but visitors can see a reconstruction of the most impressive one, painted with the four celestial creatures (dragon, tiger, tortoise and phoenix).

Halfway between the tombs and the town, the **Naseong Outer City Wall** is what remains of an 8km-long fortification protecting the ancient capital Sabi. Reconstructions of the grandiose scale of Baekje's architecture stand north of the river in the historical theme park and museum **Baekje Cultural Land** (bhm.or.kr; adult/child ₩6000/3000), a full-scale replica of what a Baekje palace and attendant village may have looked like, with plenty of space to let kids go wild in safety.

FROM LEFT: GANG CHOI/SHUTTERSTOCK, KOREA BY BIKE/SHUTTERSTOCK

Left Seodongyo Theme Park
Top right Baekje Royal Tombs of Neungsan-ri
Bottom right Buyeo National Museum

45 Paddles & Peaks of the LARGEST LAKE

LAKE CRUISE | HIKING | CULTURE

Drift past granite cliffs on a pleasure boat or test your stamina with a scramble up the craggy face of Geumsu-san. From flood-rescued Joseon gates to the lazy mist of a lakeside campsite, the experience here is as varied as the rugged shoreline. Here is how to navigate the heights and depths of Korea's largest lake.

Above Chungju-ho **Right** Oksun Peak Suspension Bridge (p220) **Far right** Canoes, Chungju-ho

CSTRIKE/SHUTTERSTOCK

How To

Getting there and around Driving or a full-day tour from Seoul is the easiest. Ferry is the best way to cruise the lake.

When to go Early June is the warm sweet spot, before the heat and rains begin.

Cost A lake ferry cruise costs adult/child ₩18,000/10,000 with hourly departures from 9am to 5pm April to October.

KOREAKHW/SHUTTERSTOCK

Cruising & Kayaking

For gorgeous views of the surrounding mountains reflected perfectly in the lake's tranquil waters, take a 'pleasure boat' cruise across **Chungju-ho**. The pace is serenely slow, ensuring plenty of time for enjoying the picturesque surrounds. With multiple ferry terminals around the lake – including Chungju Naru in Chungju, Cheongpung Naru in Jecheon, Janghoe Naru in Danyang and Worak Naru near Worak-san – there are several companies to choose from, offering a range of options for routes, duration and amenities.

For a more adventurous experience, rent a kayak or canoe from an outfitter in Jecheon. One to check out is the **Cheongpung Lake Kayak & Canoe Experience Centre**, where you can set off on an hour-long paddle in the

CSTRIKE/SHUTTERSTOCK

Camping & Glamping

One of the best ways to experience this beautiful environment is to camp. Campgrounds are abundant, ranging from popular private sites to budget-friendly public areas. For simple traditional camping, bring your own gear and look for first-come, first-served sites, although arriving early is essential. For private campgrounds or glamping, online reservations are recommended on weekends.

waters near the picturesque **Oksun Peak** and **Oksun Peak Suspension Bridge** – and the affable owner will snap plenty of photos of you for you to keep.

Lake Hikes

On the east side of the lake, the seven-section and 58km-long **Cheongpung-ho Jadeurak-gil** is a lovely trail to explore, traversing hills and valleys, and passing villages, a horse ranch and an old fortress wall. From Jecheon, start at the **tourist information centre** and pick up a map. On the west side, there's the **Chungju-ho Jongdaengi-gil**, an easy-to-navigate circular course that goes along the shore to reach a beautiful suspension bridge and cuts through forests up to the small mountain Simhang-san. From Chungju, start at the **Jongdaengi-gil information centre**. Be sure to pack water as there are no shops along the way. Eastward, the mountain **Geumsu-san** (1016m) makes for a nice

Cable Car, Monorail & Bungee Jump

In Jecheon, the **Cheongpung Lake Monorail** (cheongpungcablecar.com; adult/child ₩12,000/9000) is a quick and fun little diversion along a mountain forest track that emerges to a view of the lake. A 5km drive away is the **Cheongpung Lake Cable Car** (cheongpungcablecar.com; adult/child ₩18,000/14,000), a nine-minute ropeway ride that extends to the summit of Bibong-san (531m), offering an even more gorgeous panorama of Chungju-ho enveloped by mountains. Across the Cheongpung Bridge is the adventure sports park **Cheongpung Land** (cheongpungland.com; single ride/Top 3 package adult ₩18,000/60,000), with a 62m bungee jump, zero-gravity swing, ejection seat and zip line. Children are not permitted on most rides.

Left Cheongpung Lake Cable Car
Below Cheongpung Cultural Heritage Complex

challenging climb. While a fast one-way ascent can take 1½ to 2½ hours, plan four to six hours for a full round-trip.

Flood-Salvaged Heritage

Beside the cable car is the **Cheongpung Cultural Heritage Complex** (tour.jecheon.go.kr; adult/child ₩3000/2000), a key place to visit to better understand the chequered, complex history of this lake – while a much-enjoyed region of relaxation and recreation today, it was also the cause of mass displacement. With the construction of the Chungju Dam, an area of 66.48 sq km was flooded, submerging a number of villages and forcing some 50,000 residents to resettle.

In order to preserve some of the region's rich heritage, dozens of cultural properties, including Joseon-era pavilions, gates and historical residences, were relocated here, along with more than a thousand pieces of pottery and other artefacts. The resulting complex resembles a folk village, named for Cheongpung, the once important Joseon-dynasty town that was absorbed by Jecheon in 1914 and disappeared entirely in the 1985 flooding.

46 SURF & Sand Dunes

SECLUDED NATURE | REBORN BEACHES | EASY HIKING

The western coast of Chungcheongnam-do province hugs the long and still largely off-the-radar Taeanhaean National Park. The park's largest island, Anmyeondo, is Korea's sixth largest and is connected by a land bridge to the peninsula. Expect serene rolling hills, lush paddy fields and wide, deserted beaches.

How To

Getting there and around Buses run from Seoul Nambu to Seosan. From here, reach Taean-gun, where services continue to Sinduri and Anmyeondo. Renting a car is the best way to explore hidden beaches.

When to go Visit in May or September to avoid heavy summer rains and thick coastal fogs.

Two-wheel fun In summer, tackle the well-maintained coastal trails snaking from Sinduri south to Anmyeondo by bicycle or on foot.

Coastal Wonders

Korean Sahara The northern end of Sinduri Beach, 17km west of Taean-gun, curls into **Sinduri Coastal Sand Dunes**, a carpet of low beachside sandy hills that can be hiked and explored in a few hours. It is believed that they formed about 15,000 years ago, following the Ice Age, as sea winds blew sand towards the coast over thousands of years. The boardwalks make it easy to walk over the fine sand and across an environment mixing beach, shrubs and a backdrop of forest blending into green hills.

Surf on reborn waters

Mallipo is considered one of the best beaches on the west coast. It is 250m wide and 3km long, and in addition to bathing, it's a haven for surfers who come here to catch the strong waves. It's hard to believe it was the site of Korea's largest oil spill.

CSTRIKE/SHUTTERSTOCK

Long-established **MLP Surf** (link.inpock.co.kr/mlpsurf) offers beginner lessons for ₩77,000.

Secret beaches Anmyeondo's west coast is awash with forested, secluded beaches. The Taean Coastal Walk connects undeveloped **Sambong Beach** and its pine trails to quiet **Baeksajang Beach**, 2km north. Heading 9.9km south toward famous **Kkotji Beach**, you'll pass pine-fringed **Anmyeon Beach**, known for rock formations, and **Batgae Beach**, which offers rocky islet views and excellent shell-fishing for snails and crabs.

When Mallipo Went Black

On 7 December 2007, a barge collided with a crude carrier about 9km off Mallipo. Sludge reached the beach in a few hours, and the coast turned black. As soon as the news spread, Koreans sprang to action in what is remembered as the 'Miracle of the West Coast'. About 1.23 million volunteers from all over the nation came to Taean to help remove the oil sludge, working tirelessly to brush up the coast. The effort was tremendous: Mallipo reopened in June 2008, and finless porpoises returned in 2016.

The **Oil Spill Restoration Memorial** documents the largest ocean disaster in Korean history.

Above Kkotji Beach

47 Secret Coastal GARDENS

PINES | HISTORY | HIKING

Walk among centenarian pines once reserved for royal palaces or follow trails where the forest meets the salt spray of the West Sea. This stretch of Taeanhaean coastline offers a rare chance to see exotic species thriving in a unique maritime climate and to stay in salvaged traditional *hanok*. It is a place for quiet exploration through ancient groves and rugged cliffside paths.

How To

When to go Magnolias bloom by mid-April. Autumn has vibrant maples; winter offers stark coastal views.

Getting there Local transport is infrequent; renting a car in the region's gateway Seosan is the best way to reach the sprawling forests of Anmyeondo.

Local flavour The Taean region is famous for its *kkotgejang* (soy-marinated blue crab).

Winter colour Wander the 'Holly Garden' from November to February to see hundreds of varieties with vibrant red berries.

Meet Korea's oldest pines

Since 1978, the centre of **Anmyeondo Recreational Forest** (anmyonhuyang.go.kr; adult/child ₩1000/400) has boasted 115 hectares of Korea's only natural forest pine trees. These hundred-year-old red pines have a hard, straight trunk and look like tall umbrellas. They were used for building ships and caskets for the royal family during the Joseon dynasty and served as a primary source of timber for the reconstruction of royal palaces in Seoul, including the Secret Garden section of Changdeokgung. Observe them up close on three wooden walkways connecting to a 1km-long looping trail around a forested hill. The large reserve includes a Buddhist temple and walking trails that disappear into the surrounding hills. To its southwest, still within Anmyeondo Recreational Forest,

KBELL21/SHUTTERSTOCK

the **Anmyeondo Arboretum** offers more hiking through a pine forest, photo zones and various trails.

Seaside botanical garden
Wander through 64 hectares of lush coastal property by following the well-signposted paths that hug the shoreline at **Cheollipo Arboretum** (chollipo.org; adult/child ₩15,000/6000). To see the collection of more than 13,000 species from over 60 countries at its peak, time your visit for early to mid-April when the famous magnolias bloom. While only a fraction of the grounds is open to the public, you should allow at least two hours to explore the diverse species and enjoy the sea views that define this botanical institution.

American banker Carl Ferris Miller transformed this former farmland into a world-class sanctuary, rescuing several traditional *hanok* along the way. Stay overnight in these historic wooden homes from ₩100,000.

The Sea-Breeze Effect

What makes Cheollipo unique is its immediate proximity to the West Sea. The salt-tinged air and constant coastal humidity create a rare microclimate, allowing delicate southern species to thrive much further north than usual. This allows rare *Magnolia biondii* and the star-shaped *Magnolia stellata* to flourish. For the most evocative views, follow the garden paths west until they emerge into a grove of Korean black pines. Here, you will find the signposted 'Sea-Breeze Trail', a wooden boardwalk that hugs the rugged cliffside. The path offers a stunning vantage point over the crashing waves and the nearby uninhabited Daksum Island.

Above Anmyeondo Arboretum

The Baekje
AESTHETIC

01

02

03

01 Jinmyosu (Stone Guardian)
This pork-bellied stone animal with a single horn stood watch at the entrance of King Muryeong's tomb.

02 Ma-ae-bul (Rock-Carved Buddha)
Region-specific Buddhist sculptures famous for a subtle, warm smile, chubby cheeks and a humanistic expression unique to the Baekje heartland.

03 Gwan-sik (Crown Ornaments)
Gold diadems featuring blazing flame patterns for King Muryeong and symmetrical dangling leaves for the queen; icons of Baekje elegance.

04 Geum-dong-sinbal (Gilt-Bronze Shoes)
Distinctive boat-shaped funerary shoes with unique spiked soles to grip heavenly paths. Designed for the afterlife, they were never intended for walking.

04

06

05

07

05 Baekje Geum-dong Dae-hyang-ro (The Great Incense Burner)
Gilt-bronze master-piece depicting utopia, featuring a phoenix, dragon and, uniquely, five musicians on a sacred mountain representing harmony through music and ritual.

06 Hwan-du-dae-do (Ring-Pommel Swords)
High-status blades uniquely Baekje for dragon-and-phoenix carvings; they signify a direct gift from the king to a local lord.

07 Jo-hyeong-to-gi (Bird-Shaped Vessels)
Used in shamanic ceremonies, these clay birds were ritualistic guides intended to help the soul travel safely into the afterlife.

Listings

BEST OF THE REST

Hinterland Flavours

Saeihak Garden ₩₩

Historic Gongju restaurant near the Geum River. Must-try rich beef *gukbap* (rice soup) and the exquisite local chestnut *muk* (jelly).

Gudurae Dolssambap ₩₩

A good spot to try *dolssambap*, a set meal of hot stone pot-cooked rice with side dishes, vegetables and medicinal plants.

House of Baekje ₩₩

Try the homey specialities like grilled beef or pork rolled inside *ssam* (lettuce wraps) and *yeonnipbap* (a lotus leaf filled with sticky rice).

Jangwon Buckwheat Noodles ₩

Popular place by Gudurae Sculpture Park Pier selling bowls of buckwheat noodles and plates of shredded chicken for extra flavour.

Myeongseong Bulgogi ₩₩

Locals love the raw meat and squid bulgogi at this popular spot south of Gongju's fortress.

Korea's Best Seafood Hotpot (팔도강산 해물뚝배기) ₩₩

Century-old Boryeong restaurant for large hotpot seafood soup meals.

Social Eats

Sijang's Butcher Restaurant ₩

Judge from the number of shoes stacked by the door how popular this meat-loving BBQ restaurant is. Try the raw meat bibimbap.

Sinbulhyang Small Octopus ₩

Family restaurant serving delicious stir-fried octopus sets, iron plate-fried octopus, deep-fried king prawns and even pork belly.

SORORI ₩

Decked out like a vintage Korean classroom with top-scoring Korean classic stews and crab rice in Cheongju's stylish bistro zone.

Manta ₩₩

Excellent Italian dishes around Unridan-gil, Cheongju's trending area near the Early Printing Museum.

Brunch with a View

37.5 ₩₩

Brass- and velvet-decked Cheongju bistro serving both American and Korean style breakfast plates, like eggs Benedict, French toast and kimchi fried rice.

Dubal Cafe & Yokjang Bakery ₩

Have the best pick of local coffee, desserts and cakes near large windows with Daecheon Beach views.

Babeans ₩

There's fine espresso here, though the best feature of this coffee shop is the Daecheon Beach sea views from the 3rd-floor outdoor patio.

GANG CHOI/SHUTTERSTOCK

Seodongyo Theme Park

Black Brunch Cafe ₩

This humble coffee shop serves the best espresso on Mallipo Beach.

Cholli Coffee and Dessert ₩

Large and luminous cafeteria on the top floor of a shop overlooking Cheollipo Beach for brews and cakes.

Sunset Cliff ₩₩

Stunning clifftop location among pine trees on the northern side of Mallipo, with coffee, Western and Korean dishes.

Midnight Dining

Gomaru Gamjatang ₩₩

The speciality is *gamjatang* (pork-bone stew), a hearty and slightly spicy classic. Open all night, a rarity for late-evening drinks in Buyeo.

Mani Mani Grilled Shellfish ₩₩₩

This busy restaurant by Daecheon Beach serves hearty set meals of shellfish, seafood and meat BBQ in a large, breezy hall.

Viewpoints & K-Drama Backdrops

Love Tree

A heart-shaped, 400-year-old zelkova tree's canopy inside Seongheung-san's Garim-seong fortress. Located 20 minutes from Buyeo.

Seodongyo Theme Park

Charming *hanok* village located southeast of the city by Deogyong Reservoir. Filming location for several historical K-Dramas.

Jaondae

A massive boulder along the eastern flank of the river in Gyuam-myeong, topped by the Subukjeong Pavilion for great views.

Cheonjeongdae

Even the Baekje kings chose this stunning riverside viewpoint to perform rites for the heavens before making important decisions.

PURBELLA/IMAZINS/GETTY IMAGES

Love Tree

Jangha-ri Stone Pagoda

Lesser-known three-storey Baekje stone pagoda located in a green and quiet park on the southeastern shore of the river.

Curated Collections & Local History

Baekje Roof Tile Museum

In the Roof Tile Kiln site in Jeongan-ri, this museum highlights unique Baekje roof-tile culture through fascinating architectural displays.

Shin Dong-Yeop Literary Museum

Birthplace of the nationalist poet who was instrumental in developing lyrical poetry in Korea. A quiet, reflective spot in the heart of Buyeo.

Buyeo Life Museum

A trip down memory lane through exhibits of objects from the daily life of everyday folks.

Buyeo Ginseng Museum

Established in 2004, this factory offers visual exhibits of the history, cultivation and production of Korean ginseng.

Baekje Reservoir

The tower-like observatory and nearby Geum River Culture Pavillion offer great views and a historical overview of the area.

48 NORTH KOREA: The Final Frontier

MILITARY HISTORY | POLITICS | TOURS

Visiting the DMZ is a highlight of any trip to South Korea. A surreal, unsettling highlight, to be sure, but a highlight nonetheless. On a trip to the country's northern border, you'll learn about the peninsula's tragic history and experience firsthand the tension that persists between brother countries that remain technically at war.

CHARLES USHER/LONELY PLANET

How To

Getting there The only way to visit sites within the DMZ is on a tour. To reach Imjingak Resort, take the Gyeongui-Jungang subway line to Munsan station and transfer to bus 058B (Imjingak); the trip takes 2–2½ hours.

When to go DMZ tour schedules and itineraries depend on geopolitical conditions. Check with tour operators to get the current status.

Top tip Bring your passport and adhere to all tour rules.

STEFANGDE/SHUTTERSTOCK

Top and bottom left Imjingak Resort

Joining a Tour

Established as a buffer at the end of the Korean War, the Demilitarized Zone (DMZ) is a 4km-wide no-man's land separating North Korea (DPRK, Democratic People's Republic of Korea) and South Korea (ROK, Republic of Korea). It's the peninsula's most unexpected tourist attraction, but it's not the sort of place you can just waltz into on your own. (Nor would you want to. It's seeded with more than 1 million landmines.) To visit, you'll need to join a guided tour. Most companies offer both half- and full-day tours that depart from Seoul, and there's little variation in itinerary. Reliable outfits include **KORIDOOR Tours** (koridoor.co.kr), **VIP Travel** (vviptravel.com) and **Panmunjom Tour** (panmuntour.go.kr), which is operated by the Ministry of Unification.

Into No-Man's Land

Nearly all tours visit the **Dora Observatory**, which offers views into North Korea, and the **Third Infiltration Tunnel**, one of four the DPRK is known to have dug beneath the DMZ. At the latter, you can don a hard hat and creep down the tunnel for more than 250m. If the current relations between North and South are sufficiently friendly, tours will travel to the **Joint Security Area**, a border-straddling complex used for diplomatic negotiations. There, under the exceedingly watchful eyes of ROK and DPRK soldiers, you can look across the border and may even be able to step, briefly, into North Korea inside one of the diplomatic buildings.

Last Resort

Many tours include a stop at **Imjingak Resort**, but you can also visit this complex just outside the DMZ independently. It makes for an interesting, if bizarre, day out. On its grounds you'll find numerous memorials, a campsite, a bullet-riddled locomotive from the war, public art, the remains of a bridge that once linked North and South, an amusement park and a museum dedicated to citizens kidnapped by the DPRK. A highlight is riding a gondola over the Imjin River to visit an observatory and a museum in a former US Army camp bowling alley.

By Charles Usher
@charlesreclausher

Visiting North Korea

INSIDE THE WORLD'S MOST RECLUSIVE COUNTRY

For many travellers, few places hold the same forbidding allure as North Korea, yet just the thought of visiting the country raises a host of questions. Is it ethical to go? Is it even possible? If so, how? And if you do go, what will you find?

ABLAKAT/SHUTTERSTOCK

Left Victorious Fatherland Liberation War Museum **Centre** 2025 Pyongyang Marathon **Right** Kumgang Mountains

Division & Divergence

There are moments in history when it seems that a lever is pulled, and the world proceeds down one set of tracks and not another. One of those moments came on 15 August 1945, at the end of WWII, when US President Harry Truman approved General Order No 1. The directive instructed defeated Japanese forces north of the 38th parallel to surrender to the Soviets and forces south of the 38th parallel to surrender to the Americans. That temporary division hardened into a permanent one, and the fates of North Korea and South Korea diverged dramatically. The South grew into a robust democracy and one of the world's most prosperous countries; the North descended into totalitarianism and poverty.

Behind the Curtain

Since its founding, North Korea (DPRK) has been ruled by three generations of the Kim family. It possesses nuclear weapons. It denies its citizens freedom of movement. It imprisons people in labour camps for the crime of watching foreign TV. For many travellers, these are ample reasons to stay away. For others, the DPRK's dark reputation and its air of surreality – this is a country that once claimed Kim Jong Il didn't defecate, after all – make the prospect of seeing it firsthand all the more enticing.

But can you even go? Yes. Well, maybe. Sometimes. For various reasons, South Koreans, Americans and Malaysians are all unable to travel to North Korea at present. Everyone else is allowed to visit, at least in theory. In practice, it all depends on the whims of the DPRK government. The country sealed its borders during the COVID-19 pandemic

KIM WON JIN/AFP/GETTY IMAGES

TERIMMA/SHUTTERSTOCK

and has been in no hurry to reopen them, welcoming travellers for the annual Pyongyang Marathon, occasional visits to the Rason Special Economic Zone and little else. Even when more general tourism is permitted, it remains tightly controlled. All visitors must be part of a guided tour and accompanied by North Korean guides.

> Given the complexities of visiting, a trip to North Korea is almost by definition a trip of a lifetime.

Also, *should* you go? Some of the money tourists spend does inevitably end up with the DPRK government. On the other hand, tours are the only opportunity that most North Koreans and outsiders will ever have for a person-to-person encounter. Ultimately, the decision of whether to travel to North Korea or not is a personal one.

Northern Exposure

Given the complexities of visiting, a trip to North Korea is almost by definition the trip of a lifetime, but the country also provides some truly unforgettable sights. In Pyongyang, there are grandiose monuments to the Kims and alternative-universe attractions like the Victorious Fatherland Liberation War Museum, which presents the North's version of the Korean War. On the Chinese border, Paekdusan (2744m) is the Korean peninsula's highest mountain and the site of a stunning crater lake. Near the DMZ, the city of Kaesong is the former capital of the ancient Koryo dynasty. And on the east coast, the majestic Kumgang Mountains are widely considered the most beautiful place on the peninsula – one of the few things that Northerners and Southerners, despite being divided for more than 80 years, can still agree on.

Planning a Trip

If you're considering visiting North Korea, your first step should be finding a reputable tour company with an itinerary that suits you. **Koryo Tours** (koryogroup.com), which has been running trips to the DPRK since 1993, is especially well-regarded. Another good outfit is **Young Pioneer Tours** (youngpioneertours.com). You may also need to start saving. North Korea tours aren't cheap; plan on about €800 (US$950) for a three-day group trip. You'll also need to factor in the cost of travelling to China, where most tours depart from.

Practicalities

Right Korea Train Express (p239)

EASY STEPS FROM THE AIRPORT TO THE CITY CENTRE

Most international flights arrive at Incheon International Airport (airport.kr), which is on an island 60km west of central Seoul. There are two terminals connected by shuttle trains – T1 is used mostly for Star Alliance flights, including those of Asiana, T2 for SkyTeam flights including Korean Air. The airport is well served by restaurants, shops and other facilities.

AT THE AIRPORT

SIM CARDS

SIM cards can be easily bought at mobile network counters in Incheon's arrival halls. It's worth doing some advance research on the deals available (try trazy.com) including those on pocket wi-fi device rental. Purchases can be made online and cards or devices picked up on site.

FOREIGN EXCHANGE

While it's unlikely you'll need cash immediately on arrival, there are currency exchange counters and self-service kiosks (pictured right) in the arrival halls. Banks and currency exchange offices in Seoul and other major cities will offer better rates.

JHXFILM/SHUTTERSTOCK

FREE WI-FI

Free wi-fi is available at the airport, as well as on airport buses, public transportation and in other public areas.

ATMS

There are ATMs that accept most (but not all) overseas bank and credit cards in Incheon's arrival halls.

CHARGING STATIONS

Free charging stations are located throughout Incheon Airport. If you don't have your own charging cables, there are also wireless charging zones.

DOMESTIC AIR TRANSFERS

When booking flights involving a domestic air transfer to a regional airport in Korea, check whether the onward flight is out of Incheon or Gimpo. Schedule at least three hours between flight arrival and the next flight departure to allow for getting through immigration and customs and transferring between airports if necessary.

GETTING TO THE CITY CENTRE

AIRPORT EXPRESS (A'REX) TRAINS

The fastest service departs every 30 minutes from both terminals and goes non-stop to Seoul station. More frequent and cheaper all-stop trains take 55 minutes from Terminal 1 and an hour from Terminal 2.

BUS

Deluxe KAL limousine buses take around an hour to reach central Seoul, provide a guaranteed seat and stop at major hotels. There are also slightly cheaper city buses (5.45am to 10.45pm, every 10 to 30 minutes) that take the same time to reach the city.

HOW MUCH FOR A...

A'REX train
from ₩4,750
55min

KAL bus
from ₩18,000
1hr

City bus
from ₩17,000
1hr

TMONEY

Bus, subway, taxi and train fares can all be paid using the rechargeable touch-and-go Tmoney card, which gives you a ₩100 discount per trip. You can also use it to connect subway and bus trips as a single fare, providing less than 30 minutes has elapsed between transfer.

PRICE

A nonrefundable ₩3000 from machines at most subway stations, as well as bus kiosks and convenience stores displaying the Tmoney logo.

HOW TO USE

Beep it at all station turnstiles and getting on and off buses. Reload it with credit at any station or convenience store.

OTHER POINTS OF ENTRY

Gimpo International Airport is 18km west of central Seoul. The bulk of domestic flights (and a handful of international routes) touch down at this gateway, which is on the subway and train lines.

Gimhae International Airport is 27km west of central Busan. The Busan–Gimhae Light Rail line connects Sasang and Daejeo stations with the airport. The most economical link between the airport and city is bus 307 from Gupo station.

Jeju International Airport is 1km from Shin Jeju ('New Jeju') and 4km from central Jeju-si. The Airport Limousine bus 600 (every 20 minutes) from outside gate 5 drops off and picks up passengers at major hotels and resorts all around the island.

Daegu International Airport is just over 1km from Ayanggyo Station on Daegu subway line 1 and can be reached by bus or taxi.

Incheon has two international ferry terminals, 4km apart, that service ports in China.

Busan International Passenger Terminal is about a 15-minute walk from Choryang subway station. There are services to several Japanese ports including Hakata (for Fukuoka).

TRANSPORT TIPS TO HELP YOU GET AROUND

Much of Korea can be explored using public transport, which is frequent and reliable. Ferries to the islands can be delayed by bad weather. Outside of the major cities, a rental car or ride-sharing apps will give you more flexibility and unlock destinations not served by buses. Travel across the country quickly by KTX trains or domestic airlines.

BUSES

Buses run several times per hour between major cities and towns, and at least hourly to other destinations. Check routes, schedules and buy tickets on bustago.or.kr. Express buses link major cities, while intercity buses stop more often and serve smaller cities and towns.

KORAIL PASS

Passes cover either two or four selected days, or three or five consecutive days. They are worth considering even for a straightforward return Seoul–Busan train. Seat reservations are sensible and necessary on weekends, holidays and other busy times.

CAR RENTAL

From ₩60,000 per day

Petrol approx ₩1700/litre

Insurance ₩20,000/day

CYCLING KOREA

Ttareungi (bikeseoul.com) is Seoul's bike-hire scheme. However, poor local driving habits can make cycling in Korea a challenge. That said, hiring a bike for short trips in areas with bike paths or little traffic is a good idea. The website **Korea by Bike** (koreabybike.com) provides useful information on long-distance cycling routes, including the 633km-long Four Rivers Cycling Path from Incheon to Busan, which follows the Han, Nakdong, Geum, and Yeongsan Rivers.

AIR Korean Air and Asiana, the two major domestic airlines, offer flights to and from a dozen local airports and typically charge identical yet reasonable fares. Competition is supplied by a handful of budget airlines, such as Jeju Air.

MPASS This foreigner-exclusive Tmoney card covers use of all of Seoul's public transport network plus the A'REX trains for up to 20 rides per day. It starts at ₩15,000 for one day and is also available for two, three, five and seven days.

DRIVING ESSENTIALS

Drive on the right; the steering wheel is on the left.

There are tolls on highways. Costs vary by vehicle type and distance travelled.

Overseas bank cards are not accepted for highway tolls – have cash ready or pay via your car rental company.

110

Speed limits are 80–110km on highways, 60–80km on general roads.

Blood alcohol limit is 0.03%.

CAR HIRE To rent your own set of wheels you must be 21 years of age or over and have an International Driving Permit (a driving licence from your own country is not acceptable). Try SK Rent-a-Car (homepage.skdirect.co.kr/en), Lotte Rent-a-Car (lotterentacar.net) or Jeju Airport Rental Car (jarrent.com). Multi-language sat-nav systems are common, or use mobile phone apps Naver (map.naver.com) or Kakao Maps (map.kakao.com).

TRAINS South Korea has an excellent but not comprehensive train network operated by Korail (korail.com). Trains are clean, comfortable and punctual. The fastest train is the Korea Train Express (KTX). A grade down and around 40% less expensive are Saemaeul services, which also only stop in major towns. The cheapest fares are for Mugunghwa trains, which are comfortable but stop more often.

BOATS Ferries connect hundreds of offshore islands and the mainland. Services from Incheon's Yeonan Pier run to a dozen nearby and more distant islands, while other west-coast islands further south can be reached from Daecheon harbour, Gunsan, Mokpo, Shinan Amtaeg-namgang Port and Tongyeong Ferry Terminal.

KNOW YOUR CARBON FOOTPRINT A domestic flight from Seoul to Busan emits about 123kg of carbon dioxide per passenger. Driving in a car you'd emit around 53kg. Travelling by bus the emissions go down to about 40kg, while on a train it's 15kg.

There are a number of carbon calculators online. Try sustainabletravel.org/our-work/carbon-offsets/calculate-footprint.

ROAD DISTANCE CHART (KMS)

	Suwon	Busan	Chuncheon	Daegu	Gangneung	Gwangju	Jeonju	Jeju-si	Seoul
Busan	372								
Chuncheon	126	402							
Daegu	262	110	300						
Gangneung	214	370	165	343					
Gwangju	271	261	381	217	446				
Jeonju	177	252	289	190	362	98			
Jeju-si	499	398	628	425	696	235	339		
Seoul	43	395	102	288	219	301	218	523	
Sokcho	220	425	131	386	66	476	389	760	195

DANGERS, ANNOYANCES & SAFETY

Korea is generally a safe, crime-free country, but it still a good idea to stay aware of potential dangers. Pay heed to weather reports, especially those relating to typhoons and heatwaves. And stay away from public demonstrations.

EXTREME HEAT Between late June and the end of August, temperatures of 38°C (100°F) in some parts of South Korea are not uncommon. Alongside the humidity, it can be especially draining. Be sure to hydrate regularly and stay aware of the symptoms of heat exhaustion. Also seek out air-conditioned environments such as shopping malls and museums.

NATURAL DISASTERS Check weather forecasts regularly. While the chance of earthquakes is low in Korea compared to neighbouring Japan and China, the country does get hit by typhoons and heavy rains, especially from June to October. In July 2025, at least 17 people died in floods and landslides caused by days of torrential rain.

DEMONSTRATIONS Koreans love a noisy protest. In Seoul, you might see police in full riot gear streaming out of blue police buses with their windows covered in protective wire. Student, trade-union, environmental, ferry-disaster and other protests have occasionally turned violent. Keep well out of the way of any confrontations that may occur.

MEDICAL CARE The quality of medical care across Korea is high. You need a doctor's prescription to buy most medications and it may be difficult to find the exact medication you use at home, so bring extra.

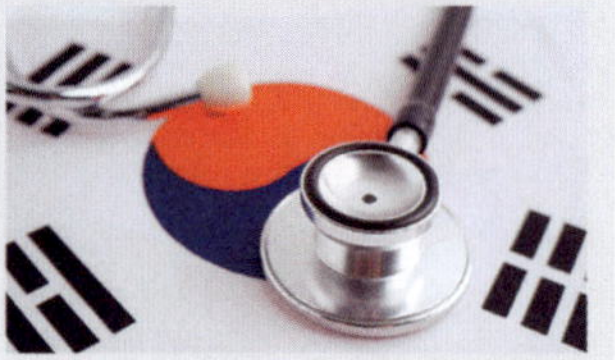

SWEET_TOMATO/SHUTTERSTOCK

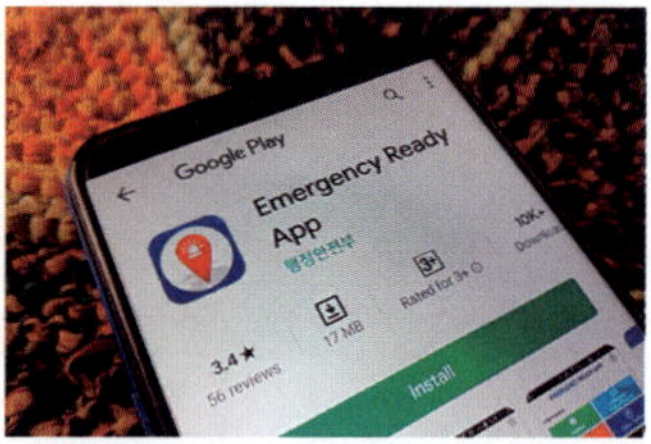

NEERAZ CHATURVEDI/SHUTTERSTOCK

EMERGENCY APP Download the Emergency Ready App for multilingual support in English, Chinese and Japanese for 36 services, including disaster alerts, safety guide, embassy information and civil defence shelter locations.

BORDER TENSIONS
The security situation on the Korean Peninsula can change with little notice. Tensions can rise after missile tests by North Korea and during the regular South Korea–US military exercises.

TRAVEL HELPLINE
If you run into difficulties communicating, try the 1330 Korea Travel Helpline, a telephone and real-time chat service. Call 1330 on your mobile phone and ask the interpreter to explain whatever you need in Korean.

QUICK TIPS TO HELP YOU MANAGE YOUR MONEY

CREDIT & DEBIT CARDS
Major international cards such as Visa and Mastercard are widely accepted, with many places – even street stalls – set up for contactless payment. Carry the physical card as Apple Pay isn't always accepted. There will also be times, such as when paying highway tolls or on buses, that your card won't work, so always carry some Korean cash.

CHANGING MONEY
Head to banks and licensed money-changers, which keep longer hours than banks and provide a faster service, but may only exchange US$ cash.

TIPPING
Not a custom in Korean culture and not required in restaurants (high-end ones may add a 10% service fee), for guides or in a taxi. You're likely to cause confusion if you try!

CURRENCY
South Korean won

HOW MUCH FOR A...

Subway fare with/without Tmoney card
₩1550/1650

Museum entrance
free, or from ₩10,000

Gimbap roll
₩5500

KOREAN TRAVEL CARD
The Korea Travel Card (koreatravelcard.com), which is similar to the Tmoney card, costs ₩7000 and is available online and from airports and CU convenience stores. As well as using it to pay for transport, the card offers benefits at thousands of tourist attractions and shops across the country.

TAX VAT is 10% on most goods and services. For purchases of at least ₩15,000 international visitors can get a refund on the tax at selected stores or at departure airports.

ATMS
Look for ones that have a 'Global' sign or the logo of your credit-card company. ATMs often operate from 7am to 11pm, but some are 24-hour such as those inside major convenience store chains.

BARGAINING
The only time it is acceptable to haggle over prices in Korea is at wholesale markets. This is best done when buying multiple items from one store in the market.

ON A BUDGET
Korea is not an overly expensive country, and there are ways to keep costs down if you're travelling on a budget. Stay in hostels or consider camping if it's summer. Many government-run museums are free or have times when admission charges are waived. A Tmoney card provides a discount on subway fares. Many supermarkets offer discounts on ready meals and other perishables towards the end of the the working day. Also look for two-for-one-type deals at convenience stores.

UNIQUE AND LOCAL WAYS TO STAY

Places to stay range from backpacker hostels and minbak (private homes with rooms to rent) to luxury hotels and resorts. Accommodation is plentiful in cities, but less so in rural areas. Staying in a hanok (traditional home) for at least one night is a unique and memorable experience, as is signing up for an overnight templestay. Glamping sites are also becoming popular.

HOW MUCH FOR A...

Hanok
₩150,000–200,000/night

Templestay
₩120,000/two-day stay

Motel
₩80,000/night

SIMON RICHMOND/LONELY PLANET

MOTELS & LOVE MOTELS

Motels are ubiquitous across Korea. The rooms are always on the small size but they are packed with facilities. However, staff rarely speak English and motels lack communal areas beyond the lobby, which is not designed for lingering.

Love motels cater for couples seeking some by-the-hour privacy, but they also accept overnight guests. If you can cope with the clandestine locations (and possibly intrusive noise from neighbouring rooms), they can be an excellent option. Some love motels, however, require a late check-in, around 9pm; earlier check-ins cost more.

JJIMJILBANG

Korean saunas are perfect places to get some rest after a long travel day. Some have a specific room where you can have a sleep. Pay the entry fee (usually under ₩20,000), use the facilities and then head for the rest room. Don't expect much in the way of bedding but there will be underfloor heating.

JULIANA KANG/SHUTTERSTOCK

HANOK STAYS

Rooms in *hanok* (traditional homes) tend to be small, and simply but tastefully decorated. You'll usually sleep on *yo* (padded quilts and mattresses) on the floor, but *ondol* (underfloor heating) keeps things snug. Bathrooms are often shared, but some guesthouses have en-suite rooms. Breakfast is included and traditional cultural experiences may also be offered.

MANEERAT SHOTIYANPITAK/SHUTTERSTOCK

TEMPLESTAYS

Korea's temples are havens of calm and quiet reflection amid the country's often non-stop activity. The templestay program provides a chance for visitors to stay in these beautiful places – either for a few hours or a couple of days – and experience the life of a Buddhist monk.

The templestay program is run by the Joyge Order of Korean Buddhism, Korea's largest Buddhist organisation. On offer are day programs, lasting around three hours, and overnight stays, including meals. No attempt will be made to convert you to Buddhism. It's a wonderful way to experience Korean spiritual culture, spend time in historic and beautifully decorated buildings, and visit some incredible locations.

Overnight stays usually last two days, but some extended periods are available. You'll be given a set of comfy cotton pyjamas to wear. Accommodation will be simple, traditionally Korean in style (ie heated floors and floor mattresses) and usually communal. There'll be more time for meditation and you'll join the monks for the communal dinner and breakfast. Additional elements could include cleaning chores around the temple, or a mindful walk.

For inspiration, read webzine.templestay.com and, if you're in Seoul, visit the Jogye-sa Information Centre for Foreigners opposite Jogye-sa.

BOOKING

Accommodation options are so numerous that there's usually little need to book ahead. The exception is *hanok* guesthouses, which typically only have a few rooms.

Book in advance for the following seasons: Lunar New Year (late January to early February), cherry blossom season (late March to early April), Chuseok (late September to early October) and autumn foliage season (early to mid November).

Seoul Hanok (hanok.seoul.go.kr) Search for *hanok* stays in the capital and find out more about this type of vernacular architecture.

Stay Folio (stayfolio.com) Lists some truly special and unique accommodation options, usually (but not always) self-catering. Particularly strong on contemporary-style *hanok*.

Templestay (eng.templestay.com) Lists the various programs available nationwide and where you can make a booking.

Homestay Korea (homestaykorea.com) Long-established homestay placement service.

Go Camping (gocamping.or.kr) Run by the Korea Tourism Organization, this site lists glamping sites nationwide.

Korean National Park Service (reservation.knps.or.kr) Booking site for campgrounds and mountain huts in national parks.

YOUTH HOSTELS

Hostelling International Korea (youthhostel.or.kr) runs 29 large modern youth hostels around the country. The dorms offer a good deal for solo travellers on a budget but they can be rather institutional and inconveniently located.

ESSENTIAL NUTS-AND-BOLTS

SMOKING
Banned in all bars, restaurants, hotels and public buildings, and not allowed while walking along the street, or outside subway stations or bus stops.

TAX REFUND
For most goods costing over ₩15,000 it's possible to get a refund on the VAT.

PUBLIC HOLIDAYS
Seollal (Lunar New Year), Buddha's Birthday and Chuseok (Thanksgiving) are set according to the lunar calendar, meaning that they fall on different days each year.

FAST FACTS

Time Zone
GMT+9

Country Code
+82

Electricity
220V/60Hz

GOOD TO KNOW

Check *k-eta.go.kr* to see if you need to apply for Korea Electronic Travel Authorisation (K-ETA) before travel.

Go to *e-arrivalcard.go.kr* to fill out the E-Arrival card online up to 72 hours before arrival.

Goods worth up to US$800 can be purchased duty-free, except liquor and perfume, which have separate limits.

The legal drinking age in Korea is 19.

South Korea's population is 52 million.

ACCESSIBLE TRAVEL

Public transport is increasingly being made more accessible but it's far from perfect.

Most Seoul subway stations have elevators and ramps, accessible toilets and Braille tiles. In subway cars, there's priority seating for those who need it.

Danurim Accessible Tourism Centre (seouldanurim.net) can arrange airport pick-up with wheelchair-ramp-equipped vehicles, as well as rental of wheelchairs and shower wheelchairs for your time in Seoul.

Korea Wheelchair Tour (koreawheelchairtour.com) is a travel agency for those with restricted mobility.

Visit Seoul (english.visitseoul.net/accessibility) has information on barrier-free tourism across the capital.

Gwangju Tourist Assistance Centre (jangtour.org) helps differently abled visitors get the most out of their trip to Gwangju.

TabiFolk (tabifolk.com/accessible-travel-groups/south-korea) is an online community dedicated to making travel accessible to everyone.

Visit Jeju (visitjeju.net) has details about accessible tourism on Korea's largest island – click on the Disabled Tourist Information button on the landing page.

WATER
South Korea's tap water is fine to drink. Even so, most people opt for filtered or bottled water.

ETIQUETTE
A short bow is most respectful for meetings and departures. Give or receive any object using both hands.

LUGGAGE FORWARDING
Zimcarry (zimcarry.net) is a same-day luggage delivery service operating across Korea.

ADDRESSES
Official addresses are road- and number-based, but some places still use an older system that is confusing to nearly everyone; for details see juso.go.kr. The best advice is to use local navigation apps Naver or Kakao Maps to locate your destination.

TOILETS
- Korea has plenty of clean, modern *hwajangsil* (public toilets; 화장실); inside the subway is a reliable place to find them in Seoul.
- Virtually all toilets are free.
- Toilet paper is usually provided, but it's wise to carry a stash around with you just in case.

FAMILY TRAVEL

Dining Many Korea restaurants are specifically set up to serve meals family-style. Bakery cafes are good for feeding hungry but picky kids.

Transport Kids under six travel free on subways and buses, while those aged 6–12 and 13–18 are entitled to different levels of discounts.

Attractions Funfairs and parks can be found in most cities, along with cinemas, video-game arcades, tenpin bowling alleys and *noraebang* (karaoke rooms).

AOY_CHARIN/SHUTTERSTOCK

LGBTIQ+ TRAVELLERS

Discrimination Korea has never outlawed homosexuality, but this is a conservative society and sexuality in general is a taboo subject.

Gaybourhoods Seoul's two most famous locations for LGBTIQ+-friendly watering holes and gathering spaces are Itaewon and the Jongno 3-ga area around Nakwon-dong.

Seoul Queer Culture Festival (sqcf.org), usually held in June, is the high point of queer visibility in the capital.

Chingusai (chingusai.net) is one of Korea's oldest sexual-minority rights organisations.

@queerscoutsbusan For events and news in Busan.

LANGUAGE

Korean belongs to the Ural-Altaic language family and is spoken by around 80 million people. Korean script, *hangeul*, is simple and accessible, as each character represents a sound of its own.

BASICS

Hello. 안녕하세요. *an·nyŏng ha·se·yo* (This expression also means 'how are you?')

Goodbye. (if leaving/ staying) 안녕히 *an·nyŏng·hee* 계세요 *gye·se·yo/* 가세요 *ga·se·yo*

Yes. 네/예. *né/yé* (Both of these mean 'yes' and they're used about equally.)

No. 아니요. *a·ni·yo*

Thank you. 감사합니다. *gam·sa·ham·ni·da*

Excuse me. 실례합니다. *shil·lé ham·ni·da*

Sorry. 죄송합니다. *choé·song ham·ni·da*
미안합니다. *mi·an·ham·ni·da*
(Both expressions are used about equally.)

You're welcome.
괜찮아요. *gwaen·cha·na·yo* (This common response means 'it's fine/no problem.')

What's your name?
성함이 어떻게 되세요?
sŏng·ha·mi ŏt·tŏ·ke dway·se·yo

My name is ...
제 이름은...입니다. *je i·rŭ·mŭn ...·im·ni·da*

Do you speak English?
영어 할 줄 아세요? *yŏng·ŏ hal jul a·se·yo*

I don't understand.
못 알아 들었어요. *mot a·ra·dŭ·rŏss·ŏ·yo*

NUMBERS

1	하나 *ha·na*	**6**	여섯 *yŏ·sŏt*
2	둘 *dul*	**7**	일곱 *il·gop*
3	셋 *set*	**8**	여덟 *yŏ·dŏl*
4	넷 *net*	**9**	아홉 *a·hop*
5	다섯 *da·sŏt*	**10**	열 *yŏl*

SIGNS

영업 중	**Open**	화장실	**Toilets**
휴무	**Closed**	신사용	**Men**
입구	**Entrance**	숙녀용	**Women**
출구	**Exit**		

EMERGENCIES

Help!	도와주세요! *do·wa·ju·se·yo*
Go away!	저리 가세요! *jŏ·ri ga·se·yo*
Call ...!	...불러주세요! *... bul·lŏ·ju·se·yo*
a doctor	의사 *ŭi·sa*
the police	경찰 *gyŏng·ch'al*
I'm lost.	길을 잃었어요. *gi·rŭl i·rŏss·ŏ·yo*

Index

000 Map pages

N

O

P

'I love going out in Hongdae (pictured left) and just letting myself get swept up in the crowd, drifting between bars and restaurants, scoping out late-night shops, catching some live music, watching buskers and b-boys – the energy there is unmatched.'

CHARLES USHER

'I'll never get tired of wandering Jeju's northwestern coast and glimpsing bottlenose dolphins jumping in the sea.'

ANN BABE

'Enjoy a superb performance of traditional Korean music and have a dance in the gorgeous Les Jardins de Médongaule.'

SIMON RICHMOND

'Ride the ferry to the island of Udo in search of its famed peanut makgeolli, burgers and ice cream (pictured right).'

ANN BABE

'I'll never forget the first time I drove over the Cheonsa Bridge and a dozen islets surrounded by morning mist beckoned at me from a calm, endless sea.'

MARCO FERRARESE

'Swoon at the fire-cracker display of autumnal leaves in Seoraksan National Park.'

SIMON RICHMOND

FROM TOP LEFT: CHARLES USHER/LONELY PLANET, PARK YOUNGMIN STI/SHUTTERSTOCK

THIS BOOK

The 1st edition of Lonely Planet's *Experience Korea* guidebook was written and researched by Simon Richmond, Ann Babe, Marco Ferrarese, Phillip Tang and Charles Usher.

This guidebook was produced by the following:

Destination editor Selena Hoy

Coordinating editor Anita Isalska

Production editor Hannah Cartmel

Cartographer Bohumil Ptáček

Image researcher Virginia Moreno

Assisting editor Liana Cafolla

Cover researcher Daisy Korpics

Thanks Ronan Abayawickrema, Soyi Kim, Charlotte Orr, Akanksha Singh, Vicky Smith